History of East Haven

C000027404

Sarah E. Hughes

Alpha Editions

This edition published in 2019

ISBN : 9789353977238

Design and Setting By
Alpha Editions
email - alphaedis@gmail.com

As per information held with us this book is in Public Domain.
This book is a reproduction of an important historical work. Alpha Editions
uses the best technology to reproduce historical work in the same manner
it was first published to preserve its original nature. Any marks or number
seen are left intentionally to preserve its true form.

DEDICATION.

_____

To the Trustees of the Old Cemetery in
East Haven, Conn.

I dedicate and donate this little work, which has
been requested by many of my townspeople, to you,
as a freewill offering of love and interest to my native
town.

The object is twofold. First, to perpetuate that
which has hitherto been written, and also to record that
which has since formed history. Second, and pri-
marily, to aid you in raising and securing a Permanent Fund for the care and maintenance of the Old
Cemetery, during all time to come.

SARAH EVA HUGHES.

TO

MISS SARAH EVA HUGHES.

We, the undersigned, as Trustees of the Old Cemetery in East Haven, do hereby gratefully acknowledge your faithful and untiring efforts in the compilation of this authentic and interesting work, and it is with pleasure we publish it to perpetuate history and the names of those who have aided in making possible the Permanent Fund.

CHARLOTTE J. THOMPSON,
ELIZABETH H. BAGLEY,
JENNIE A. FORBES,
CHARLOTTE A. HEMINGWAY,
IDA M. FONDA.

PREFACE.

By the request of several of the townspeople, a revision of the "East Haven Register," by Rev. Stephen Dodd, is attempted. This work is out of print, and only a copy now and then is to be found in the town, but a growing feeling has been expressed for its perpetuation.

The present work is merely a revision of Rev. Mr. Dodd's, with some chapters eliminated as being of little interest at the present day, viz., the "Division of Lands," "Town Boundaries," and "Public Roads"; in their places events of local interest since 1824 (the date of his publication) have been inserted. The general historical events are faithfully and fully copied from his work. In the first settlement of the town more notice of and space to the early settlers has been given, with a short biographical sketch of each one, as far as could be collected from various and reliable sources, in order to gratify the prevailing feeling of many of the present day to learn something of the first ancestors of the town. This has been carried only to 1700 and, in a few instances, lightly traced to the present day. After 1700 the children of the early settlers took the places of their fathers and bore their responsibilities and labors, manifesting the same traits of character by inheritance of the same virtues and opinions. . There is no denying the old adage that "blood will tell." No pretence is made to write a scholarly history, but a review of the past, and quotations from acknowledged authorities. The intention is to give in a pleasant and readable form some outline of the work that was done by the first settlers, the general character and customs of the people, together with some biographical sketches of interest to those who take pride in ancestry, for Ruskin says, "both moral and physical qualities are communicated by descent, far more than they are developed by education." Neither is this little work intended to compete with, nor in any way retard the publication of that of the late Rev. D. W. Havens, who has written a voluminous and exhaustive history of the town.

No quotations have been made, therefore there has been no infringement of his work in this volume; but numerous references, and some quotations, have been taken from his Centennial Sermon, as that was publicly delivered and afterwards published, which rendered it no longer private property. If omissions or mistakes have been made, it has been from inaccessibility to the facts and not from any other cause, as it has been the purpose to do "justice" to all, with "offense to none." If it is true that a work done in a spirit of love always makes for blessedness, then this work will accomplish the desired end.

The compiler wishes to express thanks to all those who have so readily and cheerfully aided in furnishing dates, records and information, and to Mr. G. A. Sanford for the photographs, and to Mrs. Clara A. Thompson of Hartford for her picture of the mountain laurel. All have made the work a pleasure, because coöperation was so freely extended.

S. E. H.

CONTENTS.

PAGE

DEDICATION iii

ACCEPTANCE v

PREFACE vii

CONTRIBUTORS TO FUND xiii

CHAPTER   I. THE SETTLEMENT OF EAST
                   HAVEN I

CHAPTER   II. PUBLIC SCHOOLS 48

CHAPTER   III. ECCLESIASTICAL AFFAIRS 67

CHAPTER   IV. INDUSTRIES 115

CHAPTER   V. DIFFERENCES BETWEEN NEW
                   HAVEN AND BRANFORD
                   SETTLED 139

CHAPTER   VI. FORMATION OF THE EPISCO-
                   PAL SOCIETY 166

CHAPTER   VII. THE GREEN 175

CHAPTER   VIII. THE CEMETERY 197

CHAPTER   IX. NATURAL HISTORY, TORNADO
                   AND CURIOSITIES 218

CHAPTER   X. LOSSES BY WAR 235

CHAPTER   XI. GENERAL AFFAIRS 286

ILLUSTRATIONS.

Facing page

SARAH E. HUGHES .... (*Frontispiece*)

ALCHEMY SPOON 4

SPEAR HEADS AND ARROW POINTS 44

THE UNION SCHOOL........................ 57

THE CONGREGATIONAL CHURCH.............. 92

THE MILL 125

LAKE SALTONSTALL....................... 130

GOVERNOR SALTONSTALL CHAIR 155

GOVERNOR SALTONSTALL'S HOUSE 156

THE EPISCOPAL CHURCH................... 171

THE HOUSE WHERE LAFAYETTE WAS ENTER-
TAINED IN 1824.......................... 178

MOUNTAIN LAUREL 189

JACOB HEMINGWAY MONUMENT.............. 204

THE COWLES MEMORIAL GATEWAY 212

EAST HAVEN RIVER AND DARROW ISLAND.. 224

FORT WOOSTER TABLET 237

FORT HALE.............................. 261

MAIN STREET 292

CONTRIBUTORS.

THE PERPETUAL CARE FUND.

Mr. CHARLES FOWLER (For Fowler and Russell family),
Ironton, Ohio $500.00
Mr. DWIGHT D. MALLORY (For Davidson family),
Baltimore, Md. 100.00
Mrs. MARIA BARNES RUSSELL (For Barnes family),
Meriden, Conn. 100.00
Mr. EDWARD BATES (For Dr. and Mrs. Bradley),
Syracuse, N. Y. 100.00
Mrs. STURTEVANT CHIDSEY LEGACY 100.00
Deacon ASA L. FABRIQUE, New Haven, Conn. 100.00
Mrs. H. MINERVA ANDREWS BLACKSTONE,
Branford, Conn. 100.00
Mrs. MARY FRANCES ANDREWS RICHARDS,
New Haven, Conn. 100.00
Mrs. TIMOTHY ANDREWS, East Haven, Conn......... 100.00
Mr. GEORGE H. TOWNSEND (General Fund),
New Haven, Conn. 100.00
Mr. ARTHUR H. BURR, New Haven, Conn. 100.00
THE MERIT HEMINWAY FAMILY, Watertown, Conn... 100.00
Mr. WILLIAM S. PARDEE, New Haven, Conn. 100.00
DR. LESTER J. KEEP, Brooklyn, N. Y. 100.00
FRANK J. LUDDINGTON, Waterbury, Conn. 100.00
PHILEMON HOLT HEIRS 100.00
 CHARLES HOLT, New York; HENRY HOLT, Bur-
 lington, Vt.; ELLA HOLT, Baltimore, Md.; Mrs.
 MORTIMER, Baltimore, Md.
ALBERT L. CURTISS, Milwaukee, Wis. 100.00
THE BISHOP HEIRS 100.00
 Mrs. JOHN H. PLATT, New Haven, Conn.; Mr. G.
 HALSTED BISHOP, Woodbridge, Conn.

CHAPTER I.

SETTLEMENT OF THE TOWN.

T this time it may be thought that the little town of East Haven has no place in history, because of its diminutive size. Let it be remembered that each little town is a world unto itself, with an individual empire of its own in associations, customs and habits of thought. Two thousand years ago the most precious title was to be a Roman citizen. St. Paul exclaims, "I am a man which am a Jew." "A citizen of no mean city." "Taught according to the perfect manner, of the law of the fathers." If St. Paul was proud of his citizenship, should we not be proud that we are of Puritan origin? He was a Hebrew of the Hebrews. His parents were both Jews of the tribe of Benjamin. Hence the similarity, for we are Puritans of the Puritans, brought up as he was, "after the manner of the law of the fathers." In all the histories of colonial times the New Haven Colony, under Rev. John Davenport and Theophilus Eaton, is called one of the most learned, refined, pious and wealthy of all the companies coming to New England. Owing to its personnel, this company was urged to locate in Massachusetts, when they first landed from England. Large concessions were made to them if they would remain, but Mr. Davenport would not consent. He wished to found a distinct colony, and we shall soon see what was wrapped in his brain.

Mr. Davenport was the head and face of the company; although Theophilus Eaton was chosen and styled Governor, yet Rev. John Davenport was the man behind the throne. He was an ordained priest in the established Church of England, preached and administered according to its rules and customs and never entirely seceded from it while in England, although he was under censure and persecution for Puritan views. He was a learned minister, celebrated for piety, and distinguished for purity of life, and esteemed by his congregation for his love of the truth, which was in contradistinction to many of his time and profession. His whole life and works may be summed up in two words, a godly man.

Like many other dissenting ministers, his people followed him to the wilds of America. He and they exemplified the same spirit of justice here that they had professed at their home. They did not take up the land of the Indian by any grant or power from England, but considered the Indians the rightful owners of the soil and treated with them accordingly. This company arrived in Boston July 26, 1637. Owing to the Pequot war, which had just taken place before their arrival, between the Massachusetts Colony and the Indians, the southern part of Connecticut had been explored and such a flattering report made of the country that Mr. Theophilus Eaton and others made a journey to the land of the Quinnipiacs, which they decided should be their future abode. They erected a hut on what is now the corner of Church and George streets, leaving seven men to winter there.

On the 30th of March, 1638, Mr. Davenport and
company sailed from Boston for Quinnipiac, arriving
about two weeks after. The 18th of April, the first
Lord's day after their arrival, the people attended
public worship under a large oak, and Mr. Davenport preached from Matthew vi. 1. Soon after their
arrival they held a day of fasting and prayer, at the
covenant, binding themselves, *"that as in matters that
concern the gathering and ordering of a Church, so
also in all publick offices which concern civil order; as
choice of Magistrates and officers, making and repealing laws, dividing allotments of inheritance, and all
things of like nature, they would all of them be ordered
by the rules which the scripture held forth to them."*
(*Trumbull.*) By this covenant they were regulated
the first year.

On the 24th of November, 1638, Rev. Mr. Davenport and others made their first purchase of land in
an open, fair and Christian spirit, with Momauguin
and his sister Shaumpishuh, called in the agreement
Squaw Sachem, who had some interest in the lands.
Probably her part was in Guilford, as the purchasers
of that place agreed with the Indians that they should
move off the lands, which they did, and she and others
came to live with Momauguin in East Haven. His
tribe now numbered only forty men, having been
greatly depleted by the cruel attacks of the Pequots
and Mohawks. "The English agreed to protect
Momauguin and his Indians from other tribes when
unreasonably assaulted and terrified. They should
always have sufficient land to plant in summer, and to
hunt and fish between Quinnipiac harbor and Say-

brook fort. The latter was situated at the mouth of
Connecticut river." (*Trumbull.*) Quite a field for
hunting and planting.

They also covenanted "that by way of free and
thankful retribution, they gave to this sachem and
his council and company *12 coats of English cloth,
12 alchemy spoons, 12 hatchets, 12 hoes, two dozens
of knives, 12 porringers and 4 cases of French knives
and scissors.*" (*Trumbull.*) This treaty was signed
and legally executed by Momauguin and his council
on his part, and Theophilus Eaton and Rev. John
Davenport on the part of the English. Thomas Stan-
ton was interpreter. On the 11th of December, 1638,
they purchased another large tract, which lay principally north of the first purchase. This was bought
of Montowese, son of the great sachem at Mattabeseck
(now Middletown). It was ten miles long, from
north to south, and thirteen miles in breadth. It
extended eight miles east of Quinnipiac river and
five miles west of it. They had the same privileges of
hunting, planting and fishing as the Quinnipiacs. For
this tract they gave thirteen coats. This tribe or company consisted of but ten men with their women and
children. These purchases included all the lands of
the ancient limits of New Haven, Branford and Wallingford, from which the towns of East Haven, North
Branford, North Haven, Hamden, Cheshire, Meriden,
Bethany and Woodbridge, with a part of Orange
have been made. Guilford lands were bought by Rev.
Mr. Henry Whitfield and his company. Milford lands
were bought in 1639 by members of Mr. Davenport's
company and both settlements were under the jurisdiction of New Haven.

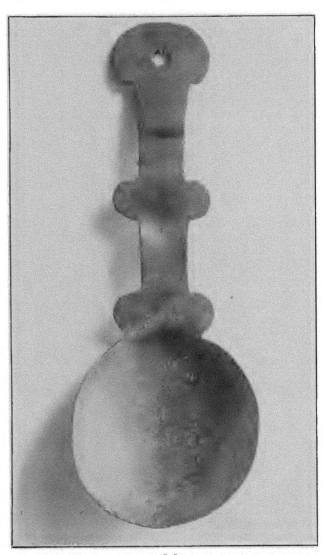

ALCHEMY SPOON, FOUND IN 1828, WHILE DIGGING THE CELLAR
OF MR. AARON A. HUGHES' HOUSE, WHERE THE INDIAN HEARTHS
WERE UNEARTHED.

It fully appears that the purchase from the Indians was clear and satisfactory. Both parties lived up to their contract and no conflict ever arose between them. The Indians and settlers lived amicably and without fear, except from other tribes.

On the 4th of June, 1639, all the free planters of Quinnipiac convened in a large barn belonging to Mr. Newman, and in formal and very solemn manner proceeded to lay the foundations for their civil and religious polity. Mr. Davenport introduced the business by a sermon from the words, "Wisdom hath builded her house, she hath hewn out her seven pillars," after which he propounded five long questions to the planters, and each one was read over twice by Mr. Newman in a clear voice, and they all with one accord gave their full consent at each reading. The sum and substance of the five questions can be simmered down to the following, viz: "That church members only shall be free burgesses, and that they shall choose magistrates and officers among themselves, to have the power of transacting all public civil affairs of this plantation, of making and repealing laws, dividing of inheritances and deciding of differences that may arise, and doing all things or business of like nature." (*Atwater.*) This being settled as a fundamental article concerning civil government, he propounded the sixth question, respecting the gathering of a church, viz: "That twelve men be chosen, that their fitness for the foundation work may be tried, he advised the names of such as were to be admitted be publicly propounded, to the end that they who were most approved might be chosen. However, there may be more than twelve chosen, yet it may be in the

power of those who are chosen to reduce them to
twelve, and it be in the power of those twelve to choose
out of themselves seven that shall be the most appropriate to begin the Church." (*Atwater.*) This was a
unanimous vote, as before, and one hundred and
eleven persons subscribed that day to this fundamental
law.

Rev. John Davenport, Theophilus Eaton, Robert
Newman, Matthew Gilbert, Thomas Fugill, John
Punderson and Jeremiah Dixon were chosen the seven
pillars of the church. October 25, 1639, the court, as
it was termed, of these seven pillars convened. A
solemn charge was given them. The purport of this
was nearly the same with the oath of fidelity and
with the freeman's oath administered at the present
time. Theophilus Eaton was chosen governor. Mr.
Robert Newman, Mr. Matthew Gilbert, Mr. Nathaniel
Turner and Mr. Thomas Fugill were chosen magistrates. Mr. Fugill was chosen secretary, and Robert
Seeley, marshal. Rev. Mr. Davenport gave Governor
Eaton a charge in open court from Deut. i. 11, 17.
It was settled that an annual meeting should be held
the last week in October, to elect the officers of the
colony, and that the Word of God should be the
only rule for ordering the affairs of this commonwealth. No trial by jury was provided. New Haven
differed from the other Connecticut colonies in its
"Fundamental Law," that "only church members
should be free burgesses," at the present time called
voters. "Fundamental" meant unchangeable, and
reads as follows: "It is agreed and concluded, as a
fundamental order, not to be disputed or questioned
hereafter that none shall be free burgesses in any of

the plantations within this jurisdiction, for the future, but such planters as are members of some or other of the approved churches in New England." At this time there were no other than the "approved churches" of the Puritans, generally called Congregational churches.

At the present time all constitutions establish a clause stating a method whereby a change can be made, but Mr. Davenport's idea was like the "law of the Medes and Persians which altereth not." We now understand why he wished to found a separate and distinct colony, one that should be governed as he saw it should be, "by the mind of God revealed in the Scripture." "1st, That magistrates should be men fearing God. 2d, That the Church is the company whence ordinarily such men may be found. 3d, That they that choose them ought to be men fearing God. 4th, That free planters ought not to give the power out of their hands."

All the foregoing may be considered as dry dust and ashes, but it seems the object for which this is written and the desires of those who requested it would utterly fail if the principles and circumstances upon which this town was founded were not set forth. We have received a rich inheritance from this source; the religious sentiment, principles and influence sifted down through all these generations, the moral strength gathered in consequence, can not be computed. It is ours, and there is no wresting it from us.

The Puritans intended to establish a purely democratic government, ignoring all hereditary titles and privileges, but, as they had no other country for a precedent but England, they fell short of their theory,

and really their form of government was a pure aris-
tocracy, yet planned and executed in a manner peculiar
to themselves. The two colonies in Massachusetts, the
Plymouth and Massachusetts colonies, like the New
Haven Colony, allowed none but church members to
vote. Connecticut was first settled at Hartford, Windsor and Wethersfield; and these river towns were the
Connecticut Colony. Church membership was never
required in the Connecticut Colony as a qualification
for the elective franchise. Herein was the distinguish-
ing difference between it and the New Haven Colony,
which led to so much opposition to the union of the
two, which finally took place after much controversy,
in 1665.

The lands of the colony were purchased of the
Indians by the principal men in trust for all the inhabitants of the several plantations or towns. Every
planter, after paying his proportionate part of the
expenses arising from laying out and settling the
plantation, drew a lot or lots of land, in proportion to
the money or estate which he had expended in the
general purchase, and to the number of heads numbered in his family, called polls. In the first division
of land in East Haven, in 1639, several enterprising
farmers turned their attention to the lands on the east
side of the Quinnipiac and began to settle there.

Among the members who subscribed to the covenant
in Mr. Newman's barn, June 4, 1639, were Thomas
Gregson, Jasper Crayne, William Tuttle, Benjamin
Linge, William Andrews, Jarvis Boykim, John Potter,
Matthew Moulthrop, Matthias Hitchcock, Edward
Patterson, Thomas Morris and John Thompson, who
settled in East Haven, or were concerned in that settle-

ment. As these were the founders, we shall try to give some idea of the men, and their relative position and character in the colony.

THOMAS GREGSON, 1639.

In 1639 Thomas Gregson petitioned for his second division at Solitary Cove, and on the 5th of August, 1644, 133 acres were allotted to him at that place. There he is said to have placed his family—the first in East Haven. One account expresses doubt about his living there with his family. He had a spacious house in New Haven opposite the Green, where the Insurance building now stands on Chapel street. Dr. Stiles, in his "History of the Judges," gives as a tradition "that Mr. Davenport, Mr. Eaton, Mr. Allerton and Mr. Gregson owned the grandest houses in town. He was a principal man in the colony at New Haven, and the first white settler in East Haven. He was elected to several important offices, such as deputy governor, a commissioner with Governor Eaton, and provisioner of meats for the colony, and was rated the third wealthiest man in the colony." In 1645 he was appointed agent for the colony to the parliament in England to obtain a patent, sometimes called a charter, which was a parchment given with the sanction of the British government, securing to the colonies the right to make their own laws and to appoint their own magistrates and governors, conforming to the laws of England.

Although he was not one of the seven pillars of the New Haven church, he was a zealous member of it and an ardent believer of Rev. Mr. Davenport's views. His family consisted of one son and five daughters. The son and eldest daughter returned and lived in England. One of his descendants, William Gregson, of London, England, gave to Trinity Church, New Haven, his homestead at the corner of Chapel and Church Streets. After many difficulties, they secured this property and built their first church upon it. He was lost at sea in 1647. As the loss of Mr. Gregson was a calamity to the early settlement of East Haven, I conclude that the following account may be introduced into this work with propriety. It is a singular affair and will be amusing to many readers. I insert it here without any comment, leaving every reader to form their own judgment concerning it. As Mr. Gregson was the first settler, it may not be inappropriate to give this account in connection with his biography. It is from the pen of Rev. James Pierpont, pastor of the church at New Haven, settled there July 2, 1685, to Dr. Mather, who requested him to sent the account:

"Reverend and Dear Sir—

"In compliance with your desires, I now give you the relation of that *apparition* of *a ship in the air,* which I have received from the most credible, judicious, and curious surviving observers of it.

"In the year 1647, besides much other lading, a far more rich treasure of passengers (five or six of which were persons of chief note and worth in *New Haven*) put themselves on board a *new ship,* built at Rhode-Island, of about 150 tons; but so walty [crank] that the master (Lamberton) often said she would prove their grave. In the month of January, cutting their way through much ice, on which they were accompanied with the Rev. Mr. *Davenport,* besides many other friends, with many fears, as well as prayers and tears, they set sail. Mr. *Davenport,* in prayer, with an observable *empha-*

sis, used these words, *Lord, if it be thy pleasure, to bury these dear friends in the bottom of the sea, they are thine, save them!* The spring following, no tidings of these friends arrived with the ships from *England;* New Haven's heart began to fail her; this put the godly people on much *prayer,* both public and private, *that the Lord would (if it was his pleasure) let them hear what he had done with these our friends, and prepare them with a suitable submission to his Holy Will.* In *June* next ensuing, a great *thunder storm* arose out of the *north-west;* after which, (the hemisphere being serene) about an hour before sun-set, a SHIP, of like dimensions with the aforesaid, with her canvass and colours abroad, (though the wind northerly,) appeared in the air, coming up from our harbour's mouth, which lyes southward of the towne, seemingly with her sails filled under a fresh gale, holding her course north, and continuing under observation, sailing against the wind, for the space of half an hour.

"*Many* were drawn to behold this great work of God; yea, the very children cryed out, *There's a brave ship!*—At length, crowding up as far as there is usually water sufficient for such a vessel and so near some of the spectators as that they imagined a man might hurl a stone on board her, her *main top* seemed to be blown off, but left hanging in the shrouds; then her *missen top;* then all her *masting* seemed to be blown away by the board; quickly after the hulk brought into a careen, she overset, and so vanished into a smoky cloud, which in sometime dissipated, leaving as everywhere else, a clear air. The admiring spectators could distinguish the several colours of each part, the principal rigging and such proportions, as caused not only the generality of persons to say, *This was the mould of their ship, and thus was her tragic end;* but Mr. *Davenport* also in public declared to this effect *That God had condescended, for the quieting of their afflicted spirits, this extraordinary account of the sovereign disposal of those for whom so many fervent prayers were made continually.*

"Thus I am, Sir, Your humble servant,

"JAMES PIERPONT."

As people of the present day are not at all given to the supernatural, it may not be amiss to say that this might have been a case of mirage, an optical illusion arising from an unequal refraction in the lower strata of the atmosphere, which causes objects at a distance to appear as in the air floating over the sea. On the Straits of Messina in Italy it is said to often occur.

JASPER CRAYNE, 1639.

Mr. Jasper Crayne had his lot and house on the east side of the Green. Jasper Crayne sold his farm of sixteen acres to Matthew Moulthrop September 7, 1652, but he had removed to Totoket (now Branford) in 1644. There is a tradition that he built on the site now occupied by Mr. H. Walter Chidsey; that he said, "he would build the best house on the east side, which would surprise them all." A corner cupboard of good workmanship now stands in Mrs. Chidsey's dining room, which was taken out of the old house by her father, the late Edwin S. Bradley.

Mr. Crayne was one of the wealthy men of the colony; if he built this house, he failed to finish off the second story, which was never done through all the succeeding ownerships. He seems to have been an energetic, active man, but of a restless turn, somewhat captious withal. At one time he was interested in the Iron Works, as overseer or agent. His house in New Haven was on Elm street, where St. Thomas's Church now stands. He was prominent in the councils of New Haven, one of its magistrates, and deputy to the General Court. He was surveyor, and laid out much of the town plot, located grants and settled dis-

puted titles. In 1666 he signed the compact to move
from Branford to Newark, New Jersey. At the time
of the union of New Haven Colony with that of Connecticut all the towns under the jurisdiction of New
Haven were satisfied, except Branford. Rev. Mr.
Pierson and almost his whole church and congregation were so displeased that they soon removed to
Newark, where Mr. Crayne became very active and
influential in state and church till his death in October,
1681. His sons, like their father, were honored and
useful, and nearly all the Craynes in that state can
trace their pedigree to Jasper Crayne.

WILLIAM TUTTLE, 1639.

William Tuttle was another of the most important of
the first settlers. It appears from the passenger list of
the ship Planter that three distinct Tuttle families came
over together. John settled in Ipswich, Massachusetts,
Richard in Boston, and William in New Haven. There
is some discrepancy about spelling the name, as "Tout-
tle or Tuttle"; then again his sons are called "Tuthill."
This latter spelling has led many to suppose the Tuthills of Southold, Long Island, and other places, were
of William Tuttle's family, which is an error. The
Long Island Tuthills were a separate and distinct
family, descended from Henry Tuthill of Tharston,
Norfolk County, England; while Devonshire was the
source of the New England Tuttles, and ever since the
settlement in America the name has been spelled
Tuttle. According to the Tuttle coat of arms granted
to William Tuttle, October 24, 1591, the name was
originally Tothill, and the crest, which was always
added after the shield was granted and was commem-

orative of some special act or office of the family, shows the last part of the name by the *hill,* upon which the dove with the olive branch in its beak stands. It is considered one of the most beautiful crests in heraldry.

In 1640 we find Mr. Tuttle everywhere called and described by the title of "Mr." Palfrey in his "History of New England" says: "There was great exactness in the application of both official and conventional titles. Only a small number of persons of the best condition (always including ministers and their wives) had Mr. or Mrs. prefixed to their names; others being called Goodman, and sometimes Brother or Neighbor, for a man, and Goodwife, or Goody, for a woman." Hollister's "History of Connecticut" says: "To be called Mr. or have one's name recorded by the Secretary with that prefix 200 years ago was a certain index of the rank of the individual as respects birth, education and good moral character. There were scores of men of good family, and in honorable stations, who still did not possess all the requisite qualities of Mr. College graduates were sometimes called Sir.

In 1640 we find his first official act was in the capacity of commissioner, to decide an equivalent to those who had received inferior meadow lands. In this brief sketch we could not follow him in all his different transactions and offices from year to year till his death; suffice it to say that in all his different offices and numerous public duties, of watchings, trainings, arbitrations between contending settlers, disputed boundaries of farms and towns, adjusting differences of contending neighbors, road commissioner, constable, and juror, he was a man of courage, enterprise, intelligence, probity and piety, a just man whose counsels were sought and judgments respected. He was largely engaged in buying and selling lands and we know not what besides. The colonial records give us an idea of the diversity of his activities and occupations, and also that he was equal socially to any of the colonists, that he lived in a manner befitting his condition, and carefully provided for his children the means of starting in life.

Mr. Tuttle was the father of eight sons and four daughters. Two sons died unmarried; the ten other children married and, with their descendants, furnish material for a genealogy of seven hundred and fifty-four pages. His numerous descendants are found in all the various professions and occupations of life. At this time of writing, October, 1907, one of his descendants, the Rt. Rev. Daniel Sylvester Tuttle, who was consecrated bishop May 1, 1867, when only thirty years of age, is the senior and presiding Bishop of the Protestant Episcopal Church, in its triennial convention in session at Richmond, Virginia. Scores of ministers and all other professions bear the name. Only one son settled in East Haven, and now the name is very sparingly represented; but there are many bearing other names through whose veins courses the Tuttle blood. Perhaps the Hughes family, particularly one branch, has more than any others not bearing the name, as the Tuttles and Hughes married and intermarried.

BENJAMIN LINGE, 1639.

Benjamin Linge is recorded as a first settler at Stoney river. It is doubtful if he ever built in East Haven, as he had no family excepting his wife. His house was at the corner of College and Grove streets. Dr. Stiles, in his "History of the Judges," gives an account of Col. John Dixwell, one of the regicides, who condemned to death King Charles I of England and, on the restoration of the crown to his son, Charles II, fled to America. "Colonel Dixwell put up with two sedate old people who had no children. Mr. Linge at his death requested Dixwell to assist his wife, and his wife to be kind to Dixwell. Mr. Linge left all his property, which was inventoried at £900, to his wife, and Dixwell assisted in settling the estate, and afterwards, not knowing any better way of assisting, married her."

Colonel Dixwell, to avoid detection, passed under the name of James Davids. Another record of Dr. Stiles says: "James Davids and Joanna Linge, widow of Benjamin, were married Nov. 3d, 1673. She died between Nov. 15th & 26th, same year, leaving her homestead to him." Colonel Dixwell, alias James Davids, married Bathsheba Howe, October 23, 1677. A son by this marriage settled as a goldsmith in Boston, whose descendants erected the monument, enclosed with an iron fence, back of Center Church, New Haven. This account of Dixwell may seem foreign to the subject of East Haven history, which it is; but as this rehash of its early times is written by request, bits of history connected with the biography of persons and events, although not directly connected with the subject, will be introduced, with the desire of furnishing something instructive and interesting. Therefore the digression is considered pardonable.

WILLIAM ANDREWS, 1639.

The first of this name to come to America was William Andrews, a native of Hampshire, England, and a carpenter by occupation. He was one of the fifty-three persons who shipped with Capt. William Cooper, on the James, of London, from Hampton, England, in April, 1635, and landed in Boston, where he was made a freeman the same year. He came to New Haven with Rev. Mr. Davenport in 1638, and in 1639 was chosen one of the twelve men to form the first church, which was constituted August 22, 1639; although he was not elected out of that number as one of the seven pillars, he was received as one of the members into fellowship as a member of other approved churches.

Mr. Andrews was a carpenter, and seems to have been a master builder, as he contracted in 1639 to build the first meetinghouse. He let out some parts of the work to others, who sublet to still other parties, who failed to make the roof of the tower and turret to keep out wet, whereupon a question arose, which the court advised them to consult together for settlement.

Military discipline was very early established in New Haven Colony, and only church members could become military officers, and when once appointed the mention of the title was never omitted, either in writing or speaking to or of the person, as it was considered a high honor. In 1642 the number of persons subject to military duty was two hundred seventeen, divided into four squadrons, each commanded by a sergeant, and William Andrews was appointed a sergeant. In

1644 a bridge was built over Stoney river, on the road
to Totoket, by William Andrews, for which he charged
the town of New Haven £3. 8s. 9d., and it was commented upon as being a fine piece of work. In 1651 it
was finally agreed and ordered that William Andrews
and others "shall have the neck of land by the sea-side,
beyond the Cove, and all the meadows belonging to
it below the Island with a rock upon it." In 1660
New Haven Colony, wishing to set out the bounds
between itself and Connecticut Colony with lasting
marks, appointed a committee for this work of which
William Andrews was a member. In seating the meetinghouse he occupied the fifth seat from the pulpit,
an honorable position.

His sons died young, except Nathan, who was born
in Boston in 1638, and removed to Wallingford in
1670. His house and home were on Main Street,
where he owned land. William Andrews died March
4, 1676. His son Nathan had two sons, Daniel and
Jonathan, and it is inferred that the present East
Haven Andrews family descended from one of them.
There was a Timothy who married Rachel Adkins.
They came from Wallingford. As the name of Nathan
has been kept up in successive generations to the
present day, there is no doubt but that he was their
ancestor. There was another Andrews family that
came from Woodbridge. There were also two Nathans
in this branch; the elder one died in 1776 in the
prison ship, in the war of the Revolution, aged 21;
the younger one fell from a mast in 1798 and died,
aged 19.

MATTHIAS HITCHCOCK, 1639.

Matthias Hitchcock signed the plantation covenant in 1639. Estate, £50; land in first division, 10 acres; 2 in the neck; 5 meadow, 20 in 2d division. All that I find recorded of him is the above (from Atwater's "New Haven Colony"). December 3, 1651, Matthias Hitchcock's name appears on the list of those who "shall have the neck of land by the sea-side beyond the Cove," etc. The Hitchcock family sold their part, and all died or removed from East Haven. There is, however, quite a long line of descendants down to 1760, and record of the death of Deacon Daniel Hitchcock in 1761, also that of his widow in the same year.

EDWARD PATTERSON, 1639.

Edward Patterson was also a plantation signer in 1639. Estate £40. Atwater says: "The name does not occur after 1646." Thomas Smith married the daughter and only child of Edward Patterson, so he became possessor of his share, which introduces Thomas Smith to East Haven in 1662. From him all the Smiths of the town are descended. Edward Patterson died October 31, 1669.

JOHN COOPER, 1639.

John Cooper was also one of the founders in 1639. He seems to have been a man of affairs, as he was employed as agent and sent to Massachusetts for securing recruits from that colony to settle in Delaware, a scheme and plan of the New Haven Colony which ended disastrously; also in 1660 he was appointed a committee "to provide a house for the schoolmaster and a schoolhouse, and therein to use their best endeavors and discretion, whether to buy or build, so as may answer the end, yet with good husbandry for the town as may be." (*Atwater.*) In 1645 he, with others, petitioned for land at Solitary Cove, which was not granted. He was one of the overseers and agents for the Iron Works in East Haven. He died November 23, 1689.

JOHN POTTER, 1639.

John Potter seems to have been a busy man in the colony. His occupation seems to have been a blacksmith, as he is first recorded in 1651 as obtaining 20 acres in the fresh meadows, then in 1662 as obtaining a piece of land on which to build his blacksmith shop. In 1680 he became interested in the Iron Works, but did not carry it on as was contemplated when he bought the farm [which eventually was owned by Jared Bradley], but in the year 1692 he and Thomas Pinion petitioned New Haven for liberty to build a Bloomary on the first spring or brook towards Foxon. We find him of a committee to treat with Branford as to land and line and finish it in 1682. Next year he was appointed one of the number to revise the village records; in 1683 he was chosen to assist in laying out the lots in the 3d division of lands; in 1686 one of three to buy Stable Point, at the lower ferry, to build housing for their horses when they went to New Haven. He died in December, 1707, and left quite a line of descendants, all of whom were worthy citizens, but the name has been extinct for many years in East Haven.

RICHARD BERKLEY, 1639.

Atwater and Savage spell the name Beckley. Sergt. Richard Berkley, with others, petitioned for land beyond Solitary Cove in 1645, but their petition was not granted. In 1651 Richard Berkley renewed the application for himself, but the town refused to grant him the land because other men had applied for it. On December 3, 1651, the application was again renewed and it was finally *"agreed and ordered that* William Andrews, Richard Berkley, Matthias Hitchcock, Edward Patterson and Edward Hitchcock shall have the neck of land by the sea-side, beyond the Cove, and all the meadows belonging to it below the Island with a rock upon it. They are to have the neck entirely to themselves by paying to the Town one penny an acre for 500 acres for every rate, and for their meadows as other men do." This was the settlement at South End. It has been stated that the Rev. Nicholas Street often called it "the garden of his parish." By 1689 these men had sold their lands, so that nearly the whole of South End was owned by James Dennison, John Thompson and Thomas Smith, the latter inheriting his through his wife, who was the only child of Edward Patterson. The Thompsons and Smiths have held possession of the land until the passing generation. Richard Berkley moved to Wethersfield in 1668.

JARVIS BOYKIM, 1639.

Jarvis Boykim, a carpenter by trade, who first came to Charlestown with one servant in 1635-6 from Charrington, in Kent, England, and removed to New Haven with the Davenport company, was one of the signers

of the colony constitution in 1639. He had resided in
Charlestown, Massachusetts, some time before coming
to New Haven, but no further account is recorded of
him.

We now have given all the information available,
at the present time of the very early settlers of East
Haven, which we will style "Thirty-niners," because
they signed the colony constitution at that time. Some
others signed in 1639, but did not come to East Haven
till a later date than the above mentioned.

On the 7th of March, 1644, the colony constitution
was revised and enlarged, and then were added the
names of Matthew Rowe and John Tuthill; and in
July following, Alling Ball, Edmund Tooly, Thomas
Robinson, Sr. and Jr., William Holt, Thomas Barnes,
and Edward Hitchcock; and in August, Peter Mal-
lory and Nicholas Augur. On the 4th of April, 1654,
George Pardee, John Potter, Jr., and in May, Matthew
Moulthrop, Jr., were added. February 7, 1657, John
Davenport, Jr., Jonathan Tuthill and John Thompson
subscribed; May 1, 1660, Nathaniel Boykim and
Thomas Tuttle.

Matthew Rowe, 1644.

Matthew Rowe's death is the first one recorded of
the early settlers. He left two sons, John and Stephen.
From them have descended quite a long line. Next to
the Brown farm, Matthew Rowe, Jr., had his farm.
This Matthew was a grandson of the settler. The
lots about Dragon Point between the Davenport and
Ferry farms were laid out, but lay dormant several
years. The transaction relative to that subject stands
thus on record:

February 13, 1670, "the town by vote granted that those that have land on the east side, about Dragon point, shall have liberty to lay their lots together, and to begin at which end they please. And the townsmen are hereby appointed to settle it with them both in respect to convenient highway, and also how far their lots shall run in length from the river." In 1703 these lots were occupied, and Matthew Rowe, Jr., had his farm there. This may be called the settlement of Fair Haven.

The term Dragon (which will hereafter be called Fair Haven) was so called from a sandy point of that name about forty rods below the bridge, on the eastern side of the river. The tradition is that at the time of the first settlement of New Haven this point was a place of resort for seals, who lay here and basked themselves in the sun. At that early period these animals were called dragons, hence the name Dragon Point.

The Rowe family has always been characterized for its enterprise, activity and intelligence, and has generally led in business matters and mercantile pursuits of the place. One line produced a succession of deacons for several generations.

ALLING BALL, 1644.

In 1649, "It was ordered that Mr. Davenport, pastor of the Church, shall have his meadow, and the upland for his second division, both together on the East side of the East-River, where himself shall choose, with all the conveniency the place can afford for a farme, together with the natural bounds of the place, whether by creeks or otherwise." He accordingly laid out a tract of land about a mile square and containing about 600 acres above the point. In 1650 Alling Ball became his farmer, and was exempted from military service while he continued in Mr. Davenport's employment. Probably those of the name of Ball descended from this early settler.

WILLIAM HOLT, 1644.

William Holt, born in England in 1610, came to New Haven as early as 1644, where he signed the constitution of the colony in that year, but removed to Wallingford about 1675. His death occurred in 1683. His line of descent seems to be John, Joseph, Daniel, who apparently was the first Holt born in East Haven in 1711. Mr. Holt was one of the prominent men of the town and took much interest in public affairs. He died June 11, 1756.

Dan Holt, son of Daniel, born in East Haven in 1744, was a lieutenant in a company that went to the assistance of New York during its occupancy by the British in 1776. He died in 1829. Philemon Holt, son of Daniel, born in 1775, was a very prominent man, of rare business capacity and integrity. He filled all of the various town offices, from time to time, and represented his town in the state legislature four terms. The name is now extinct in East Haven.

THOMAS BARNES, 1644.

Thomas Barnes signed the colony constitution in 1644. He and his brother Daniel settled on the plain south of Muddy river. His son Thomas seems to have been the founder of the Barnes family in North Haven.

The name is now nearly, if not quite, extinct on East Haven soil, but all the different branches of the Barnes family trace their origin to Thomas of New Haven, 1644.

PETER MALLORY, 1644.

Peter Mallory signed the plantation covenant in 1644. It is a matter of regret that no record of this family has been found, but it is presumed all the New Haven and Fair Haven families descended from this follower of Rev. Mr. Davenport.

GEORGE PARDEE, 1654.

George Pardee was apprenticed to Francis Brown, tailor, 1644, to stay five years, and was married to Martha Miles by the governor, October 20, 1650. "Marriages were not solemnized by a minister of religion, but, according to the Puritan view of propriety, by a magistrate. The requirement that marriage should be contracted before an officer of the civil authority was a protest against the position that marriage is a sacrament of the Church, which the Church of England believes; and at this early date a minister had no legal authority to pronounce a couple husband and wife, though the bride be his own daughter." (*Hollister.*) This Francis Brown is recorded as being one of the seven men who remained in Quinnipiac the winter after Mr. Eaton had explored the country and decided to return and settle there the next spring.

The ferry at Red Rock had been operated by Francis Brown, but in 1650 George Pardee took it.

Francis Brown, the first of that family, died in 1668. George Pardee was afterwards allowed to build a house there at his own expense, and in 1670 the Ferry farm was granted to him, which was left by him to his son George, and it continued in the line of his descendants until about 1870, when the name was extinct and the property was divided and streets cut through and lots sold for residences. We must conclude George Pardee made good use of his time while an apprentice, besides using the thimble and goose.

A colony school was established in the autumn of 1660, but it was hard work to keep it up and it was thought best to discontinue it, so "the town of New Haven negotiated with Geo. Pardee, one of their own people, to teach the children English and to carry them on in Latin so far as he could. £20 were allowed this year out of the town treasury, and the rest to be paid by patrons of the school." (*Atwater.*) When the time for which he was engaged had expired, the colony of New Haven had been absorbed into the colony of Connecticut and thus lost its jurisdiction. July 18, 1678, Mr. Pardee bought 33 acres at the Cove of the Gregson estate, and in 1716 his son George, Jr., bought the remainder of the farm, which remained in the name until after 1824. George Pardee died in 1700.

The name of Pardee has always been an honorable one in East Haven, and its members have filled various offices of church and state down to the passing generation. Mr. Isaac Pardee was one of the staunch men of his time, firm and sound in principle, a worthy example. He was succeeded by two sons. Mr. Joseph

Pardee was town treasurer for many years, and Mr. Bradley Pardee was selectman and held other offices for years.

WILLIAM LUDDINGTON, 1662.

The first mention that is recorded of William Luddington in colonial records is that he died at the Iron Works in East Haven in 1662. He was the first of this name and family. He left a son William from whom a long line has descended, many of whom have filled various offices of church and state all through these succeeding generations. Thomas (son of the first William) removed to Newark, New Jersey. His eldest son was John.

MATTHEW MOULTHROP, 1662.

Matthew Moulthrop is named among the planters of New Haven, but for some reasons unknown, in the list of persons numbered, estates and land division, a blank is registered against his name. In 1651 14 acres were granted him in East Haven in the fresh meadow. In 1667 he bought land of the widow of William Andrews at South End. He died December 22, 1668, and was succeeded by his son, Matthew, who appears in various offices of the town. The name is now nearly, if not quite, extinct on East Haven soil.

THOMAS SMITH, 1662.

Atwater's "Colonial History" says: "In consequence of the decision of Thomas Nash, who was a gunsmith, to settle in New Haven, serious inconvenience was experienced for want of a smith till 1652.

Thomas Smith came from Fairfield on the invitation of the planters, who gave him a considerable tract of land on condition of serving the town in the trade of a smith upon just and moderate terms for the space of five years." He married the daughter and only child of Edward Patterson, one of the South End men, and so became possessor of his share. Capt. Thomas Smith, the father of the Smith family, died November 16, 1724, aged about 90.

JOHN THOMPSON, 1662.

The three Thompson brothers, Anthony, John and William, came from Lenham, county of Kent, England. In 1887 Rev. E. E. Atwater, while searching out the Atwater genealogy in England, came across the baptism of Anthony Thompson, August 30, 1612, in Lenham, in Kent. This discovery led him, through his own connection and descent from the Thompson family, to prepare a paper on the birthplace of Anthony Thompson, one of the planters of New Haven, which was read before the New Haven Colony Historical Society October 6, 1887, and which stated that the house of his birth was still standing.

Anthony Thompson signed the colony constitution at New Haven in June, 1639. February 7, 1657, John Thompson subscribed. Thomas Harrison, one of the proprietors who bought land at South End, sold his share at South End and land at Muddy river to John Thompson. From this ancestor has descended a large family, influential in the town since its settlement.

The first settler, John Thompson, father of the East Haven Thompsons, died December 11, 1674, twelve

years after coming to East Haven. He was succeeded by his son John, whom we find active in settling
boundary questions, in the division of land, revising
village records, as selectman, collector of rates, and
various other duties, up to the time of his death,
February 13, 1693. The Thompson family has, in
all its different branches, held offices of trust and
confidence down to the present time.

Stephen Thompson, born December 25, 1723, who
was one of the building committee of the "Stone
Church," and was badly injured (as told elsewhere),
was the father of four sons. He built a house for each
one, which are all standing to-day (1907), two of
which have never been out of the name and descent.
His son Amos' house is on the east side of the Green,
Moses' house was built on the southeast corner of
the Green on the site of Rev. Jacob Hemingway's
house, which was burned. This house now stands on
Hemingway avenue, having been moved there in 1898.
Stephen's house stands on the corner of Main street
and Hemingway avenue. The fourth house he built
on the corner of Main street and Thompson avenue,
where he died, and his youngest son, James, came into
possession of it, in which he reared a family of ten
children, nine of whom were boys. This son, Capt.
James Thompson, filled all the different offices of the
town, and among others was elected to the state
legislature as representative of his town ten terms,
always serving with ability and distinction. He was
succeeded in this office by his son James, and three
grandsons, the late John Woodward Thompson, James
S. Thompson and Edward Foote Thompson, who is
now serving his second term as county commissioner.

His residence is that of his father, grandfather and great-grandfather, where five successive generations have lived.

SAMUEL HEMINGWAY, 1662.

Samuel Hemingway, son of Ralph and Elizabeth (Hewes) Hemingway, was born in Roxbury, Massachusetts, in June, 1636. Ralph Hemingway was active in town affairs and a member of Roxbury Church. He brought a large property with him, and in 1638 was one of the largest taxpayers and land owners in Roxbury. His wife was also wealthy. His eldest son, Samuel, settled in New Haven and later moved to East Haven, in 1662, where he married Sarah Cooper, a daughter of John Cooper, the agent of the Iron Works in East Haven. We find him a very busy and influential man, serving the town in many and some difficult capacities, such as settling boundary questions, securing mill grants, revising village records, selectman, looking after village grants and privileges, town clerk and other minor duties. He was a neat and handsome penman. His house was not far from the furnace, and as he was interested in the milling business, probably never changed it. He was the first man to send a son to Yale College. He was rated the third richest man in the town, which was only a few pounds less than the highest. He died September 20, 1711, aged 75 years, and was succeeded by his two sons, John and Abraham, who took the stand and place of their father in public affairs.

We have only to look over the town records of East Haven to see the frequency of the Hemingway name in all the varied policies and happenings of the place.

The name of John has been continued by generations succeeding each other to the present day. John 4th was widely known and justly popular throughout the state, while the name of his son Merit of Watertown, Connecticut, is daily carried into and read in nearly every household in the Union, on the spools and silks bearing the name of "M. Heminway & Sons, silk manufacturers, Watertown, Conn." The house where Merit Heminway (as he holds to the old spelling) was born in 1800 is still standing, in a good state of preservation, on Main street, near the Branford line.

The descendants of Abraham and Enos settled in the north part of the town, near the North Haven line, and have displayed the same characteristics of family down to the present day. "Enos Hemingway served in the state legislature of Connecticut from 1797 to 1809, the longest term in its history." His twin son, Willis Hemingway, was legal eye and ear for Fair Haven for forty years or more. No man ever lived who enjoyed the love and confidence of his townsmen more than his eldest son, Samuel Hemingway, particularly those of small means. If they had anything to invest Samuel Hemingway was the man to whom it was intrusted, and this confidence always returned them a good percentage. The reputation of his financial ability, and the strictest integrity, elected him to the presidency of the Second National Bank of New Haven, long years before his sudden and widely lamented death. His mantle has fallen upon his two sons, Samuel Hemingway and James Smith Hemingway. The former is now president of the Second National Bank, and the latter treasurer of the New Haven Savings Bank. The sons of Col. Willet

Hemingway, the twin brother of Esquire Willis, are all noted financiers and successful business men of the highest integrity and social standing.

RALPH RUSSELL, 1664.

Ralph Russell came to East Haven about 1664, at the establishment of the Iron Works. John Russell, his brother, was a potter in the furnace. In 1664 a piece of land was granted to Ralph Russell by the advice of the town, probably to induce him to become a settler, as all trades were considered benefits to the young colony. Ralph Russell died in 1679 and in the same year the Iron Works were given up. It is a tradition in the Russell family that the death of the principal workmen produced this change. Some authorties say the ore in North Haven was exhausted. His descendants became large landholders in the vicinity of what is now called Russell street, and the land is still (1907) in the possession of his line of descent. The East Haven Russells seem to be in no way connected with the Branford and North Branford Russells. The latter descended from Rev. Samuel Russell, who was pastor of Branford Church forty-three years and in whose study Yale College was founded, of which he was librarian thirty years.

Lieut. John Russell, eldest son of Ralph, was one of the committee chosen April 25, 1706, to attend to church matters. When the first meetinghouse was built in 1706, John Russell was one of the overseers; when the second wood house was built, Capt. John Russell was one of the building committee. In "seating the meeting house," Capt. John Russell was one of the six chosen to perform that honorable duty.

Capt. John Russell died February 13, 1724, aged 59 years. Lieut. John Russell succeeded his father in public affairs. He is called ensign in 1703, when he was chosen, with others, to manage the concerns of the village. April 24, 1707, the village voted to sell 600 acres on the lower end of the half-mile, and John Russell was one of the six men who bought this land and divided it among themselves. He was active in surveying and laying out roads. Lieut. John Russell died October 18, 1774, aged 80 years. The name of Russell has been historic in England ever since Henry VIII created the first Lord Russell, whose title was transformed to Earl of Bedford, and from that to Duke of Bedford, which title stands next to royalty. The Duke of Bedford is the acknowledged chief of the house of Russell. Not that there is any connection between this house and the American Russells, but stranger things than this have happened.

THOMAS MORRIS, 1671.

Thomas Morris signed the plantation covenant at New Haven in 1639, and was admitted a free inhabitant July 3, 1648. That is why he is not mentioned in the first division of lands, having no right of commonage in the order in which they were drawn, but living on one of the small lots which had been freely given to thirty-two householders. Atwater says: "Thomas Morris dwelt on the bank side (that is on East Water street) and east of the four proprietors, whose land extended from Union to Chestnut streets (New Haven)." When the first meetinghouse in New Haven needed repairs Thomas Morris was one of the committee to decide "how it may be done, for most

safety to the town and least charge." Doubtless these
men composing the committee were master workmen
having under them journeymen and apprentices. Mr.
Morris wrought as a shipbuilder, but his appointment
on this committee indicates he did not confine himself
to shipbuilding alone. On March 16, 1671, he
bought the little neck having Gregson's farm on the
north and the meadows along Fowler's creek on
the east. His design was to carry on shipbuilding, the
timber there being very suitable for that purpose, but
two years afterwards death put an end to all his
purposes. The date of the deed of the land is on
the house, 1671.

EXTRACTS FROM THE MORRIS TREE.

"Tradition in the family affairs affirm that a singular incident
made Mr. Morris acquainted with the value of the soil, and
the excellence of the timber for ship building on the tract
of land now known as Morris Point. It seems he once left
his cart, with a load of wood on it, standing near the edge of
the bank where he lived, the base of which met the water of
the harbor. A company of young people who were visiting
at his house coveted the sport of seeing the cart roll down
the bank, and put it in motion. They did not calculate the
velocity it would acquire in the descent, nor the distance to
which it would move. They soon beheld it floating at too
great a distance to be reached and drifting in the direction of
the Cove, on the East Haven side, where it was fortunately
driven ashore and recovered. It was his excursion to obtain
the cart that brought the quality of the timber and the land
to his notice.

"His negotiations for the purchase of the Point were in
1688, but he did not receive the deed from the court till 1671.
From him it passed into the hands of his son Eleazer, by whom
it was inherited by his son John. John had no children and
gave it to Amos, one of the sons of his brother James. This
Amos was the first proprietor who resided upon the farm,

and it has never ceased to be in the hands of his descendants. He was a man of extraordinary enterprise, and of undoubted piety, a Puritan of the best type, a deacon in the East Haven Church. He had in his own possession the means of carrying on commerce abroad, and his papers show that he trafficed with some of the West Indian ports. His wharf accommodated vessels of considerable size and his warehouse often contained large quantities of goods. He also carried on the manufacture of salt, and had a building with five boilers for that purpose. His enterprise and public spirit are still further seen in the fact that he bought the land and constructed at his own expense the causeway across the salt march that leads from the Cove to the road by which the meetinghouse is approached (now Thompson avenue) from all that section of the town."

It was a gigantic work to be undertaken by a single man in those days, yet when the town assumed the road they voted to allow him nothing for it. However, after much altercation and the appointment of several committees, the town voted to allow him $40. His history reaches the Revolution and affords much interesting matter.

JOHN AUSTIN, 1673.

A petition dated October 6, 1656, was presented to the New Haven government by the inhabitants of Greenwich to be received under their care, John Austin being one of the signers. In 1676 he bought land of William Fowler on the east side. He seems to have had his house on the north side of the Green, and to have been a man of considerable means, from his list. He, with others, obtained a deed from the Indians for Stable Point, for housing for their horses when they went to New Haven, which is the point just north of Tomlinson Bridge. He died February 22, 1690, the father of the East and New Haven Austins. He was succeeded by his son Joshua, who seems to have been quite a man of affairs.

John Chidsey, 1681.

The first mention of this good man in New Haven is in 1656, when an honorable seat in the meetinghouse is assigned him. In 1681 Deacon John Chidsey, a tanner and shoemaker, settled on the north side of the Green, on a three square lot of about three acres, between John Potter and John Austin. Afterwards ten acres were granted him by the village on the west side of the fresh meadows, which ever since has been known as Chidsey's field and Chidsey's hill. Mr. Havens, in his centennial sermon, credits Chidsey's hill as the one on Main street now opposite Forbes place, which is an error. Chidsey's hill commenced at the corner of Peat Meadow road and Main street, and ran west to nearly the Four Corners. The field was later bought by the Woodwards. In March, 1683, he "proposed to the village to have a third division of land among us equal to ten heads, and £100 estate, which he doth apprehend to be 60 acres; and for the future he will be engaged to pay towards the expenses of the village after the rate of £200 rateable estate, until his estate shall amount to £200, and then to rise as his estate shall rise."

He was deacon of the church in New Haven, residing only seven years in East Haven and dying December 31, 1688. He was succeeded by his two sons, Caleb and Ebenezer. The North Guilford branch of Chidseys descended from his son Joseph. His son Caleb succeeded him in the deaconship, but he filled this office in East Haven, being one of the church's first deacons. He died February 20, 1713. At a village meeting December 23, 1703, the inhabitants voted that they would take up their village grant. In April, 1704, Caleb Chidsey was chosen moderator, and Ebenezer Chidsey clerk. Caleb Chidsey was one of the committee chosen to go to New Haven and discourse about the differences they speak of between them and us. He was treasurer of the money coming from the sale of the "half-mile." Ebenezer Chidsey was clerk of the village from 1702 to time of his death, September 26, 1726.

The two brothers were chosen with John Potter to treat with Mr. Hemingway to become their first minister, also respecting forming the church in 1710, and so we may continue to trace the good offices of the Chidsey name through the town records all along down to the present day. The late Mr. Samuel Chidsey was one of the active men of the town up to his death, and his son, Samuel R. Chidsey, is following in the footsteps of his father; besides many others of the name are to be found doing their duty as interested and capable citizens, descendants of a worthy ancestor.

Isaac Bradley, 1683.

The first mention made of Isaac Bradley is on Branford records in 1674. He is then noticed as a "sojourner at New Haven," and the town granted him a home lot of two acres at Canoe Brook. The term "sojourner" would imply that he did not intend to make New Haven his permanent abode, and the subsequent grant of land to him in Branford, that he was a man desirable for the colony; otherwise he could not have obtained two acres at Canoe Brook. At that period no man could obtain land, which had not been previously taken up, without the consent of the town, and, in many instances, could not sell it to another, even if it had been granted to him. This was done in order to keep out undesirable inhabitants. Mr. Bradley being a carpenter, the town no doubt considered him a valuable acquisition. After nine years he removed to East Haven.

The village had granted one acre of land to Joseph, son of Ralph Russell, west to Stoney river, which he soon sold to John Potter, and John Potter the same day conveyed it to Isaac Bradley, on which he built his house. On the post road near Stoney river were Daniel Bradley and his sons, Stephen, Timothy and Jacob. Ebenezer Chidsey bought Isaac Bradley's house north of Daniel Bradley. Isaac Bradley, father of the East Haven Bradleys, died January 12, 1713. Isaac Bradley, Jr., died, unmarried, July 10, 1716.

From his three sons, William, Samuel and Daniel, descended one of the largest number of families of one name in the town (excepting the Smith family, which is an exception everywhere). In influence, social position and wealth, they took a high rank, and the town records are plentifully sprinkled with the name of Bradley in every capacity. Josiah Bradley was the squire of the town from 1787 to 1806. At one time the name was so numerous that it was a synonym for East Haven, as it was often remarked in other towns, "to say Bradley was to name the whole of East Haven." Like many other old colonial families, the name has been greatly depleted by death, removals and the usual decline in the number of children, in families, until at present there are comparatively few families left; but those few still retain the characteristics of the family and are valued citizens. Among the younger members is Mr. Henry H. Bradley.

THOMAS GOODSELL, 1692.

Thomas Goodsell appears on Branford records in 1679. He married Sarah Hemingway, daughter of Samuel, June 4, 1684, and moved to East Haven in April, 1692. Little is recorded of him, although what is signifies he was a man of note in the community. His home was where the present Bailey house stands, and the small rise of ground just west has always been called Goodsell's hill. His estate is rated among the highest in town, therefore we must take it for granted that, with the high social position of his wife and his own good name and character, coupled with his wealth, he was a man of influence. He died May 16, 1713, and left three sons, two of whom, Thomas and John, graduated from Yale College in the same class, in 1724, John being only nineteen. The name has long been extinct in East Haven. Rt. Rev. Daniel Goodsell, Methodist Episcopal bishop, whose summer home is at Granite Bay, is a descendant of this Goodsell family of East Haven.

All the information obtainable of the first settlers up to 1700 has now been given. There are three others after that date of which mention will be made. Doubtless many moved into the town, remaining only a short time. Emigration was as rife then as at any subsequent period, much more so than one hundred and fifty years afterwards.

John Woodward, 1716.

Rev. John Woodward was graduated at Cambridge College, England, in 1693, was ordained pastor of the church at Norwich, Connecticut, December 6, 1699, assisted in the council that compiled the Saybrook Platform in 1708, was dismissed from his pastoral charge September 13, 1716, and was admitted an inhabitant of New Haven, December 24, of the same year. He obtained liberty of the town to buy of the Indians one acre of land to accommodate his house and bought various pieces of land around him, thus becoming possessed of a convenient farm. In 1738 he was chosen moderator of the society meeting. This is his first appearance on the village records. He seems to have lived a retired life after coming to East Haven, not taking any very active part in the affairs of the day, but devoting his attention to agriculture. No record is found of acting in his professional calling after coming to East Haven. He died February 14, 1746, and was succeeded by four sons, all of whom married and settled in East Haven. Their families being mostly daughters, the name did not become numerous, but those who did retain it became among the largest landed proprietors of the town, and in point of wealth, popularity and influence took high rank, which, with their ancestral domains, they hold to the present time.

Samuel Forbes, 1728.

Samuel Forbes is mentioned in 1728 and was employed in shipbuilding on the point below the mill.

This is all the early record that was given of him. It has always been a tradition in the family that he was a Scotchman. Certainly the thrifty, cautious, skillful and successful habits of his descendants, male and female, display the acknowledged traits of the "canny Scot." As a people, they rather avoid participation in public affairs; but when once enlisted they always show the same fidelity of purpose and exact observance of duty that they manifest in their own concerns. At the present time, Mr. Frederic Forbes is one of the successful business men of the town. Mr. Albert Forbes, who so lately has been called from us, filled many offices of public trust for many years, and was one of the solid men of the town.

DEODATE DAVENPORT, 1729.

Deodate Davenport came from Stamford and appears first on record, 1729. He was the great-grandson of Rev. John Davenport of New Haven, 1639. Mr. Davenport's grant of six hundred or more acres on the east side of the Quinnipiac had lain dormant till this great-grandson came to New Haven, and had the land which the Davenport family owned surveyed and located. He was the son of John Davenport, 3d, who was the third pastor of the church in Stamford. The farm, or tract of land, was in the northwest part of the town, what has since been called "Hemingway town," Dana Bradley's farm and vicinity. He was one of the early deacons of the church and a public-spirited man. The name has been extinct for many years.

JOSEPH BISHOP, 1751.

Joseph Bishop came from Guilford. Only one son, Ichabod, is accounted to East Haven. His sons were men of great activity and enterprise. His son Elias was known in several states as an extensive dealer and shipper of horses and mules; his son John was a lifelong resident of East Haven on the old homestead in South End, a very worthy and reliable man, warden of St. James Episcopal Church for a long period. One grandson is Professor William H. Bishop, formerly professor at Yale, author, and now consul general at Palermo, Italy; another grandson is J. Halsted Bishop of Chicago. None of the family is in town now.

All the early settlers have been sought out and recorded as far as possible; facts have been looked up from different reliable sources, and if any have been overlooked, who seem entitled to notice, it is because nothing could be found of them. That there are many names of families who are not mentioned is very true. In every community there are scores and scores of good men, capable in every way, men of family, wealth and social position, who never drift into public affairs,— they do not like the notoriety, they shrink from the responsibility, they cannot bear public criticism, by nature not being adapted to it. It is not their fault; we see this difference between brothers in the same family. On the other hand, others without any apparent effort float along on the stream of public activities, as easily as a duck takes to water, the more they are buffeted the better they like it, and it seems to stimulate them to greater action.

We have now seen that East Haven was settled by the very best people of the New Haven Colony. They were all men of principle, not only that, but of piety as well. They walked as they believed. They had left country, home and relatives to found a new government on new principles founded upon the law of the Scriptures, as they saw the right. Besides, they were a class of intelligent, religious, heroic men. "God sifted a whole nation that he might send choice grain over into this wilderness."

There are some expressions which it may be well to explain. One is "granting land" to individuals. At the present time it has the smack of pauperism; not at all so in early times. It was not receiving anything from the town; it was giving title to land bought. It must be remembered that all the land bought of the Indians was in trust for all the people, and no sale could be made without the consent of the town, or court as it was sometimes called. The expression freeholder, or inhabitant, may not be understood. No person could be an inhabitant till he was the possessor of real estate; that made him a freeholder, but he could not be a freeholder unless he was a church member; and if he was a church member, then by a vote of the town he could be granted real estate, or land. Thus he had a voice in both church and state. This was the pet idea of Rev. John Davenport, which he formulated in Holland while an exile before coming to America. The New Haven Colony consisted of New Haven, Branford, Guilford, Stamford and Southold on Long Island. This church member rule was in use in the Massachusetts and Plymouth colonies.

Some dissatisfied with this law came to Connecticut and settled at Hartford, Windsor and Wethersfield, and other towns, which became the Connecticut Colony, where church membership was not required.

In 1639 the first constitution for the Connecticut Colony was made, permitting all men to vote who had taken the oath of allegiance to the commonwealth. All men were equal before the law and each man had a voice in the government. This is why Connecticut is called the "Constitution State," and upon which principle the United States constitution is founded.

It has often been a source of inquiry why Rev. Mr. Davenport left his people in New Haven, after many of them had followed him to Holland, and then with many more had crossed the ocean to New Haven. When New Haven Colony submitted to the union with Connecticut, it gave Mr. Davenport a shock of disappointment which fell upon him like a blow. He could not bear to see the extinction of the little sovereignty whose foundation he had laid, and for which he had so strenuously contended. He lost interest in his dearly loved colony. His cherished idea of church membership government was sacrificed and New Haven no longer was attractive to him. It was rather the monument of a great defeat and sorrow. In a letter to a friend he writes, "Christ's interest in New Haven Colony is miserably lost."

Just at this time he received a call to the First Church in Boston to champion the cause of orthodoxy against the "half-way covenant." His church was loth to give him up and never did give a full consent. He determined to accept the invitation, contrary to the wishes of his church and congregation, and arrived in

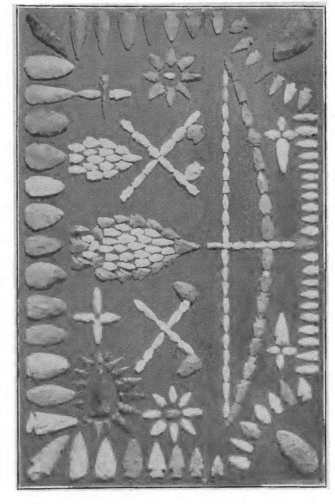

SPEAR HEADS AND ARROW POINTS FOUND ON THE HUNTING GROUNDS OF THE QUINNIPIAC INDIANS. COLLECTED AND OWNED BY CAPTAIN GEORGE EDWIN LANCRAFT.

Boston May 2, 1668, but his ministry was of short duration. He died in Boston, of apoplexy, March 15, 1670, in the 73d year of his age. Thus passed away East Haven's first minister. He was as much theirs as New Haven's, as he was the only minister and East Haven was New Haven.

Mr. Davenport was succeeded by the Rev. Nicholas Street, who was the great-grandfather of Rev. Nicholas Street of East Haven. He was born in Bridgewater, England, a graduate of Oxford in 1624, came to New England between 1630 and 1638, and was a colleague of Mr. Hooker in Taunton, Massachusetts, and afterwards had sole charge of the church there till he came to New Haven, November 23, 1659, when he was installed teacher. Dr. Bacon says, "The distinction between pastor and teacher was theoretical, rather than of any practical importance. Both were in the highest sense ministers of the gospel; as colleagues they preached by turns on all public occasions and had an equal share in discipline. The pastor's special work was to attend to exhortation, and therein to administer a word of wisdom. The teacher was to attend to doctrine, and therein to administer a word of knowledge. The pastor and teacher gave themselves wholly to the ministry and their studies, and accordingly received their support from the people. They might properly be called clergymen at the present day, pastor and assistant." [*Bacon's Hist. Dis.*] This custom was a relic from the Church of England, where three grades of ministers are often found in one parish, viz.: rector, vicar and curate. After the first ministers in New England died, only one person offi-

ciated as minister of the parish, and was generally
called pastor. Properly speaking, Mr. Street was the
second minister of Center Church, New Haven, from
1668 to the time of his death, April 22, 1674.

This family has always been a noted one in the
annals of New Haven Colony, and to his great-grandson, Nicholas Street of East Haven, stands one of
the grandest monuments of his labors which can be
found in the whole of Connecticut, if not in the whole
of New England, "The Old Stone Church," erected in
1774. Typical of the Puritan by its solidity, strength
and endurance; of the times by its refined absence of
ornament.

Rev. Nicholas Street left four sons, two of whom
had no sons to perpetuate the name. The sons of
Nicholas Street were Philip, Edwin and Owen. The
former died in early life, leaving no family. The latter,
Rev. Owen Street, graduated from Yale in 1837 and
was a successful pastor of several churches, finally
settling in Lowell, Massachusetts. He was present at
the "Centennial Celebration" of his grandfather's
church in East Haven, 1874, gave the invocation
prayer, and contributed two original hymns, which
were sung at the time; also an after-dinner address of
much historical interest.

Four of the sons of Mr. Elnathan Street settled in
East Haven. Mr. Benjamin Street answered the call
of his country in the trying times of the Civil war.
After 1850 Mr. Augustus Street settled in East Haven,
was chosen town clerk in 1894, serving in that capacity
till his death, April 30, 1902. Previous to that time he
was town treasurer for many years, also treasurer of
the East Haven Congregational Church. He was a

popular town officer, his name sometimes appearing on both political tickets. He left an only child, Miss Lottie E. Street, who was appointed assistant town clerk previous to her father's decease. Mr. Thaddeus Street was a very successful farmer and dairyman in East Haven, where he spent his whole life. He was elected deacon of the Congregational Church August 30, 1872, and died January 16, 1882. He left three sons, Samuel H., Frederick B. and Clifford Street, all active business men.

CHAPTER II.

Public Schools.

UR schools in East Haven are under the management of the Town School Committee, consisting of nine members, three of whom are elected every year to continue in office for three years, the change from the old district system having been made in 1898. This committee is again divided into three sub-committees of three members each, one of which, the Committee on Schools, takes the immediate oversight of the schools, examines and recommends the teachers and the amount of salaries to be paid them, and attends to the various other matters relative to attendance, course of study, and discipline. Three more form a Committee on School Buildings and Fuel. These recommend the janitors and look after all details concerning the buildings. The third sub-committee is the Committee on Books and Supplies.

The town, in its annual meeting, fixes the length of the school year, but the committee as a whole decides as to the date of beginning and closing, and determines the length of the three terms.

Schools and Education.

As the Puritan colony of New Haven brought their schoolmaster with them, and a school was opened before the church was established, it may not be amiss

to give place to education for our second chapter.
When the public school building on the corner of
Lombard and Fillmore streets, New Haven, was
erected and named, the question was often asked,
"Who was Ezekiel Cheever?"

Probably to Horace Day, Esq., who was well versed
in colonial lore, and who was connected with the public
schools of New Haven for over fifty consecutive years,
the name was suggested, as Ezekiel Cheever was the
first schoolmaster in New Haven. He came over with
Mr. Davenport and company, in the ship Hector, from
London. He lived at the corner of Grove and Church
streets, and opened a school in his own house. He
was born in London January 25, 1615, coming to New
Haven in 1639, and was thenceforth the schoolmaster
of the plantation, receiving for some time a yearly
stipend of £20, which in 1644 was increased to £30.
He was one of the chosen twelve for the foundation
work of the church and state, and occasionally
preached, although never ordained. He was an author
of several books, and was chosen one of the first seven
magistrates for the plantation; was a deputy to the
General Court, in 1646, and was probably the third
man of influence in the colony; but, dissenting from
the judgment of the church and its elders in respect
to some cases of discipline, he commented on their
action with such severity that he was himself censured
in 1649. Soon after this he left New Haven and died
in Boston, August 21, 1708, in the 94th year of
his age.

There is no account of schools on record until
the beginning of the last century (1700). Their
deficiency in regard to even a common education was

very great. Some of their public men,—men who sustained various offices and appointments of trust, were unable to write their names.—Their mark is made at the bottom of several instruments on record. Experience taught them the necessity of paying more attention to the education of their children. January 13, 1707, a committee was appointed at a village meeting, "to see after the schools, and agree with a man to keep school in East-Haven, to teach children to read and write." The committee accordingly agreed with Mr. Hemingway to take charge of the school. (This Mr. Hemingway is supposed to be the Rev. Jacob Hemingway.)

In 1728 the village was divided into four districts, and the public money into as many parts, according to the number of children over five years and under fifteen years of age. The next year they agreed to employ a schoolmaster as near the middle of the village as was convenient—some part of the time at South End, and some part at Foxon, according to the number of children from eight to eighteen years of age. In 1732 it was fixed between six and sixteen years. At that time Foxon district included all the families north of the Bloomary brook, and a line running west to Claypit brook. A school was begun in Dragon district (now Fair Haven) in 1730.

The first schoolhouse was on the "Green, or Marketplace," and afterwards east of the present meetinghouse. One stood on the hill near Matthew Moulthrop's house, west of Foxon; and in 1767 one was built a little north of Bloomary brook.

In 1742 the school money was divided thus: Two thirds for the schools below the Bloomary brook, and one third north of that line, and so west, over to Nanny Capel's brook. Foxon district was then very thrifty and populous, but has since declined in wealth and population.

In 1743, "It was voted that the Southend children shall have their proportion of the school money from the age of 4 to 18." In 1769 the village was divided into six school districts. The public school money was derived from the sale of the public lands in Litchfield County.

Though the people of this town have been favored for more than a century with a college at their door, they have not availed themselves of that advantage to give their sons a public education. Only six have enjoyed that privilege, viz.:

Jacob Heminway graduated in 1704.
Thomas Goodsell   "   " 1724.
John Goodsell   "   " 1724.
Jared Potter   "   " 1760.
Asahel Morris   "   " 1789.
Amos Pardee   "   " 1793.

Agreeable to the new law respecting the school fund of this state, a census of the children between the ages of four and sixteen has been taken every year in the month of August.

As soon as the town was divided into districts, the inhabitants of each erected a schoolhouse in accordance with the times. These were considered then very commodious, but at the present day would be thought little better than common storehouses for miscellaneous articles. The houses were oblong in shape, with a narrow hall at one end and a huge stone chimney at the other. Inside was a wide-mouthed fireplace of six feet, to burn the four-foot "back logs and fore sticks." All around the three sides of the room was a shelving desk, fastened to the wall, for writing and "ciphering." The seats were made of the outside slabs of sawmill logs, rounding side down and not infrequently covered with the natural bark. On one side of the chimney was the "dungeon," for the smaller refractory juveniles; on the other, a closet for the teacher's belongings. The smallest children sat on lower movable benches without backs, in front of the older scholars. Another row of movable benches was placed near the fireplace, to accommodate relays at the fireplace during the day, in answer to the frequent request, "Please may I go to the fire?"

The school hours were from nine to twelve A. M. and from one to four P. M. School opened with prayer, then the reading of the New Testament by all who could possibly read words of five or more letters, two verses apiece, round and round the room, reading, writing, "ciphering," with some grammar for the most advanced. The teacher wrote out all the copies in the writing books and made all the pens from goose quills brought by the scholars. All the working days of the week were school days, Saturday afternoon being devoted to learning and reciting the Congregational catechism and a preparation for Sunday.

The teachers "boarded around," that is, each family boarded the teacher so many days for each child of their own, and frequently in case of sickness in the family, or other causes, boarded the teacher for their friends or neighbors. This practice, although quaint and obsolete, was not without its advantages to teacher, parents and pupils. The school year was divided into two terms: the winter term commencing the "Monday after Thanksgiving," taught by a man teacher till about March or after; the summer term, commencing after "Training day in May," and closing during September, taught by a woman teacher. After the boys reached the age of twelve they were employed on the farm, but generally the girls, except the older ones, attended school the year round; the boys all gathered into school when the man teacher took charge, and often continued till they were twenty years old. The women teachers followed the same schedule of instruction, with the addition of sewing, muslin embroidering and "marking samples," with oftentimes lace embroidery, and the ladies of that period were as expert with the needle as they were with the spinning wheel.

After 1800 it was necessary to enlarge the number of studies and geography was introduced. New schoolhouses were built, and in place of the fireplace "Franklin stoves" were introduced, which stood nearer the center of the room, with a huge stovepipe running from the top of the stove across the room and entering the little chimney on the opposite side. This was considered a great improvement, and doubtless it was, but we of to-day would not think of heating the ceiling at the expense of the floor. In winter the scholars had to bury their inkstands in the hot ashes, or put them under the Franklin hearth, to keep them from freezing. No provision was made for water. The scholars in summer brought their penny for a water pail and drinking cup, if the previous season's supply had given out. There were no refrigerators in those days, and the good housewife hung her butter, meat, etc., down the well in pails. Often after the children had drawn a pail full of water from the well, with pole and sweep, which was no small task for their strength, it was caught up by the neighboring owner and thrown away, and the children told not to come again, because they had disturbed the improvised refrigerator.

Things worked along another generation, when the school days were reduced to five and a half, or five days one week and six the next, the day omitted always being Saturday. History was added to the number of studies, and a great improvement made in the text-books used. In 1830 Daboll's Arithmetic, the English Reader, and Murray's Grammar were no longer in use. Readers simplified and better adapted to the taste and understanding of the young were introduced, but Webster's Spelling Book held its own for a long time; and great prominence was given to the study of "fore part of Spelling Book," respecting the use, accent, etc., of letters, also abbreviations, and Roman numbers. That died out in the forties, as well as the every other Saturday custom, and five school days per week was the allotted time. People now began to realize the most unprofitable time of the year for study was during the hot summer months, and gradually the terms were changed to the present length.

It is supposed that the average life of the first schoolhouses built in East Haven was about thirty years, as it is known that the West or Woodwardtown second schoolhouse was built about 1800, and is still standing as a small dwelling house. A record has been found as follows: "A Committee consisting of Ichabod Bishop, Samuel Holt and Daniel Hughes fixed the

site for the old yellow school house on East Haven
Green Apr. 29th, 1799." It is inferred that the people
could not agree as to location, as each man appointed
was a non-resident of the district. This house was
burned in 1862, and the district remained without
a schoolhouse until about 1868. For several years
a school was taught in the old Esquire Bradley house
on Main street, in a very large room on the first floor,
which had served the purpose for town meetings, voting places and justice courts, in the Squire's day. It is
now owned by Mrs. Wyllis Baily. It was built in the
first settling of Stoney river about 1645 by William
Tuttle for his son John, who sold it and the home lot
to John Potter in 1662. Josiah Bradley lived there in
1824. From there the school was moved up to another
old house, corner of Hemingway avenue and River
street, adjoining the Old Cemetery. In 1868 they
erected a new schoolhouse on Main street on the west
side of the Green, which has been enlarged and
remodled into a dwelling house, the residence of Mr.
S. W. Tarr.

In the middle district the old red schoolhouse gave
place to a new one about the middle of the last century,
standing on the same site on High street, which is now
used as a freight house by the railroad. In 1882,
when the west side of the town was annexed to New
Haven, it took off the Quinnipiac, the west or Woodward, and a large share of the South End district,
which left only three districts and a remnant of the
South End district to East Haven. In 1894 occurred
the death of John Woodward Thompson, who left a
substantial legacy to the district, with the proviso that

the east and middle districts unite in one and build a schoolhouse within three years after his death.

John Woodward Thompson, son of James, Jr., and Leura (Woodward) Thompson, was born in East Haven July 22, 1833. He was descended from two of the prominent families of the town, for he was a grandson of Capt. James Thompson, and on the maternal side a direct descendant of Rev. John Davenport of 1639 fame. He was educated in the public schools of the town in his very early years, and later was under the instruction of the late James Frisbie, a graduate of Yale and for many years principal of Branford Academy, so he was well prepared for an active business life. In his personnel he was attractive and gentlemanly, very genial in his nature and agreeable in association; he also liked a good joke, "which is relished by the wisest of men." He retired from business comparatively early, and for several years was an amusing correspondent of the Shore Line Times.

In disposing of his estate, after remembering each of his cousins with a small legacy, and giving to St. Andrew's Methodist Society $1,000, in memory of his mother and grandmother, whose home was the site of the church, he gave the bulk of his property to charitable institutions, and the residue to the Union School district, with the proviso, as stated above, that the east and middle districts consolidate and build a new house within three years after his death.

The first school meeting of the legal voters of the Union School district was held at the Town Hall on Thursday evening, January 24, 1895, by virtue of a notice issued according to the requirements of law, on Friday, January 18, 1895, by S. W. F. Andrews,

THE UNION SCHOOL.

Emeline A. Curtis and William H. Chidsey. At this meeting the legacy of John W. Thompson was accepted, and L. F. Richmond, E. F. Thompson and R. H. Coe were appointed a committee of investigation relative to a suitable site. On February 14 an adjourned meeting was held and the committee reported on five different sites, three on High street, one on Main street, and the lot owned by D. W. Tuttle, next to the Dillon place. A vote was passed thanking the committee and they were discharged as a committee on site, but were continued to investigate disputed claims against the Thompson estate. D. W. Tuttle was appointed to secure legislative action relative to bonding the district. March 21 Henry T. Thompson, Albert Forbes and E. Gilbert were appointed a building committee. The Street lot on High street, just north of the Stone Church on the east side of the road, was selected. The said plot of ground was to cost $2,000 for 120 feet front. At this meeting it was voted to build a brick schoolhouse with not less than four rooms.

On April 18 a vote was taken rescinding a previous vote selecting the Street lot, and May 2 the New Haven Board of Education was appointed, as the law directs, to select a site. July 13 the New Haven Board reported that they had selected a site on the northwest corner of a proposed highway extending west of East Haven Green, and on the Hemingway-Kirkham land. July 24 the site as fixed was changed, by more than a two-thirds vote, to the farther south end of the Hemingway lot, the lot to be 100 by 200 feet. September 26 a special meeting was called and held to reconsider and rescind all former votes relating to a new site and a new schoolhouse. This proposition was defeated by a decisive majority, and at a meeting held January 16, 1896, it was voted that the treasurer give bonds in the sum of $5,000.

A special meeting was called February 5, 1896, "to change the site as now fixed." The proposition was defeated. On February 25 a meeting was held to consider plans and specifications, and March 19 the building committee was given *carte blanche* powers to build a new brick schoolhouse with four rooms, to cost approximately $6,000. The committee was also instructed to furnish the same. The members of the Board of Education of New Haven, by a committee consisting of S. R. Avis, F. A. Betts, J. T. Manson and W. I. Conner, rendered their services gratuitously, for which a vote of thanks was passed.

The following is a copy of Mr. Thompson's letter:

"EAST HAVEN, CONN., Apr. 27th, 1896.

"TO WHOM THIS MAY COME:

"Ground was broken for the school building on Wednesday morning, April 22nd, 1896, by Leonard B. Smith, and the excavation was made by him and Edmund B. Woodward. Brown & Berger are the architects, and R. Redfield & Son subcontractors for the building of the foundation walls; L. V. Treat and Sons, mason builders; D. C. Sperry, carpenter and joiner; and the Fosket & Bishop Co., plumbers and dealers in heating apparatus; all of whom are the contractors with the Union school district for the building and all of the superstructure. Ebenezer Gilbert and Albert Forbes are associated with me as building committee.

"HENRY T. THOMPSON,
"*Chairman of Building Committee.*"

[*From the New Haven Journal and Courier.*]

THE CORNER STONE LAID OF EAST HAVEN'S EIGHT THOUSAND
DOLLAR SCHOOL BUILDING—A SPLENDID SITE AND A FINE
BUILDING—THE SCENE AT THE CORNER STONE LAYING YESTER-
DAY AND THE EXERCISES—THE CONTENTS OF THE BOX IN THE
CORNER STONE.

Yesterday was an ideal spring day, and although the sun
was not altogether in a cloudless sky, yet the weather was well
nigh perfect.

At 11 oclock in the forenoon, April 28th, 1896, the corner
stone of East Haven's new school building was laid with the
assistance of Mr. Redfield, one of the contractors. The princi-
pals were Messrs. Thompson, Andrews and Bradley, chairman
of the building committee, and presiding officer of the Union
school district officials, and secretary of the board of education, in the order named.

L. D. Chidsey, a native of East Haven, born within a stone's
throw of Lake Saltonstall, gave the box, which was covered
by a granite slab from the East Haven shores of Long Island
Sound.

The services were unostentatious. When the box was
placed in position heads were uncovered, and the secretary of
the school board said: "May God's blessing attend those who
assemble here."

When the school building is completed and formally set
apart for school purposes, which will be in September next, the
exercises will be of a noteworthy character.

A portion of the contents of the box, which was prepared
gratuitously for the occasion by Sheahan & Groark of New
Haven, is as follows:

The name of every scholar in the public schools (attested
by the autograph of the teachers, Misses Lord and Woodhull)
at 9.15 o'clock on the morning of the 27th inst.; a letter from
Henry T. Thompson, Esq., chairman of the building committee;
the roster of the New Haven Grays; state report of the state
board of education; a statistical account of the public schools
in East Haven by C. W. Bradley, secretary; a document from
the state board of health; an original notice of a school meeting dated January 30th, 1896; list of officers and students of

Yale University; catalogue of the State Normal Training School; manual of the Congregational church in East Haven; list of church officers, with the names of the two pastors, Rev. Mr. Cook and Rev. Mr. Clark; annual town reports of New Haven, East Haven and Branford; public acts, State of Connecticut, 1895; Connecticut School Register; Fast Day proclamation of Governor Coffin; class day exercises Hillhouse High School; Beckwith's Almanac 1896; a copy each of the Journal and Courier, Evening Register, Morning News, Daily Palladium, Evening Leader, New Haven Union, Shore Line Times, Branford Opinion, Connecticut Republicaner, Catholic News, New York Tribune and Journal of Commerce; a list of the East Haven town officers; a democratic town ticket, also a republican ticket; a program of Washington's birthday anniversary exercises celebrated at the Hyperion theatre on Saturday, February 22; the names of large tax payers in New Haven, April 27th, 1895; the autograph of Mrs. Andrews, postmaster in East Haven; and a copy of the Daily Florida Citizen, sent from Jacksonville by Mrs. Grace A. Bradley, sister of L. S. Bagley, and formerly a teacher in the public schools in East Haven.

PASSING OF THE OLD SCHOOLHOUSES.

THE OLD YELLOW SCHOOLHOUSE.

The old yellow schoolhouse was not the crown
That capped the highest hill in town,
It stood on the public square,
And although its gables were not so fair,
Yet it calls to mind those former days,
Our grandsires trod on learning's ways;
'Twas where they ciphered numbers through,
And solved by Dibble's aid deep problems hard to do,
Then found, in games to boyhood dear,
Escape from study too severe;
In forest shade, and on Saltonstall mountain the wolf to spy,
Adown the hills and on Thompson's meadow the sled to fly;
In near-by field with ball and bat,
To play at "two and three old cat";

And then as fox, with pace not slow,
To chase Mrs. Tyler's geese across the green and through the
    snow.
That men should teach the winter school,
Became the universal rule;
Much brawn the teacher must possess,
Though he might have of knowledge less,
The switch was large and toughened through
And freely plied whenever due.
One thing promoted discipline,
And held the roguish nature in,
It was the never failing rule:
Two strokes at home, for one at school.

The old yellow schoolhouse was a place where met
Staid learned men of every set;
The doctor came, the lawyer, too,
And clergyman, each with his cue;
But 'twas the school committee man
Who terrified the little clan.
Just twice he came in every term
To tell them what and how to learn,
And show the school, and teacher, too,
How very, very much he knew.

How generous teachers then were found
They aired sparebeds the district round!
To spend those long cold wintry nights,
Oft teachers went on queer "invites."
At close of school one winter's day
A bonny lass was heard to say:
"We've butchered pigs and killed the fatted cow,
We're ready for the teacher now."

This boarding round was not all vain,
The child's and parents' hearts they'd gain;
And were they what they ought to be,
The family life, in some degree,
Would rise, expand, and nobler be.

Among our teachers, not a few
Were noble souls as e'er we knew;
In school they more than science taught,
They taught manhood's worth in life and thought,
And if we could, we'd let them know
How through our lives their teachings flow.
But they'll not lack their meed of praise;
Their work will live in other days,
And with an influence sublime,
Will leave its mark throughout all time.

By CHARLES W. BRADLEY,
Secretary School Board.

UNION DISTRICT SCHOOL HOUSE.

Monday, August 31st, 1896, 2 o'clock p. m.

PROGRAMME.

William H. Robinson, Chairman

Music .... Branford Military Band
Invocation .... Rev. D. J. Clark
Music .... Branford Military Band
Presentation of the Building .... By the Building Committee,
Henry T. Thompson, Chairman.
Acceptance in behalf of the District .... Dwight W. Tuttle
Approval by the Board of School Visitors ... Grove J. Tuttle
Music .... Branford Military Band
Remarks .... Horace L. Day
Address .... Charles H. Fowler
Closing Ode. Tune: "America."

COMMITTEES.

Dedication.

Mrs. William H. Robinson.   Albert H. Page.
Miss Lottie E. Street.   Henry T. Thompson.
William H. Robinson.   Dwight W. Tuttle.
Frederick L. Hawkins.   Ebenezer Gilbert.

Reception.

Ebenezer Gilbert.   William H. Robinson.
John S. Tyler.   Edmund B. Woodward.
Leonard R. Andrews.   Augustus Street.

Programme.

Miss Lottie E. Street.   Dwight W. Tuttle.
          Henry T. Thompson.

Music.

Mrs. William H. Robinson.   Henry T. Thompson.

Collation.

Albert A. Page   Frederick L. Hawkins.

In the library of the new school building are twenty-five new volumes of "The Encyclopedia and Dictionary of Arts and Sciences and General Literature." This work is a very valuable and timely addition to the new equipments of the school. There is something more to say, of a pleasant nature, about these books. Information is given that they are the gift of William H. Robinson, Chairman of the Union District School Committee.

The parting of the ways, from the old to the new, had now come. A new era and a greater interest in schools were manifested on all sides. After eleven years of successful operation, the people saw and felt the necessity of just doubling the size of the house and number of rooms of the Union schoolhouse. When school opened in September, 1907, eight rooms were the number instead of four. East Haven now numbers only two school districts, the first, or Union, and the Foxon. The remnant of the South End district, left after annexation of the west part of the town, was taken by the Union district through legislative action. An abstract from the school report of the year ending July, 1907, says:

"With the completion of the new addition to the school building, and affairs adjusted to meet the enlarged facilities, it is confidently expected that the town will have a school plant that will compare favorably with the New Haven schools. In fact, it is absolutely essential that we should maintain the same standard, as in no other way will it be possible for our scholars to pass the examinations for the High School. In reviewing the events of the past year, it is with a feeling of sincere sorrow that we record the death of Frederick L. Hawkins, which occurred June 1st, 1907. He had been a member of this Committee from its inception, and for six years was its Secretary. His high sense of duty, strength of character and many personal charms made him one of the most respected and efficient members of the Committee and community. All with whom he came in contact will hold only the most pleasant memories, and those who knew him best realize keenly that the loss is almost irreparable."

"L. W. Thompson,
"Secretary Town School Committee."

It must not be supposed that East Haven people have been unmindful of the benefits of educational advantages. The public schools have been kept up with regularity and efficiency, so far as circumstances would permit. The schools of the town have always been largely supplemented by those outside its borders. There is scarcely a family but what has had representatives in the city schools and private institutions, at a greater or less distance from home.

More space has been given to this subject than may be thought necessary, but the regret has been so often expressed and the fact deplored, that so little has been recorded of the details and records of building the Stone Church, that it is thought pardonable to transmit to posterity a more minute narration of a movement second only to the church. East Haven is becoming more thickly populated, and with the increase of inhabitants greater advantages of all kinds will be secured, and with its good beginning schools will take first rank in the future. Mr. Charles W. Bradley, secretary of the Board of School Visitors, in his last report before he removed from town, gave a parting shot, which it may be well to remember. He said, "If there was sufficient gratitude in the district, there would be an educational institution known as the "J. Woodward Thompson School."

YALE GRADUATES, EAST HAVEN,

INCLUDING FAIR HAVEN, TO 1882.*

Academic Course.

	Class.	Professions followed.
Dana Goodsell,	....	Theology.
Owen Street,	1837	Theology.
Samuel Miles Brown,	1844	Teaching.
Charles S. Hemingway,	1873	Teaching.
Charles Ives,	1874	Law.
F. Howard Hemingway,	1875	Business.
James Smith Thompson,	1877	Law.
Charles H. Levermore,	1879 .	President Adelphi College.
Edwin C. M. Hall,	1880	Medicine.
E. Otis Hovey	1882	Natural Science, Geology.
Lincoln D. Granniss,	1906	Educator.

*In 1882 Fair Haven and the western part of East Haven were annexed to New Haven. After 1882, East Haven graduates only are recorded.

YALE UNIVERSITY.

Law Course.

Charles Holt Fowler,	1861
Dwight Williams Tuttle,	1867
Grove J. Tuttle,	1875
S. W. F. Andrews,	1875
Rev. Edwin E. Hall,	1875

Scientific Course.

Frink Mansfield Smith,	1887	Civil Engineering.
Irwin Granniss,	1896	Medical.
Charles W. Holbrook,	1896	Medical.

CHAPTER III.

Ecclesiastical Affairs.

HE inhabitants on the east side of the Quinnipiac, from their first settlement, attended public worship at New Haven, but with great inconvenience, labor and danger. They were obliged to leave home early in the morning, travel through the woods on unmade roads, and then cross the ferry, which was often dangerous. During the Indian wars and commotions, the women and children, on the Sabbath, were collected together at one house in the neighborhood, under the protection of a guard, while some part of the families attended public worship in New Haven, and for many years the men were required by law, under the penalty of a fine, to appear at meeting with their arms, ready for battle. Similar inconveniences attended the transaction of their business at New Haven. It was natural for them, therefore, to anticipate advantages from being organized as a distinct parish from New Haven. With zeal they prosecuted this object. In the year 1678 they petitioned New Haven for their consent to become a distinct village, and for some other privileges. Not succeeding that year, on the 18th of August, 1679, they renewed their application, which resulted as follows:

"At a town meeting held in New-Haven 29th Dec., 1679—and for the village on the East side those inhabitants gave in

their propositions to the Committee, which they desired might
be granted, which were—

1. That they might have liberty to get a Minister amongst
them for their meeting, and keep the Sabbath in a way as
they ought.

2. That boundary might be granted them as high as Muddy
River.

3. That they have liberty of admitting inhabitants among
them, for their help in the work and maintenance of a
Minister.

4. That they may have liberty to purchase some lands of
the Indians, near Mr. Gregson's, if the Indians are willing
to part with it.

5. That what land of the Quinnipiack is within Branford
stated bounds, the right of the purchase may be given them.

6. Lastly, that they may be freed from rates to the Towne
when they shall have procured a Minister."

This business was referred to a committee, to report
at the next meeting.

"At a Town Meeting, held in New-Haven, 29th Decr. 1679—
the inhabitants of Stoney River, Southend, and some others,
on the East side of the River, having formerly made a
motion, and for several reasons therein expressed, to have
liberty among themselves, to procure a minister to preach
the Word and administer ordinances among them, and several
other particulars, as in their petition more fully appears;
the Towne at their request appointed a Committee to examine
and prepare matters against some other meeting; and after
some consideration of the business, did prepare an answer,
and made return to the Towne at the aforesaid meeting which
is as followeth.

"1. That they be encouraged and have liberty granted to get
a Minister to settle amongst them as soon as it doth appear
they are in a capacity to maintaine a Minister and uphold the
ordinances of Christ.

"2. That when they are settled in a village way with
Ministry, they have liberty to admit their own inhabitants for
the future, but to attend to such cautions and considerations

for the regulation of their settlement, as may consist with the interest of religion, and the Congregational way of the Churches, provided for, to be upheld. ·

"3. As to the purchase of land of the Indians near Mr. Gregson's farme; New-Haven being bound in covenant to supply the Indian with land for planting when they need, how far liberty to purchase lands of them may consist with that engagement, unless with due caution, is to be considered.

"4. For the Quinnipiack land now within the town of Branford, and was at first bought by us, and never payed for by Branford to us, that the Towne would grant unto them our right, the better to enable them to treat with Branford for enlargement on the purchase money due, with the consideration that New-Haven hath been long out of purse.

"5. For the payment of rates to New-Haven, that they be freed from it when they are settled in a Village way with Ministry.

"6. For Commonage, that the stated Commonage be at liberty on that side of the River within their limits, for the use of New-Haven as hitherto, and what shall remain for commonage within be agreed upon.

"7. That the inhabitants of New-Haven, that live in the Towne, and have propriety in land on the Indian side, whilst they so continue, pay their rates to New-Haven as hitherto.

"8. That their bounds shall be the north side of Alling Ball's farme, by a line from the River as his line runs untill it meets with Branford line, above Foxon's; and that the farmers above that line be left at liberty to contribute to the Ministry with them, and such not to pay to the Ministry at New-Haven, whilst they so do, until further orders."

After the town had heard the considerations of the committee in answer to the inhabitants on the east side respecting the village, the town approved and confirmed it to be their order by vote.

Agreeable to this grant, the village applied to the General Court for a law to locate and incorporate them as a society. That transaction will appear from the following documents. So early as May, 1667, they had requested this privilege of the General Assembly, when they resolved,

"Upon the Motion of the Deputies of New Haven, this Court grants the Towne liberty to make a Village on the East side of the East River, if they see it capable for such a thing, provided they settle a Village there within four years from May next."

"A General Court of Election held at Hartford, 13th May, 1680. In answer to the petition of John Potter, Samuel Heminway and Eliakim Hitchcock, that they might have liberty (they having obtained consent of New-Haven) to become a Village and to set up a distinct Congregation there, with liberty to invite and settle an orthodox Minister amongst them." (*Col. Rec.*)

According to this grant, the village immediately proceeded in making arrangements to obtain a preacher.

"17th January, 1681, They appointed John Thompson and Samuel Heminway to speak with Mr. James Alling to know his mind in reference to his settling with us in the work of the ministry.

"At the same meeting the Village granted 100 acres of land to the encouragement of the Ministry amongst them. The one half of which they give to the first minister that shall settle with them in that worke. And the other half for the standing use of the University here forever. And that this last fifty acres, given to the Ministry, shall not be given away to any, either by major vote or otherwise."

The committee applied to Mr. Alling, who served them several months, but contemplating a long journey, he declined their invitation to stay longer with them. The committee reported this to the village meeting, and "they then agreed to look out some other meet person, to carry on the worke of the ministry here. They directed their Committee to renew their application to Mr. Alling and if unsuccessful, then goe to Mr. Harriman, and treat with him, and desire his help in the Ministry amongst us, and further, to give him an invitation to a settlement in the worke of the ministry amongst us. It was also ordered that Matthew Moulthrop, and John Potter doe set out five acres of the land upon the Green, formerly granted, the one half for the Ministry, and one half for the first Minister that shall settle with us, and they are to leave the spring clear for a watering place for cattle. It is also agreed that the 95 acres to the Ministry, and the minister that shall settle with us, the one half of it shall be laid as near home as may be, and the other half upon Stoney River."

Mr. Harriman was employed, and the village raised by tax £50 for his support—"current money with the merchant." And they gave him a formal call in November, 1683.

"They also voted to proceed immediately to build a house for the minister, and to finish it in a year." This they attempted to accomplish by a subscription, which is a specimen of the public spirit of the village at that period.

"A Catalogue of the persons, together with the several sums they (this day) promise freely to contribute towards building the minister's house and fencing the home lot which are as follows:

James Denison £20 00 00
John Thompson 20 00 00
Samuel Heminway 20 00 00

Nathaniel Hitchcock 10 00 00
Thomas Smith 10 00 00
Eliakim Hitchcock 6 00 00
George Pardee 5 00 00
William Luddington 5 00 00
Thomas Pinion 2 10 00
James Tailor 1 10 00
William Roberts 1 10 00
Robert Dawson 2 00 00
Isaac Bradley 1 00 00

"Matthew Moulthrop will do what he can. John Potter also. Joseph Abbot, 25 rods of rail fence about the home lot."

"The house is to be 36 feet long and two stories high. And to be set on the side of the Green, west of Matthew Moulthrop's." The house, however, was not built at that time, and it is probable that Mr. Harriman did not continue long with them, as they seem not to have proceeded in the Society plans after 1684 or 5. For in 1686, they are mentioned in a land affair, as having returned to their former connection with New Haven. Unhappily, there is a chasm in the village records from April, 1685, to December 23, 1703. At a meeting held at the last-mentioned date, "The Inhabitants voted to take up their Village grant; and appointed a committee to manage the concerns of the Village in order to a settlement, according to the General Court grant, and informed New-Haven of their design." They pursued that object, and in September the next year, appointed a committee to prefer a petition to the General Assembly, to meet in October at New Haven. A petition was presented and met with success.

"At a General Assembly at Hartford, May 1704. This assembly having considered the petition of Capt. Alling Ball and John Potter, inhabitants on the East side of the East River, in the Township of New Haven, moving, that whereas this Assembly did formerly grant that they should be a distinct society, and have liberty to call and settle a Minister amongst them, when they should find themselves able to maintain the ordinances of God in a suitable manner, and that they doe apprehend that they are able so to doe, that, therefore, this Assembly would please to grant them certain privileges, and other matters and things for their encouragement, and enabling them to goe forward with that worke; this Assembly for divers weighty reasons doe see cause to referre the further consideration of their petition to their General Assembly in Oct. next. And if the inhabitants of New-Haven doe not appear, at the said General Assembly, and there make their pleas, then the petition shall be granted, with this restriction, that the propriety of lands shall not be concerned with." (*Col. Rec.*)

While these matters were pending, they were making preparation, and looking about them for a minister. Jacob, the youngest son of Samuel Hemingway, and born in the village, graduated at the college at Saybrook (now Yale University), under the presidency of the Rev. Abraham Pierson, 1703, and was then about twenty years of age. To him the people turned their attention.

"At a meeting of the Village 20th Nov. 1704, Voted to look out for a minister to carry on the publick worship of God amongst us; and it was voted—
"1. To seek to Sir Heminway that he would give them a taste of his gifts in order to settlement in the worke of the ministry. And—
"2. Voted to desire John Potter, Sen. Caleb Chedsey, and Ebenezer Chedsey, to treat with Sir Heminway, to get him, if they could, to give them a taste of his gifts in preaching the Word."

1

At another meeting of the village, the 19th of December following—"They having had some taste of Sir Heminway in preaching the Word, did declare their desire to have him go on in the worke of the Ministry amongst us, in order to settlement; and towards his encouragement they engage to allow him after the rate of £40 by the year in pay. And, Voted that George Pardee and Caleb Chedsey signify our desires and propositions to Sir Heminway, and take his answer and make returne."

The committee immediately consulted Mr. Hemingway, and reported at the same meeting, "That Sir Heminway does comply with their motion, God's grace assisting, and does accept the proposition, and desires some consideration with respect to wood."

The next month they voted to give him £50 a year. They continued in this state until the close of the year 1706, when, at a meeting, the village appointed "William Luddington and John Potter to treat with Sir Jacob Heminway, to see whether he will goe on in the worke of the Ministry amongst us."

When Mr. Hemingway commenced his labors, the village had no meetinghouse. But at a meeting June 10, 1706, "The Village agreed to build [a house], 20 feet long, 16 feet wide, and 17 feet between joints, and set it across the east end of the School House." William Luddington and John Russell were overseers of the work, and were allowed 3s. 6d. per day, other men 3s. and team 6s. This house served them until the year 1719.

December 2, 1706, Mr. Hemingway reported his answer to their 2d arrangement.

"Gentlemen, Whereas you have given me notice by two men, that you desire me to carry on the work of the Ministry in order to settlement among you. I do, therefore, hereby give you notice that so far as God shall enable me thereunto, I am heartily ready and willing to gratify these your desires upon these conditions—1. That you give me £50 yearly, and my wood. 2. That you build me a good convenient dwelling house, within 2 years time, or give me money sufficient to do the same, one half this year ensuing, and one half the next. 3. That when it is in your power, you give me a good and sufficient portion of land.

From my study 2d Decr. 1706. Yours to serve.

JACOB HEMINWAY."

On the 26th of the same month, the village met and voted, "We do promise Mr. Heminway, if he will carry on the work of the Ministry in said Village, to build him a house, if we can in two years after this date, and give him £50 pay, and his wood. And in the mean time, if he wants a house to hire him one." To accomplish these objects they laid a tax of fourpence farthing.

In the year 1707, the village built a house* for Mr. Hemingway, 40 feet long and 20 feet wide, on a five-acre lot, on the southeast corner of the Green. One half acre was allowed to set the house upon, adjoining to Mr. Hemingway's home lot. The wages

* It has been asserted that Jacob Hemingway's house, which was built for him on the southeast corner of the Green, was the one removed in 1898 to Hemingway avenue now owned by D. W. Tuttle, Esq. This is an error. The Rev. Jacob Hemingway house was burned, and Mr. Stephen Thompson built the house removed for his son Moses, on the site of the parsonage. This corner has formerly been called "ministers corner."

in working at the house were three shillings a day for a man, and six for a team.

The terms proposed were adjusted and ratified in 1709. They gave to him the house and lot it stood on, also 12 acres on the cove road, 12 acres in the bridge swamp, 30 acres in the half mile, £50 per annum, and sufficient wood, "if he performs the worke of the Ministry so long as he is able; or if it be our fault that he is forced to leave us, it shall be his. But if it be his fault, or he leaves the place, or is hindered in the worke, then the property is to return to the Village. And he is to have the use of the Parsonage land."

The same year, "3d May, 1709, voted to petition the General Assembly that we may embody into a Church state."

"May 12, this Assembly do grant their consent, and full liberty to the inhabitants of the village of East Haven, in this colony, to embody themselves into a Church state, with the approbation of their neighboring churches."

The care and solemnity with which they proceeded in preparing for that transaction is worthy of notice.

April 25th, 1710. "Upon some considerations about setting up the worship and ordinances of Christ in this place, and in order to a suitable attendance upon so great and weighty a worke, the village made choice of, and desired sundry persons, whose names are underwritten, as a Committee, to take advice and search for the right way, as near as may be ascertained, to prosecute the aforesaid worke, under hopes of the blessing of God to accompany and succeed such a worke for soul good to us, and ours after us, to many generations." The persons chosen for this object were William Luddington, Thomas Goodsell, Lieut. John Russell, George Pardee, Caleb Chidsey, Sergt. John Potter, and Daniel Collins.

With such views the church was gathered and constituted a Congregational Church, and became a member of the consociation of New Haven County; that body having been organized according to Saybrook Platform, in 1709.

The church was gathered on October 8, 1711, and Mr. Hemingway was ordained pastor of the church the same day. Unhappily no church record can be found of the transactions of that day, nor of the affairs of the church until 1755. It, however, appears, that Caleb Chidsey was one of the first deacons; he died in 1713. Joshua Austin was deacon in 1718 and he and Thomas Smith were both deacons at the time of Mr. Street's ordination, but were then very aged.

As early as the year 1714 the village "voted to build a [the second] meeting-house 30 by 40 feet, 20 feet high, and jutted one foot at each end, with a strait roof." The next year they voted a sixpenny rate for the expense. In 1718 they began the house. Capt. John Russell, Nathaniel Hitchcock, Abraham Hemingway and Samuel Hotchkiss were the building committee. The next year they were charged "to hurry the work." The form of the seats and the pulpit were to be like those of the Branford meeting-house: and a pew was to be built for the ministry. Wages from the 10th of September to the 10th of March, to be 2s. 6d., and the rest of the year 3s.; team 5s. and Indian corn 2s. 6d.

The house being sufficiently advanced to occupy, the 19th of October 1719, the village met and "voted that the new Meeting-house should be seated*:—that the first short seat should be reckoned equal with the second long seat and so on:—that Mr. Shepard, Mr. Tuttle, and William Luddington, should sit in the first short seat. [This was near the pulpit and among the highest in dignity.] And old Mrs. Heminway, Mrs. Bradley, Mrs. Denison and Mrs. Smith, shall sit in the first seat of the square body. Mr. Pardee, Mr. Morris, Capt. Russell, Sergt. John Thompson, Samuel Russell, and Samuel Clark, shall sit in the fore seat of the square body. These six men are chosen to seat the rest of the meeting-house, or the major part

---

* An explanation of this term may be a pardonable digression from the continuous history:

SEATING THE MEETING HOUSE.

Dr. Bacon in his "Historical Discourses of New Haven" says, "This affords us a glimpse of the associations and relative social importance of the first settlers of New Haven. One of the earliest matters was the building of the meeting house, followed by the solemn and weighty matter of 'seating' it. It was considered a mark of honor to be chosen one of the seating committee. They were grave men appointed for the purpose, who graded and dignified the seats, according to some rule of nearness to the pulpit by which they were esteemed more or less honorable. The people were then voted into them one by one, in accordance with the following rules. 1st, Dignity of descent. 2nd, Place of Public Trust. 3rd, Pious Disposition. 4th, Estate. 5th, Peculiar service of any kind."

The sexes were seated apart, the men on one side and the women on the other side of the middle alley. Children followed their parents to the door but were not allowed to sit with them in the assembly, and were placed under a

of them to do it, according to their rates in 1717, and that by Monday next ensuing."

About thirty years afterwards, the meetinghouse wanting repairs, it was motioned to build a new house, but they continued to repair the old one for about fifty years, when they began the erection of the stone house. [The second meetinghouse stood on the "Nole" opposite the northwest corner of the Green, on Main street opposite Hemingway avenue, and the slight elevation was called Meetinghouse hill for many generations.]

In the meantime, the people growing remiss concerning the wood with which they had stipulated to supply Mr. Hemingway, they voted to give him £50 in lieu of wood, provided it was not delivered in a specified time, for which they would be allowed 3s. per load.

20th Feb. 1722, "Voted, that Mr. Heminway shall have a piece of land for pasturing, adjoining to the west end of his home lot, as it is set out by Deacon Austin, Thomas Alcock and William Bradley. He to have the use of said land so long as he shall continue in the worke of the Ministry amongst us in this place, he paying to the Village one shilling per year, yearly, as long as he improves said land for pasturing.

"tithing-man." The young unmarried men were in one gallery and girls in the opposite gallery. Soldiers, however, sat on both sides of the alley, nearest the door. The custom of young unmarried people sitting in opposite galleries was a custom followed in New England in much later generations. The people had no choice in their own church, everything being settled by vote, and they might be considered as so many pegs, driven in their proper places, upon which to hang their titles.

The bounds of the land set out by the aforesaid three men, is about 13 rods on the Southend, on the westerly side 17 rods, and northerly 10 rods."

In January, 1737, they voted to sell the parsonage, and constitute a permanent fund with the avails. This measure, however, was opposed, and John Hemingway, Joseph Granniss, Samuel Russell, Matthew Rowe, John Dawson, Moses Thompson, James Dennison, Isaac Penfield, Samuel Smith, and Isaac Howe entered their protest against selling the parsonage land.

In 1752 "Voted that Mr. Heminway shall name the Psalm in public; Nathaniel Barnes shall tune the Psalm, and in his absence Jacob or Isaac Goodsell."

Mr. Hemingway continued in the ministry fifty years, and died October 7, 1754, in the 71st year of his age, having preached seven years before ordination.

In March, 1755, Mr. Nicholas Street was invited to preach for the Society on probation, with the consent of the Rev. Association.

"At a Society meeting, 5th July, 1755, voted unanimously to give Mr. Street a call in the worke of the Gospel ministry with us, and appointed a Committee to treat with him on the subject."

And in August

"Voted that we will give Mr. Street for his settlement amongst us £1500 money, Old Tenor; to pay £500 in one year; £500 in two years and £500 in three years. And if he changes his principles from what he was settled upon, then he shall return the £1500 in money, to the Society."

This was equal to about £126 proclamation money.

"Voted to give Mr. Street for his yearly salary £60, in New-York money, dollars at 8s. or any other money equivalent thereunto, for the first year; sixty-five in the same money for the second year, and seventy in the same money for the third year, and so to continue yearly so long as the said Mr. Street shall preach with us."

"Voted, also, that Mr. Street shall have the use of that piece of parsonage land by the two springs, three years after he is ordained."

"Voted, also, that Mr. Street shall have the use of the two biggest pieces of land, so long as he shall continue in the work of the Ministry amongst us."

At the same meeting Mr. Street personally appeared, and accepted the aforesaid proposal, and was ordained by the consociation of New Haven County, October 8, 1755.

In 1768 the society again voted to sell all the parsonage lands and give Mr. Street £80 salary. From the 100 acres that had been set apart to the encouragement of the ministry, 50 acres were given to Mr. Hemingway as the first minister, and a part of the remaining fifty was sold to Mr. Hemingway to pay up arrears of his salary, and some of it was sold to defray the expenses for building the first meeting-house. In 1739 the parsonage lands were all resurveyed and another piece was added south of Samuel Hotchkiss' farm.

The next year, January 30, 1769, it was "Voted to sell all the parsonage lands. The monies arising and accruing to the said Society from the sale of said lands shall be kept as a fund for the support of a regular Calvinistic Ministry, upon Saybrook Platform, especially as to the doctrines thereof, in East-Haven; and that the interest of said fund shall annually be paid to such a ministry and no other, according to the original intention in the sequestration of said lands."

The sales amounted to £390 9s. 9d. In 1779, it became convenient for some of the purchasers to make payment in the depreciated continental bills, when they were already reduced four to one, i. e., one dollar was worth only twenty-five cents in silver. A vote of the society was obtained to call in the money; and thus all that fund sunk in their hands to about $300. For the sake of this fund, Mr. Street had previously relinquished the parsonage and his wood, and accepted £80 salary.

The same year the society voted to build a new meetinghouse, and in voting where it should stand, 37 votes appeared for the Green, and 27 for the end of Mullen Hill. A large committee was then appointed to fix upon the place; but they could not agree. The next year, they chose Capt. Eliakim Hall, Colonel Chauncey, and James Wadsworth, a committee for that purpose, who met, and their doings were reported to the court. But the people were not yet satisfied. The same result attended another committee in March, 1771.

In December of the same year they tried another vote; when 20 votes appeared for the Green, 2 for Thompson's corner, and 29 for the end of the hill. Being convinced that they could not agree, in February, 1772, they voted to apply to the County Court, and request that two of the judges and another man be of the committee. They met and fixed the stake on Thompson's corner. In this decision the society acquiesced, and began to make preparations to build.

The end of the hill was the center of the society, and nearly in the center of the population, north and south. The Green would be more convenient for the

south and east part of the society. The South End
people had to go round by the Cove and come out on
the Green. The road was crooked, long, and some
part of the way very uncomfortable. The present
road from the meetinghouse to South End was laid
out after that period.

John Woodward, Amos Morris and Stephen Morris,
and afterward Stephen Thompson, Joel Tuttle, and
Stephen Smith, were of the building committee. Isaac
Chidsey and Dan Bradley were chosen in 1774. "27th
April, 1772, Voted to build a stone house 60 feet long,
and to lay a six-penny rate for it." The committee
were authorized to purchase the land of John Thompson, and pay for it out of that rate. The house was
begun without a steeple, but a few enterprising men
were determined to have one, and finally obtained a
society vote for it, and also to add eight feet to the
length. The outside of the walls now measured 70
feet by 50, exclusive of the steeple. In 1773 and 4,
the walls were raised and covered. The seats were
then removed from the old house into the new, and
public worship commenced in it in September, 1774.

It was a great and honorable work, and stands as
a lasting monument of the enterprise, public spirit,
wisdom and perseverance of the undertakers, and
especially of the leaders. And not only to these men,
to whom all reverence and gratitude are due, but also
to the architect and master builder of this strikingly
chaste and beautiful house of worship. The history
of this widely known and justly admired church would
seem incomplete if we allowed further oblivion to
cast its shadow over the name and work of George
Lancraft, under whose guidance and dictation every

stone was laid. Mr. Lancraft was born in 1724, was a native of Holland, Province of Flanders, and at the time of this building was in the prime of life, height of activity, energy and good judgment, as his successful work shows. Let us for a moment consider the disadvantages and difficulties under which this lone man labored, and our admiration for the work accomplished will be increased. He was the only skilled workman employed in its erection, and that he was a perfect master of his business, in every particular, a glance at the structure at the present time is positive evidence. He had no foreman to whom he could entrust any part of the work. It was his eye to criticise, and his hand to control. True, there might have been some among his helpers who could do a fairly good job, but his workmen were the men and farmers of the town, who donated their services, whenever their own affairs would permit, ever ready to do what they could without any social distinction; even to the building committee, all lent a hand. Sometimes his workmen were numerous, which only increased his oversight, and at other times were few. Every stone must be measured by his rule and placed by his level, under his immediate eye. At this early date everything had to be done by hand. There were no dummy engines to do the hoisting of materials, and swing the heavy stones into place; all was manual labor.

There is a tradition, and not without good foundation, that his first work in East Haven was the building of the stone house on Forbes avenue in 1767 which is now the parish house of the Chapel of the Epiphany. Owing to the recent remodeling of this house for

church purposes, much of the ancestral work has
been displaced, and in no instance has been improved
by its modern workmanship. Certain it is that the
people had full confidence in Mr. Lancraft's ability,
which to-day stands such a lasting monument to his
skill. Mr. Havens in his Centennial Sermon says,
"It is less surprising that they should have undertaken
to build a stone meeting-house, than that they should
have wrought it in the manner and form they did.
There was not another in all the English Colonies of
America, which furnished them a pattern." No, there
was not. Can it be conceived that these home-born,
and town-staying men, unacquainted with architectural
designs and beauty could possibly rear such an impos-
ing structure, with such nicety of line and finish, and
such exactness of construction without the guiding
hand of a master architect and builder? No indeed!
And that designer and constructor was George Lancraft, of Holland,* Province of Flanders, where massive buildings of architectural beauty and grandeur
were everyday sights throughout his former life.
Nothing in this line was new to him, and, as he had
taken stone masonry for his life's work, doubtless he
had made it his study until he stood master of the
science. The work was done with such faithfulness
and efficiency that, after the lapse of one hundred and
thirty-three years since its completion, scarcely a stone
has started from its original bed, and that its walls

* A convincing proof of his country was the earmark of
his work by the date which he placed over the door. This
was a well-known custom in Holland as well as early New
York, before the English took possession, so much so it has
been noted in history.

are as plumb and level as when laid was the verdict of experts less than a year since.

It now bears the record of being the "oldest stone meetinghouse" standing in New England, and first "stone meetinghouse in Connecticut." At the time of Rev. Mr. Havens' Centennial Sermon in East Haven he stated "there were but two meeting houses of any kind standing in the State older than the East Haven stone meeting house: the brick meeting house in Wethersfield and the wooden edifice in Farmington."

It was a cheaper building than one of wood. They had stone and lime, and teams and laborers enough to do the work. A stone house saved them money. The stone was within easy distance of the house, and quarried from the Russell farm and vicinity. The papers containing the accounts of the building are lost, and the expense of it cannot now be ascertained, but it is supposed that when they began to meet in it, it had cost ten or eleven thousand dollars.

The steeple and inside of the house were not finished for several years on account of the Revolutionary War. The society has never seen a more favorable period for this great work than the one preceding the war. They were then united as one people and the society, probably, never contained a company of men of more enterprise or greater resolution and public spirit than that generation contained. When the war was terminated, divisions began to appear and considerably diminished the active ability of the society to perform such a work again, and in a few years a number of those influential and enterprising men were removed by death. Although there is yet a considerable portion of wealth in the society, it is not accompanied with the same resolution and enterprise which the Fathers possessed. But it ought to be considered, that the hand of the Lord was in the work. The time had come when the "Lord's house should be built," and then men and means were prepared to execute the work of the Lord, and fulfill the divine purpose. *"Except the Lord build the house, they labor in vain that build it."* And when the work was done, the people had occasion to say *"the Lord hath done great things for us, whereof we are glad."*

A serious calamity, however, befell the builders. The workmen were raising the last window cap, on the north side, when the scaffolding gave way, and three men with the stone in their arms fell to the ground. Tony, a negro servant of Capt. Amos Morris, was considerably injured, but in two weeks was so much recovered that he ran away. Mr. Stephen Thompson (one of the building committee) had his skull fractured, was trepanned, and after much suffering, recovered. Mr. Joseph Hotchkiss had one leg crushed by the stone, passed through ten months of suffering, and never fully recovered from the effects of the injury.

The society resumed the work of finishing the house in 1791, for which they laid a tax of one penny half penny. Nothing decisive was effected till March, 1793, when Samuel Davenport, Esq., Amos Morris, Jr., Joseph Russell, John Woodward and Dan Holt were "authorized and empowered to indent and agree with any gentleman or gentlemen, to finish the meeting-house, of said society, in said East Haven, in such a manner as they, or the major part of them shall think best; said house to be finished by the first of December 1794." Though objection was made to building a spire at the same time, on the ground of the increased burden it would impose, it was finally concluded to make one business of it. The people gave themselves to the work with characteristic energy and carried it through to a successful end in 1796. Hence the first spire was erected in 1796. Previous to this the style of the steeple was called "Squaw's Cap," which was no spire at all but a kind of roofing.

The society had scarcely become comfortably seated and settled in their finished house when a great calamity befell it. October 8, 1797, a terrible tornado passed over the town. "On Sunday evening last, between six and seven o'clock we experienced a violent gale of wind from the westward, attended with heavy rain and thunder. At East Haven the steeple of the meeting-house was blown down which falling on the roof, broke through the side where it fell leaving only one rafter standing and penetrating the floor, greatly damaged the seats."

The entire cost of repairing the damages caused by the tornado amounted to $1,000, which added to the $2,500 just expended, in finishing the meetinghouse, was a large sum for so small a society, but they were, as usual, equal to the emergency. The repairs were immediately commenced, with the expressed stipulation that everything should be done in the most thorough manner. The new spire which replaced the fallen one was a tall and graceful one, far superior in form and style to the one just destroyed, which remained standing sixty years. In 1798 the society

"voted to procure a bell, to place in the new steeple."
The necessary funds were appropriated and a committee appointed to carry out the vote. Dr. Bela
Farnham, "The Beloved Physician," one of the
committee, was present at the melting of the metal,
and he threw into the molten mass nineteen "Spanish
milled dollars," to give the bell a sharp and silvery
tone. The committee were also present at the mysterious process of casting, and with great satisfaction
saw it come forth from its smoking mold, in full per-
fection of beauty and tone. Now that bell has tolled
the passing knell of all that committee, and of all
the former pastors of this church, as well as more
than three generations of its people (1907).

There were some public-spirited, energetic, and
liberal men in the society, with whom the determination to do a thing was the same as doing it. Upon
their request the society passed a vote, giving permission "to Edmond Bradley and others, to affix a
clock in the steeple, in such a manner, as to strike
the bell that is about to be fixed in said steeple; provided that said clock is affixed without any expense
to the society." The clock was procured and placed
in position, and has ever been a faithful servant
to the people. Thus the "Old Stone Meetinghouse,"
after a lapse of 29 years since the first vote taken in
1769, stood complete in all its appointments, and Mr.
Havens in his Centennial Sermon pronounced it "by
far the finest church edifice in New Haven County,"
at that time.

Just previous to the agitation of building a new
house of worship in East Haven, the Old South
Church in Boston had been completed, and was con-

sidered a wonderful work of architecture, finished in
the latest style, and a tradition has always been extant
that some members of the society went to Boston to
see this renowned edifice as a model for their new
house. Certainly there is a striking resemblance
between the two, in the general style and outline of
the houses. However, if the tradition of this visit is
true, it certainly did not shake their confidence in Mr.
Lancraft to erect them a house of stone, which Mr.
Havens says," has saved them the outlay of thousands
of dollars, and will save thousands more, in centuries
to come."

Events went on to 1822, when square pews were
passing into history. In these pews some of the
people sat facing the minister, some back to him, and
some sideways. East Haven people taking the
recently erected Center Church of New Haven for a
model, in the arrangements of seats, took out the
square pews in the body and north side of the house
and replaced them with slips. They left two square
pews each side of the east door, also south and west
door, with an aisle in front of them, and the middle
aisle running from the south door to the pulpit.

Until about 1820 none of the meetinghouses in New
England were warmed even in the severest weather.
Some of the elderly ladies carried foot stoves, about
a foot square, containing a brass or copper receptacle
for holding coals or charcoal, and it was the common
practice to pass it around from one to another, and frequently from one pew to another, as a footwarmer.
Others carried heated soapstones, or bricks encased in
ornamental bags or covers. About 1825 two wood
stoves were placed in the "old stone house." As no pro-

vision had been made for heating, there was no chimney to the house. One stove stood in the northeast corner, and the other in the northwest, with the stovepipe running out of the window. In 1840 coal burners were instituted, and were in use about twenty-four years.

In 1847 there was a change in the ministry and the meetinghouse, although retaining its symmetry and beauty on the outside, was antiquated, inconvenient, dilapidated, and positively repellant on the inside. The walls were stained with the accumulation of moisture, from the stones being plastered upon without lathing; the slips and square pews were uncomfortable, and to add to their dreary appearance had in some former time been painted a dismal green, which asserted its right to cling to every adjacent object, till the good ladies, to prevent being permanently attached to their pews, had lined them with as many kinds of material, in different shades of green, as there were pews. The high-perched pulpit was on a level with the galleries. Mr. Havens says, "It must have been at the hazard of a stiff neck on Monday, if those seated in the body of the house kept their eyes on the preacher during the delivery of the sermons on Sunday." The greatest wonder was the "Paul Revere" pepperbox-shaped sounding board suspended over the preacher's head. He further says, "Upon what principle of acoustics such a machine was constructed, it is difficult to imagine. The only earthly use it did subserve, was to rivet the attention of children, and keep them quiet."

An obstacle which stood in the way of improving the interior of the church was the peculiar manner in which the pews had become the property of the holders by deed. Taxation to defray current expenses had now passed away, and a plan was proposed to make a permanent sale of the pews, and with the avails create a fund to support the ministry. This scheme worked well for a while, but had now outgrown its usefulness, and was a detriment instead of a benefit. Mr. Havens says, "It was fortunate that the society contained a few energetic and public-spirited men, who taking the matter in hand, with the tacit consent, rather than active coöperation of the majority carried it through this crisis." Having secured the rights of the pew owners, in one way or another, the work of remodeling the "Old Stone Meetinghouse" was commenced May, 1850, and completed the following October. The men having the work in charge were as follows: Architect, Sidney M. Stone; builder, Newton Moses; mason, Robert Edmonson, all of New Haven. Foreman carpenter, E. Sturtevant Chidsey, and carpenter, Daniel M. Church of East Haven. Other carpenters, Horace Treat, West Haven; James Prindle, New Haven, and Robert W. Hill, Waterbury, now a professional architect.

A great change had now been made; nothing but the solid walls, tower and spire with bell and clock, were left unchanged. Even the walls in some measure had been altered. The upper tier of windows was lowered, the door and windows on the east end had been filled up, also the south door, the south side of the tower, and the window behind the pulpit on the north side. New frames and windows were inserted, and the building brought into its present shape. The

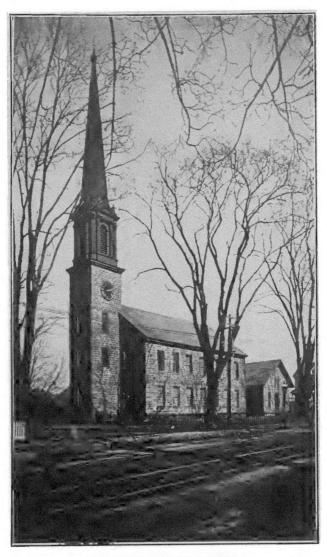

THE CONGREGATIONAL CHURCH.

most sweeping change was on the interior. The west end was pierced with doors, one on each side of the tower. The pulpit was placed at the east end; new galleries were built on the north, south and west ends. The walls upon which the plaster was originally laid, without lathing, were furred out and covered with hard finish. Everything in the interior was now new and up to date.

The furnishing of the interior was done by the ladies of the society, who displayed their characteristic energy, zeal and wisdom, as they always have done in the past, and it is perfectly safe to predict they always will in the future. For years they had been busy with brain and hand, accumulating and storing up for this event, which they foresaw, and wished to come. Their hopes were now realized and a beautiful well-appointed church outside and inside was the climax. So extensive were the changes made that it seemed no other than proper and befitting that the "Old Stone Meetinghouse" should again be dedicated to the worship of God. The services were held October 16, 1850, when a discourse was delivered by Rev. Joel Hawes, D.D., of Hartford. The entire cost of the work was about $6,000.

In 1853, the society saw and felt the need of a parsonage for its minister. No parsonage had been built since the one in 1706, which they presented as a free gift to their first pastor, Rev. Jacob Hemingway. Each succeeding minister had built his own house, which left the society without a parsonage down to 1853, when the society bought the residence of the late Haynes Hemingway, Esq., on Hemingway avenue, which was purchased for $2,000, and was occupied for a parsonage nearly twenty years.

In 1859 the steeple which was erected in 1798 had become so dilapidated as to be in danger of falling. Immediate measures were taken for replacing it with one of more modern style and greater architectural beauty. This work was committed to Mr. Daniel M. Church, a native of East Haven, as well as a lifelong resident, and a noted steeple builder, having built fourteen in the state of Connecticut, besides being engaged on many others outside of the state. Mr. Church was assisted in his work by Mr. Edwin Russell, who was also a native and resident of East Haven, an expert house carpenter.

Mr. Havens in his Centennial discourse says, "The lofty and spacious belfry, the neat and graceful spire, corresponding with the stern simplicity of the building, and towering above to the height of 196 feet from the ground, makes it a conspicuous object and an ornament to the village, in the center of which it stands. It is not surpassed in symmetry of form, excellence of workmanship and good taste by any structure of like magnitude in the Commonwealth." A just tribute to home talent. The cost of this new steeple was about $2,000, which could not have been built since at twice that amount, owing to the advance of price for materials and labor.

In 1868 it became apparent that refinishing and further improvements were necessary for the interior, to keep pace with the times. The society, sustained by the unanimous sentiment of the congregation, commenced the work with unusual promptitude, and it was completed in about three months. The inner walls and ceiling were painted in fresco,

a new and tasty pulpit replaced the old one, the lower
floor was recarpeted, the pews new cushioned, and
new lamps provided. The cost was about $3,000.
Another great improvement was made at the same time.
For several years some of the ladies had been gathering funds for an iron railing around the grounds.
Incited by their energy and perseverance, a number of
public-spirited gentlemen came forward with their aid,
and an ornamental and substantial fence was built on
Main and High streets, also a broad concrete walk
continuous with the fence was laid, at an expense of
about $1,300 including both.

When these improvements were completed the
question came up, "How shall the meetinghouse be
heated?" The day of stoves had gone by and a furnace was impracticable because there was no basement.
After much discussion it was finally decided to introduce steam. The funds came very readily; perhaps the
first cost was larger than for other modes of heating,
though in the end no greater, because of a less amount
of fuel used, with a much more equable pleasant heat,
as well as being more cleanly and easier to control.
This was the first church in the state that was heated
by steam. The cost was about $1,300.

In 1873 the people desired to provide their future
pastors with a residence in conformity with the age
and fashion of the day. With this view they purchased the house formerly built by their third pastor,
Rev. Saul Clark, on High street. They enlarged and
remodeled it, and made it one of the most beautiful
and commodious rural parsonages in the state. The
cost was about $8,000. Since 1873 various improv-
ments, as water, gas, telephone, and modern house-

hold conveniences have been introduced, as they have appeared one after the other.

The necessity of a chapel as an adjunct to the church had long been agitated. A portion of the ladies had been laboring with might and main for the "Chapel Fund," and ten years before the object seemed almost complete, but unforeseen difficulties arose, which required time to remove. The enterprise was greatly aided by a liberal bequest of the late Mrs. Eliza Andrews Dodd. In 1874, the centennial year of the "Old Stone Meetinghouse," the object was consummated, and a "Centennial Chapel," a monumental building, was reared in honor of the men who built the Stone Church, and of the generation they represented, as this chapel will be a century hence of this generation. This coincidence of time, this connection of the close of one century with the commencement of another, links together the history of the two, and sends them down the ages clustering with like associations and memories. It not only forms a connecting link between the centuries, but by a most singular and notable coincidence, a stronger and more lasting memory of the architect and constructor of the Stone Church, Mr. George Lancraft, is revived and strengthened by his successor, Mr. William M. Lancraft, who was his great-grandson, and the contractor of the 1874 chapel. And still another link of the past with the present was the donation of the architectural plans of the "Centennial Chapel" by Mr. Robert W. Hill, a professional architect, who was a great-grandson of Deacon Stephen Smith of Foxon, deacon of the Stone Church thirty-eight years. The donation was solicited by his friend Ephraim Sturtevant Chidsey.

Now we have gone through the tangible history of the church and its buildings, there is but one more event to chronicle: the Centennial Celebration which took place Wednesday, September 16, 1874, at ten o'clock in the morning. The invocation was by Rev. Owen Street of Lowell, Mass., a grandson of Rev. Nicholas Street. Reading of Scripture, Rev. Burdett Hart, D.D., of Fair Haven, whose large and prosperous church was a daughter of the Old Stone Church. Singing, original hymn, by the pastor, Rev. D. W. Havens. Prayer, Rev. Leonard Bacon, D.D., of Center Church, New Haven. Singing, original hymn by Rev. Owen Street. Historical Discourse, part first, by Rev. D. W. Havens. Singing, original hymn, by Rev. Owen Street. Historical Discourse, part second, Rev. D. W. Havens. Singing, original hymn, by Rev. D. W. Havens. Benediction, Rev. O. Evans Shannon.

At one o'clock P. M. a collation was served. The blessing was invoked by Rev. George I. Wood of Ellington, Conn. After dinner addresses were made by Rev. Owen Street, Prof. George E. Day, D.D., of Yale Divinity School, Rev. Leonard Bacon, D.D., of New Haven, John G. North, Esq., of New Haven, and Rev. S. S. Joscelyn, of Brooklyn, New York. Remarks were made by Joseph C. Farnham, Esq., of Brooklyn, New York, Joseph D. Farren, Esq., of Lawrance, Kansas, Mr. Charles H. Fowler of New Haven, and Samuel T. Andrews, Esq., the chairman. The concert in the evening, under the direction of Dr. J. G. Barnett, was well attended despite the storm. The reception at the parsonage, after the concert, was a

very pleasant occasion, although affected by the
storm.   Thus ended a day memorable in the history
of this venerable church and its people.

Mr. Havens says, "During the last quarter of a
century a larger amount has been expended upon and
around the Church, than all it had previously cost,
including the original erection.   The minimum value
of the society's property can not be less than $75,000.
If by any chance, it should be destroyed it is doubtful if it could be replaced for twice that sum."   Now
(1907) the church stands complete, beautiful in its
solidity, charming in its simplicity, which is its beauty,
and its beauty is its simplicity, unadorned, and thus
adorned the most—a perfect specimen of colonial
architecture, which is so much copied and dwelt upon
at the present day in one form or another.   "Other
styles may be better,—purer, more picturesque,—but
the colonial style is our traditional style, and is a heri-
tage too precious to be thrown away.   No style
expresses us so well as a people.   Our architectural
old clothes fit us, and become us better than the new
modes from Paris.   With a well-established tradition
for the colonial style it would be a gross mistake not
to continue it."   [*Geo. D. Seymour.*]

Unless destroyed by accident or the convulsions of
nature, it will endure for centuries, and the interior
can be remodeled and improved from time to time as
fashion and taste dictate.   But the whole of the
exterior should never be disturbed, not one stone
should ever be displaced, for fancied improvement
which would only be a destruction of the beautiful—
even more, an act of sacrilege and vandalism.   East
Haven people are so used to this structure of beauty

that they do not realize the admiration it calls forth from strangers. As a western man of much travel and observation remarked, "From the tip of the vane on the spire above to the ground underneath it is simply beautiful, not only in proportions and construction, but in material and color as well." Here let us remark that Mr. Seymour recommends red as a color for the coming "City Beautiful" (of which he is one of the committee). This color is also recommended for the great national cathedral of St. Peter and St. Paul, which is to be built at Washington, D. C., and is to be one of the grandest buildings in the Union. With red stone a church has a warmth of color and a look of the absence of newness that is very pleasing. All these requisites are combined in the Old Stone Church—what could we ask for more?

Now one hundred and ninety-six years have been enrolled on the great scroll of time since the first church was established, and the first minister ordained in East Haven. Let the first half of the century passed stand as a memorial to Rev. Jacob Hemingway and his labors of gathering and planting this church on this wild and hitherto barbarous soil. It may be thought his work was light, as his people were all Puritans. The fact must not be overlooked that human nature is the same in all ages of men and in all places and countries; although they were all Puritans they were not all saints.

The second half of that century bears witness to Mr. Street's labors, faithfulness, anxieties, sacrifices, and final accomplishments, in the erection of the beautiful Stone Church, which stands as a memorial and monument to this saintly man.

Rev. Saul Clark, 1808 to 1817.

Rev. Saul Clark was ordained pastor January 13, 1808. He was a young, enthusiastic, progressive man, of an ardent, sanguine, hopeful temperament, fully abreast of the times, if not in advance of them. With the independence of the country had also come a greater independence of thought and action, a wider scope of views, and a broader outlook for future development. Being young himself, he took a deep interest in the young people, and he soon drew them to his standard. He was deeply interested in educational matters, and devised and recommended many improvements. He instituted weekly neighborhood prayer meetings in all the districts of the town, and as he was an untiring, fervent worker, the result was that a greater religious interest grew up in his parish, a revival followed, and he gathered nearly the whole town into his church.

The early dawn of temperance was now breaking over the land, and he espoused the cause with his accustomed fervor. He organized the first temperance society in Connecticut and was insistent that his converts should abstain totally from all intoxicants. Not that his people were any more intemperate than the world which surrounded them, but those days were more given to hospitality, and there were very few houses with any pretentions to respectability without their sideboard, with its array of decanters, sling tumblers, and flip mugs. It was considered a great act of discourtesy on the part of the host or hostess if the social glass was not passed around at an afternoon or evening visit, or even a morning call. Cider was coequal with water at all their meals, and even the poorest families had their cider, and often the poorer the family the greater the number of cider barrels. The good dames at their "spinning spells," and even the young ladies at their "quilting bees," sipped their "sling" before supper. It is related that at a quilting held at Colonel Bradley's, one of the most exemplary homes in the town, "cordial" was passed round made of jelly and spices with hot water instead of the usual sling, because they belonged to Mr. Clark's temperance society, and many were the smirks and winks exchanged among the company. The great wonder of the present day is that with these customs there was any temperance at all in those days.

Mr. Clark contended, that that which is not actually good is directly evil. His preaching was of that high Calvinistic order, delivered with all the fire and oratory of an ardent nature and youth, that often grated on the nerves of some of his hearers. He discovered faults in his church which he thought should be purged from it and he set his face unflinchingly to the work. He was a man who when once he had taken a stand in the cause of right pursued it with an unyielding will and purpose, from which his temperament could not, and would not allow him to recede. He placed his principles and those of the church preëminently before his individual interest, which he sacrificed. The course he pursued caused intense feeling, and a division in his church was daily widening which he saw would not be healed by his continuance with the people, so he called for his dismission, which was granted.

Fifty-seven years after, Mr. Havens in his Centennial discourse fully vindicated and sustained Mr.

Clark in his views and acts, with these words: "After a few years, it was seen that the principles for which Mr. Clark contended were precisely those embraced by all evangelical churches. In respect to these principles he was merely in advance of the people, just as seventy-five years earlier Jonathan Edwards was driven from Northampton for adherence to a principle, which was afterwards adopted by all the churches in New England. The crisis was passed, the church was saved but the pastor had sacrificed himself." Still he had the good of the church at heart, and in his farewell sermon advised them, among other things, to settle a minister as soon as possible, before the people became disaffected by listening to different preachers. His love for his first church never seemed to be abated, for in death he wished to be buried with his first people, and he and most of his family now rest in the Old Cemetery.

REV. STEPHEN DODD, December 10, 1817, to
April 20, 1847.

Rev. Stephen Dodd was born in Bloomfield, New Jersey, March 8, 1777. Married Phebe Pierson, November 29, 1799. She died February 27, 1815, and he married Abigail Ann Law of Cheshire, Connecticut, February, 1816. He was ordained to the gospel ministry September 28, 1803, and supplied two congregations for seven years in the town of Carmel, Dutchess County, New York. In October, 1810, he removed to Waterbury, Connecticut, and became pastor of the Congregational Church of Salem, Connecticut. He resigned in May, 1817. He then supplied the congregation in East Haven, and on December

10, 1817, was installed pastor of the Congregational Church in East Haven, which pastorate he held twenty-nine years and four months, resigning at the age of 70 years.

Mr. Dodd found his people in a considerably perturbed state; but by his calm, firm, judicious manner, they gradually settled their ruffled feathers, and in due course of time they were all securely tucked under his mantle. Not being new to the work, his experience taught him how to avoid contention and secure harmony. His preaching was perhaps less ultra in doctrine than that of his immediate predecessor; but his sermons were always plain, sound, and practical, truly evangelical, and purely orthodox, earnest and forcible in delivery. He was very faithful to his people, and an industrious writer, seldom exchanging his pulpit for others. In his personnel he was of stout and sturdy build, and at once impressive in his firmness and fixedness of purpose; although he might be cold and austere even to severity, yet beneath that broad and ample waistcoat beat a heart warm with love and sympathy for his own people. He had no affiliation for any one outside of his creed, not even courtesy, and especially none for his neighbor who preached in gown and bans, which he characterized from his high-perched pulpit as "heathenish garments, the rags of popery."

He was not only the spiritual leader and guide of his people, but their temporal counselor and instructor also. He rejoiced with his people in their prosperity, lamented with them in adversity and grieved with them when they mourned. He never intruded himself in family affairs, but when his advice was sought

it was given in a calm Christian spirit which many
times smoothed the troubled waters of family dissen-
sion. He was a firm and fearless advocate of temperance in all times and places and under all
circumstances. He took a commendable interest in
schools, and always visited every school twice each
term. Children are keen observers of men and man-
ners, and those outside of his flock well knew there
was no word of praise for them no matter how
deserving.

We must not censure the men for such prejudices,
but lay the blame at the door of the times in which
they were born and lived. This sentiment had
descended from the settlement of the country, and was
intensified from generation to generation until now it
was double distilled and purely refined. It is a happy
thing that this• "middle wall of partition" is now
crumbling away between those of differing creeds;
that the bitterness of feeling and asperity of speech
between various schools of belief is softening. They
were all alike one to another, for each said acrimon-
ious things of the other, and each one had some
epithet of ridicule to apply to another. How much
more Christian in spirit to have a wholesome and
hearty respect for each others' opinions, to be united
in the brotherhood of Christ and the fatherhood of
God!

In politics he was an uncompromising "Whig" in
those days. If he had lived to the present time he
would have been a true Rooseveltian. During high
political contests, it was often remarked outside of
its limits, that East Haven was governed by the steeple
rather than by the state, which we have no desire to

contradict. It this was true, is it not a high compliment to the man who stood under the steeple? We often see a fine preacher of admirable sermons, but when he leaves the pulpit his work is done; he can not affiliate with the people, he is not adapted to the work by nature, and therefore is not a pastor. While on the other hand we meet a more indifferent sermonizer but a complete pastor, one who holds the people as it were in his hands.

In Mr. Dodd we find the rare combination of preacher, pastor and governor. It is wonderful what command he held over his people. This may be illustrated by the following incident: In the fall of 1842 Second Adventism came into view, then called "Millerism." At a social gathering of one of his prominent members, one who was present related the remarks of a very prominent physician of New Haven; neither one was an Adventist. One after another commented on the subject, and finally the hostess, who had been an earnest listener, remarked, "Well, I shall think just as Mr. Dodd does," and that expressed the whole: as pastor, so was the people, and as the people so was the pastor, one and the same. Like Solomon he believed in the healthy use of the rod with his people, and he often gave them a sound thrashing, from his red-cushioned pulpit. Some might laugh in their sleeve, but none took offence, and they with one accord laid it on the back of erring human nature, which needed wholesome correction, and before the next Sunday they had all settled back into their accustomed groove—shall it be called rut? He stood high among his clerical brethren, and in the councils of the consociation his advice was sought and his decisions revered.

Mr. Dodd was a natural genealogist, and early in his pastorate sought out and compiled a history of the town, supplemented by a genealogy of all its families. The work was much appreciated and every family owned a copy, but in the lapse of years and the scattering of families the work has been carried to all parts of the Union; it is now out of print and only a copy here and there is to be found in the town.

During Mr. Dodd's pastorate a change of the arrangement of seats was made, in 1822, when the sheep-pen pews were removed from the center and north side of the house, and slips substituted in their places, leaving a tier of the old square pews all around the three other sides. "Also the first fence of which there is any account was put around the meeting house lot. This was due to the energy and liberality of the ladies of the congregation. It was a substantial structure and for thirty years added greatly to the beauty and general appearance of the church surroundings."

Mr. Dodd was happily seconded and aided in his pastoral duties by a very discreet and worthy wife. She sought no distinctions only those which come from a faithful discharge of womanly duties to home, church and community. She was every way suited and adapted to the views and ways of her husband, being very plain and neat in dress; neither could be accused of leading the fashions of the day. He was a man very much afraid of expense for his people, as well as the town, and this extreme conservatism prevented him from keeping pace with the progress of the times. Utility and service before fashion was the predominant idea of this worthy couple in all temporal things. His wife was always solicitous for his welfare, even to selecting her successor, in case of her demise, which she did to the general knowledge of the town, years before she passed on to the great hereafter, which event occurred October 17, 1847. Mr. Dodd was now left alone, never having enjoyed the happiness of being called father. East Haven people regarded it as one of the events of Providence that the good lady's wish should be consummated, so after a reasonable and proper time had elapsed, Mr. Dodd proceeded to complete the wish of his late wife, with the perfect sanction and congratulations of the whole town, when he made his third matrimonial venture with Miss Eliza Andrews, July 12, 1848, Rev. D. W. Havens officiating.

Miss Andrews was a sister of the late Deacon Samuel T. Andrews, by whose advice and counsel many a point in town affairs was settled and carried to a successful issue.

This pleasant union continued about eight years, when Mr. Dodd passed on to the reward of the faithful on February 6, 1856. Mrs. Dodd continued on in the even tenor of her way, doing good as she had opportunity until September 21, 1868, when she was called home to enjoy the fruits of a well-ordered Christian life.

Rev. Daniel William Havens, June 16, 1847, to
July 2, 1877.

Times had now greatly changed. Education was
making strides in the land. Books, magazines, and
newspapers were daily read; knowledge of topics
formerly unknown to the general public were subjects
of common discussion. The minister, the doctor, the
squire and the schoolmaster were no longer the brains
and intelligence of the community. Everyone read,
thought, and reasoned for himself in all matters—
theology not excepted. It was a crucial test of a young
minister's ability, tact and perseverance, to be a
successor to one of a long pastorate. The calm, even,
smooth ways of the past must now give way to the
rush of the present. This distressed the old, and not
unfrequently disturbed the conservative younger
people, while the young clamored for the vanities of
the passing hours.

Amid all this din of conflicting opinions many a
young minister resigned after a few years, and sought
fields anew. Scarcely one of the neighboring towns
but went through this experience. It speaks well
for both people and pastor that in East Haven two
consecutive pastorates of thirty years each followed
one another. Mr. Havens was a young man fresh
from the school of theology, without experience, yet
we see him avoiding the pitfalls which befell many
of his cloth and age. He could not have done this
without the aid and support of his people. He was
a man who met all with cordiality and courtesy, in
all walks of life. He very early showed his interest
and coöperation for the benefit of the community in

the active part he took in the work of improvement and adornment of the Old Cemetery (elsewhere recorded).

No doubt Mr. Havens met with trials—what person does not when dealing with the public? But one has only to read over the upheavals, reconstructions, revolutions, improvements and additions to the church edifice to see he was sustained by his people. All these could not have been accomplished without the united strength of pastor and people.

He was born in Norwich, Connecticut, January 24, 1815, son of Capt. Daniel and Desire (Howes) Havens. In early life he was converted in New York City, where he connected himself with the Murray Street Presbyterian Church. Soon after he decided to study for the ministry and entered Yale University, graduating in 1843, and from East Windsor Seminary in 1846. June 16, 1847, he was ordained pastor of the Congregational Church, East Haven. Soon after his ordination in 1847, he married Miss Elizabeth Hemingway, daughter of Capt. Harvey and Elizabeth (Woodward) Hemingway, both natives of East Haven, belonging to its oldest families, although at the time she resided in Brooklyn, New York. She died in 1885. Three children were born to them: Mrs. T. A. Fairchild, Miss Bertha M. Havens of Holton, Kansas, and Mr. Wm. H. Havens of Meriden, Connecticut. In 1887 Mr. Havens retired from the ministry and returned to Meriden, Connecticut, to the home of his son. August 31, 1889, while on a visit to East Haven, he died at the home of his brother-in-law, F. Foot Andrews. His remains were borne through the gateway of the Old Cemetery which he had been so instrumental in erecting just forty years before, there to await the glorious coming of the Lord.

This brings us down to the present day, to the pastorate of Rev. Daniel J. Clark, who is the sixth regularly ordained and installed pastor of this venerable church. In three years more will be its bicentennial; also the rounding out of Mr. Clark's thirty years' ministrations to a united and appreciative people. In the providence of God it is devoutly hoped that pastor and people may be able to unite in the celebration of the event. If so, it will be the third consecutive pastorate of thirty years duration. It is doubtful if such a record can be shown in the history of any other people in New England.

Mr. Clark is of old New England stock, a native of Ludlow, Vermont. He prepared for the ministry at Wesleyan University, Middletown, Connecticut, class of 1876; was married to Miss Alice Cornelia Deming of Newington, Connecticut, October 27, 1878; graduated from the Hartford Theological Seminary, class of 1880; was ordained pastor of East Haven Congregational Church, July 7, 1880, thus serving the church nearly twenty-eight years.

The following statement from Mr. Clark will be of interest:

"During this period the church has grown from a membership of 167 in 1880 to that of 366 in 1908, over all losses by letter and death. During the same period several very important changes and improvements have been made. The chapel has been twice frescoed, at an expense of $300; the church and chapel have been renovated, recarpeted and painted at a cost of over $2,000, and a piano has been placed in the chapel, for which $300 was paid. The parsonage has been made more comfortable by installing a furnace, and the introduction of all the modern improvements, at an expense of nearly $1,000.

"A steam-heating system for church and chapel has been recently introduced, costing $1,200. A slate roof has been placed upon the church, for which $400 was paid. Three thousand dollars have also been expended for a beautiful pipe organ, which adds largely to the effectiveness of the services. All these improvements have called for an expenditure of over $8,000.

"During the period under consideration, the church has received legacies of over $15,000.

Edwin Granniss	$11,000
Edward Ellsworth Thompson	1,000
Edward Akland Walker	1,000
Albert Forbes	1,000
John Woodward Thompson	500
Barbara Perkins	580
Total	$15,080

"But after all, facts and figures can but poorly tell the story of a church's work and life. The best of the story as well as the largest part of it, must ever be that which no eye but God's can read. What the services of this church have been, Sabbath after Sabbath, and year after year, to many weary and burdened hearts, to many darkened and troubled homes; and what the fellowship of believers has been to all who have had a part in its work and worship, is known only to God. Though much has been done, yet much land remains to be possessed. While to-day we may rejoice in the fact that 'Hitherto hath the Lord helped us,' as we look away from the past and into the future let us 'thank God and take courage.'

"DANIEL J. CLARK."

East Haven, Conn.,
February 29, 1908.

CONGREGATIONAL DEACONS.

Caleb Chidsey, died February 20, 1713.
Joshua Austin, died March 29, 1760.
Thomas Smith, died 1762.
Daniel Hitchcock, died 1761.
Deodate Davenport, died December 3, 1761.
Samuel Hemingway, chosen 1758; died October 25, 1777.
Abraham Hemingway, chosen 1761; removed.
Amos Morris, chosen 1776; died December 30, 1801.
Stephen Smith, chosen 1778; died January 22, 1816.
Samuel Davenport, chosen 1797; died July 9, 1810.
John Morris, chosen July, 1800; removed 1806.
Levi Pardee, chosen July, 1800; died November 21, 1813.
Enos Hemingway, chosen 1806; removed June 13, 1830.
Amos Morris, chosen 1816; resigned 1818.
Bela Farnham, chosen July 1, 1832; resigned March 5, 1852.
Amos Morris, chosen July 1, 1832; resigned March 5, 1852.
Samuel H. Hemingway, chosen July 1, 1832; died September 30, 1849.
Ruel Andrews, chosen March 5, 1852; died April 30, 1864.
Alfred Morris, chosen March 5, 1852; died September 20, 1876.
Aaron L. Curtis, chosen September 2, 1864; died June 26, 1872.
Edwin Street, chosen May 1, 1868; resigned June 17, 1878.
Asa L. Fabrique, chosen May 1, 1868.
Samuel T. Andrews, chosen August 30, 1872; died August 22, 1884.
Thaddeus Street, chosen August 30, 1872; died January 16, 1882.
Frederick B. Street, chosen April 7, 1882.
Merrick M. Russell, chosen April 7, 1882; resigned April 11, 1884.
Julius H. Morris, chosen October 10, 1884.
Collis B. Granniss, chosen October 10, 1884.

ST. JAMES'S EPISCOPAL CHURCH.

The population of Fair Haven increased yearly. The village now had two churches, viz.: The Grand Street Congregational and the Methodist, both on the

west side of the Quinnipiac; but there was no church
on the east side. The Episcopalians of the place had
hitherto attended services in East Haven or New
Haven, principally Trinity Church, New Haven. They
now thought their numerical strength would warrant them in supporting a church of their own.
This was greatly seconded and aided by the late
Capt. Isaac Brown, who donated the site for
the church, also the stone from his quarries to
build it, and a liberal contribution for its erection. St.
James's parish was organized March 30, 1843. It was
decided to take steps to build a church immediately.
The building committee was Esquire James Barnes,
Daniel Foote, George P. Thomas, Samuel M. Tuttle,
Ralph Warren.

Ground was broken for the foundations in May,
1844. The corner stone was laid by Rev. Dr. Harry
Croswell, July 8, 1844, and the church was consecrated
in July, 1845. The first baptism in the church building was August 3, 1845, and the first confirmation on
November 12, 1845. At this service Rev. William E.
Vibbert was ordained to the priesthood. He was
elected rector while in his diaconate period, March 28,
1845, and continued its universally beloved spiritual
guide and leader until August 1, 1892, when a stroke
incapacitated him from further duties. He was rector
emeritus until his death November 9, 1895, aged 82
years. An eloquent, forcible, practical, orthodox
sermonizer, every discourse fraught with weight, contained food for reflection and consideration. A zealous, loving, sympathetic, watchful rector for forty-
seven years and four months was laid away among
his people November 12, 1895.

By the vote of annexation in 1882, the territory where this church stands ceased to be East Haven soil, therefore its subsequent history belongs to New Haven.

PILGRIM CONGREGATIONAL CHURCH.

In 1830 the Grand Avenue Congregational Church, which was a scion of the Old Stone Church, East Haven, was established, and a new, commodious brick church was built on the site of the present Strong Public School. This church so increased with the population that in 1852 it was necessary to either build a new church or enlarge the old one. After due consideration, it was thought best for the Congregationalists on the east side to form a new church society, which they did March 25, 1852. A very amicable and pleasant division took place from the parent church, and the new society proceeded to build a new church on the corner of East Grand and Lenox streets. It was dedicated the summer of 1853. Rev. Nathaniel J. Burton was its first pastor. It has become a large and influential church. Like its Episcopal neighbor opposite, this part of the town was ceded to New Haven in 1882, when East Haven history ceases.

CHAPTER IV.

Iron Works and Mills.

HE transactions relative to the Iron Works are contained in sundry resolutions and orders. This was probably the first establishment of the kind within the present bounds of the state. This business was introduced in the following manner:

"General Court, N. H. 12th Nov. 1655.

"The Towne was acquainted that there is a purpose that an *Iron Worke* shall be set up beyond the farmes at Stoney River, which is considered will be for a publique good; and Mr. Goodyear declared Mr. Winstone and himself did intend to carry it on; only he desired now to know what the Towne desired in it; much debate was about it; but no man engaged in it at present; but divers spoke, that they would give some worke toward making the Damm, whose names and number of days worke were taken, which amounted to about 140 days: so it issueth for that time."

"29th Nov. 1655.—The Governor informed the Towne that this meeting was called to consider something further about the Iron Worke, sundry who engaged to worke, last Court, have not yet performed, tho' all others have; and it was now concluded, that those that are now behinde, should be called upon to perform what they promised.—It was also now desired that men would declare, who will engage in the worke, and what estate they will put in. But few speaking to it, it was desired that those who are willing would meet at the Governor's this afternoon at 2 o'clock, to declare themselves therein, and it was now propounded whether the Towne will give up their right in the place, and what accommodation is necessary for the best conveniency of the said *Iron Worke;*

in this case all the Towne voted to give a full libertie for the *Iron Workes* to go on, and also for wood, water, ironplace, oares, shells for lime, or what else is necessary for that worke, upon the Towne lands upon that side of the great river, called the East River; provided that no man's propertie laid out, or to be laid out, be entered upon, nor no planter prohibited from cutting wood, or other conveniency upon the said common, in an orderly way; and that Branford doe make the like grant, according to their proportion they have in the worke, that future questions about this thing may be prevented.

"19th May, 1656. Upon motion of Mr. Goodyear and John Cooper, in behalf of the Collier that comes to burn coal for the Iron Workes; he had 12 acres of land granted him as his own, if the Iron-workes go on, and he stay three years in the worke. Provided that all minerals there be reserved, and that he attend all orders of the Towne for the present, and in disposing of said lands hereafter, if it shall so fall out, to have it. The place propounded for is a piece of land lying betwixt the Great Pond, and the Beaver Meadows, a 100 or 2 acres, about 2 miles from the Iron worke. Against which grant or place none objected, so as to hinder the same."

This is now called the Farm. It was first in the possession of Theophilus Eaton, the governor. It was given to his daughter Mary, who married Valentine Hill, merchant, Dover—Pisquataqua. He sold it to Nathaniel Micklethwaite, merchant, London, November 2, 1660, for £230 sterling, or $1022.22. He sold it to Thomas Clark of Boston for £100 lawful money, February 28, 1665, and in the township of New Haven. The farm contained 300 acres of upland and 60 acres of meadow.

"14th Sept., 1657. The Governor informed the Court that Mr. Winthrop has let out his part of the

Ironworkes to two men in Boston, Capt. Clarke and Mr. Tayne, as they have agreed."

This plan met with a general disapprobation. Debating followed. It was contended that as this establishment was made for the purpose of trade, there was danger of the entire alienation of the trade and the property. And there would also be a collection of disorderly persons which would corrupt the morals of the neighborhood and cause great trouble in the town. The subject was "referred to the Court and the Townsman John Cooper to consider it, upon what terms to let out the workes and whether they should cut wood upon our ground."

That reference reported thus: "An agreement made by the Committee appointed to consider about the Iron Workes was read to the Towne and by vote confirmed and ordered to be entered."

"At the Governor's house, 1 Dec. 1657.

"1. It is agreed that the Iron Workes propounded to and allowed by this Towne, and to which they granted several priveleges, was, and is only for this Furnace now made in the place intended, and expressed, as appeareth by the records, with a Forge, or two, if necessary for the Iron which this furnace produceth, which are to be improved by the Townes jointly within the limits allowed by this Court.

"2. This Iron worke and all the privileges thereunto belonging, were intended and granted for the good of New-Haven and Branford, for bringing and setting up trade there, which in whole or in a great measure they are like to be deprived of, if any part of it be alienated either to strangers, or others out of their jurisdiction. They, therefore, think it not safe that any part of it be sold, or leased out, without particular and express law and licence from the Towne, or Jury, or a Committee, as is appointed for house lots or lands.

"3. That our neighbors and friends of Branford provide and supply their part of wood, which is 3-8ths parts, with other things of a like nature, from the land within their own limits, and that New-Haven do the like for their 5-8ths parts.

"4. That all servants, women and others employed in any respect about the Iron workes, shall attend and be subject to all orders and laws already made, or which shall be made and published by this towne, or jurisdiction, as other men.

"5. That the grant made by the Iron workes be forthwith delivered to the Secretary here, that it may be read and considered; as the grant made by New-Haven shall be to them; that the two plantations may receive and bear their due proportion in profits and charges, as was at first provided for."

How far these resolutions were carried into effect does not appear. About eight years afterward, Benjamin Linge prosecuted John Cooper, agent of the Iron Works, for the damage he had sustained from the water of the dam. And the people employed there, being many of them corrupt foreigners and strangers, were so immoral and vicious as to require the frequent interposition of the civil authority.

"The General Court, therefore, ordered that complaint should be made to Capt. Clark about the disorderly persons that came to the Iron Works. And also ordered that the master, clerk or overseer, and other officers shall not admit any, without a certificate from persons of known reputation, under the penalty of 40 shillings for every offence; and if any come to tarry there without such recommendation and permission, shall be liable to the penalty of forty shillings."

As a further check to these increasing evils, Matthew Moulthrop, Sr., was appointed conservator of the morals of the people about the Iron Works.

Of so much consequence was this establishment, that after the union of New Haven with Connecticut, a special order was made regarding the people employed in the work, to free them from taxes for seven years, as appears from the following:

"13th May, 1669, Upon the petition of Mr. William Andrews on behalf of Capt. Thomas Clark, master of the Iron works of New-Haven, for encouragement of the said worke, for the supply of the country with good Iron, and well wrought according to art, this Court do confirm a grant formerly made by New-Haven: That the said persons and estates constantly or only employed in said work, shall be and are hereby exempt from paying country rates for 7 years next ensuing." (*Conn. Col. Rec.*)

At this period, and until the business was relinquished, Thomas Clark of Boston appears to have been the principal owner. Business was carried on here both from New Haven and Branford. It continued until about 1679 or 80. Why the business was relinquished cannot now be satisfactorily ascertained. The furnace was supplied with bog ore from North Haven. It was chiefly carted, but sometimes brought from bogmine wharf by water round to the point below the furnace; and from that circumstance the point to this day is called *Bogmine*.* There was a great mortality in the village in the year 1679, when Ralph Russell and some other principal workmen died, which may have obstructed the operation; and probably the expense was too great to realize sufficient profits. It is a tradition in the Russell family that the death of the principal workmen produced this change. Another authority says the vein of ore in North Haven was exhausted. Jasper Crane and John

* *Bogmine* was also the *nom de plume* of the late John Woodward Thompson.

Cooper were overseers and agents. Richard Post was founder, and John Russell was potter in the furnace.

On August 19, 1680, Thomas Clark sold to Sergt. John Potter, "All that farm lying and being within the township of New-Haven, and near and adjoining, to a brook called by the name of Stoney-brook, which Thomas Clarke bought of Nathaniel Micklewaite of the city of London, merchant, containeth by estimation 300 acres of upland, be it more or less, and 3 score acres of meadow, be it more or less, adjoining thereto; excepting always all the uplands that hath been formerly sold from the said farme or Iron workes, reserving only all the Iron worke plates of Iron, and the moveables to himself, that are upon the premises." John Potter was to pay £40 per annum for 21 years, in wheat, pork and peas. The farm soon passed into the hands of William Rosewell, whose only child married Gurdon Saltonstall, afterwards the governor of Connecticut.

Sergt. John Potter did not resume the iron business, as was contemplated when he bought the farm, but in the year 1692 he and Thomas Pinion petitioned New Haven for liberty to build a Bloomary on the first spring or brook towards Foxon. In April

"Some of the townsmen having viewed the brooke that runs into Stoney river at that place, or thereabouts, which was moved for by John Potter, formerly, to set up a Bloomary; the town by vote approved of his design of a Bloomary; and for his encouragement allow him the use of said brooke and 20 acres of land, not exceeding 30, near the *first spring,* the west side of Stoney river, and grant him the liberty of what Iron mines there are within the town bounds, and the use of what wood he needs in the commons for the work, if it proves effectual. The aforesaid land is to be laid out and bounded to him, by the surveyor, and one or two of the Townsmen. Always preserving the necessary highways, if there be any." (*N. H. Rec.*)

This Bloomary was established, but I can not find how long it was in operation. The site of the furnace was sequestered for a gristmill, as appear from the following curious document on East Haven records:

"Articles of agreement made between the Inhabitants of Stoney River of the one party and Samuel Heminway of the other party, 2 July, 1681, is as followeth, concerning setting up of a Grist-Mill at the Furnace Dam.

1. "The said Village doth for his encouragement give the Furnace Dam, with the use of the water damed therewith, and do promise to defend the said Heminway in the possession thereof, (so far as in their power) without let or molestation from any, either New-Haven or Branford, or any other; reserving liberty for John Potter to have a convenient place for water from the same pond, to set up and manage a Bloomary Furnace of Iron, if the said Potter shall at any time, hereafter, see cause to enter upon such a design."

2. "The said Village doth give to the said Heminway the land that liest next to his house between Stoney River and the Farme, to the quantity of an acre or two, if it may be spared from the highways, as they shall see good to set out to him, and 16 or 17 acres of land elsewhere, that may be convenient for the said Heminway.

3. "The said Village do free the said Grist Mill from paying taxes to the said Village or Town.

4. "The Inhabitants of the said Village do engage to bring the corn that they would have ground into meal, to the said Mill.

5. "The said Inhabitants do engage to perform the whole work of what is necessary for the setting down said Mill, and to repair it, that the Dam may be secure from breaches at the setting down said Mill. But said Heminway is to secure it at his own charges for the future, when some extraordinary, or unsuspected accident shall happen to it.

6. "The said Inhabitants of the said Village do engage to assist him to raise the Mill Stones, and to get them to the said Mill, and to give the said Samuel Heminway liberty to use what timber and stones may be needful for building and repairing the said Mill, as shall be most convenient for him in that business.

"And in consideration of the premises the said Samuel Heminway doth engage as followeth:

1. "That the said Heminway will, before the next winter, in November next ensuing, set up a sufficient Grist Mill, at the above place, and keep the said mill in good repair, fit to make good and sufficient meal of corn, that is dry and fit for grinding.

2. "That he the said Heminway will set up a house over the Mill sufficient to secure the inhabitants' corn from damage by the neighbours hogs, or other creatures, that might otherwise devour it—within his compass.

3. "That the said Heminway or somebody for him, shall attend at the said Mill, one day in a fortnight, if there be need, to grind for the inhabitants their corn. And shall spend more time, and give attendance on the same, if need be, that is, till he hath ground all that is brought to be ground the said day.

4. "That the said Heminway will take no more toll for the grinding our corn into meal that what the law allows.

5. "That he will either keep this mill himself, or if he shall let it to any other, it shall be to such an one, as the Inhabitants of the Village shall approve of.

6. "The said land, the said Village do give to the said Heminway, to be for the use of said Mill, and so continue, except the 16 or 20 acres given him.

"The first article is thus to be so understood, that the said Heminway doth engage to bear his share with the other Inhabitants of the said Village in any damage that may fall by the Dam or Stream, or by any trouble for the same, by New-Haven or Branford, or any other. And as for the land about the house, mentioned in this agreement, it be understood, that the said Heminway is to have what can be spared there from highways and across on the other side of the pond.

"The abovesaid articles of agreement concerning the Mill, made between the said Samuel Heminway and the Inhabitants of said Village, 2d July, 1681, is confirmed by Vote to be their doings." (*E. H. Rec.*)

The grant of 16 or 17 acres, the town of New Haven refused to ratify. About 25 years after this transaction, the sons of Samuel Hemingway, viz.: John and Abraham, obtained a grant of the mill privilege from Branford, as follows:

"Branford, 23 Augt. 1706.—At a meeting of the Proprietors, warned according to law, John and Abraham Heminway, of New-Haven Iron works, desire us to grant them liberty to erect a Dam on the Furnace pond, where it formerly was, and to get stone, and timber and earth to erect the same, on our side.

1. "We having considered the public benefit such a Mill may be, doe on the terms following grant the desire of the said John and Abraham Heminway, viz. that they shall raise the said Dam no higher than it was formerly, nor no higher, than shall be allowed by Mr. William Maltbie, Deacon John Rose, Sergt. Nathaniel Foot, of Branford, when they shall view said Mill place."

2. "John and Abraham Heminway, and all who shall after them possess and improve said Mill, shall at all times, hereafter, grind what corn shall come from this Towne, in turn, as it shall come to said Mill, not preferring others before them."

3. "The said John and Abraham Heminway, their heirs and assigns, shall erect and maintayne a sufficient Mill, at said place, at all times, hereafter forever; upon those aforesaid conditions, we grant the request of said John and Abraham Heminway. But if they or any, who shall at any time hereafter possess said mill, shall refuse or neglect to perform any or all the abovementioned conditions, then this grant

shall be void and of no effect, that we, or our successors, may set up a Mill ourselves for the public benefit on this side."

Voted and passed Test, by William Maltbie, Clerk. (*Branford Rec.*)

The manner of expression in this document intimates that the mill had not been erected by their father, as was expected when he obtained the village grant. The water privilege where the forge stood was disposed of afterwards. Samuel Hemingway applied to the town of New Haven for it and obtained the following order.

"April 26th, 1687. Samuel Heminway moved to have liberty to set a fulling mill where the forge formerly stood. After much debate the towne granted liberty to the said Heminway to set up a fulling mill in the forementioned place, provided that he make no dam that shall make a pond to raise the water above two feet deep upon Austin's highway. And that he consider beforehand, whether such a dam, but of such a height as aforesaid, will answer his purpose."

Upon this grant and one that was made by the village in 1706, John and Abraham Hemingway, and John Marsh, jointly erected a fulling mill in 1709, on the premises.

In 1684 it was contemplated to build a sawmill on the first spring. That plan was relinquished and one was built on Claypit brook, below Danforth's swamp, which was abandoned many years ago.

As East Haven was the first place in Connecticut where an attempt was made to manufacture, it seems fitting that the circumstance should have a place in history.

If, perchance, it was not the first place, it certainly was the first where the Iron Works were established

THE MILL.

in Connecticut, which has already been described. It is proposed to follow along this changing line to the present day.

They brought the bog ore from North Haven round to "Bogmine point" where the furnace stood, and smelted it at the furnace. It was then taken to the Bloomary (which was near where the present grist-mill stands), and run through this forge, which is the first one after it is melted from the ore. It was now ready for the blacksmith. No attempt was made to manufacture anything but what was done by hand on the anvil under the strokes of the smith. This business was given up after about twenty-five years. The site of the furnace was sequestered for a grist-mill, which was run without interruption till it was burned down in 1878. The site of the bloomary or forge, commonly called the "old iron mill," was now used for a fulling and carding mill. At this time, two hundred years after the grant was made for its erection, the question may arise, What was a fulling mill?

We must go back to this time and remember there were but two materials used in America for clothing and household purposes; both products of the farm, one vegetable, the other animal:—flax and wool. We must not forget that every thread of wool or flax had to be run between the thumb and finger of some female member of the household on either the flax or wool spinning wheel—linen for summer wear, and woolen for winter, for male and female, as well as all the household necessities.

After the spinning and weaving had been done in families, the flannel was then taken to the fulling mill, where by some process of heat and sweating the cloth was thickened and made compact and firm for men's wear, blankets, etc. If it was woven plain it was called kersey; if twilled it was cassimere. The finer portions of wool were woven for women's wear.

Sometimes it was a mixture of wool and linen called "linsey woolsey," which was not fulled but dressed and pressed. In summer all wore linen, variously colored, plain, or plaid or striped. The men's everyday wear was plain, or twilled, the coarser kind called tow cloth. The dyeing was made from roots and barks principally. It is true, silks and broadcloths were known, and some possessed them to a limited extent, but they were only used on state occasions. Yet with all this work of housekeeping, spinning and weaving, many of the women of that period were expert needlewomen, and their embroideries on lace and muslin are not excelled by those of the present day.

Connected with the fulling mill was the carding apparatus, used for combing and making wool into long fleecy rolls, about an inch in diameter and three-fourths of a yard long, ready for the wool spinning wheel. A machine was used also for opening and breaking flax into long silky heads, about half a yard long for the little or flax spinning wheel. This carding could be done by hand; but it was a slow, tedious process and was generally done at the fulling or carding mill. The business of the fulling mill was not given up until about 1840, when it had dwindled to nothing, and the mill was afterwards turned into a gristmill run by Mr. Jeremiah B. Davidson, into whose family it had passed several years before. At the present time it is the site of the Forbes mill. At this time there were two gristmills running at the same time.

The old grant made to Samuel Hemingway, the first settler of that name, July 2, 1681, remained in the family, descending from father to son just one hundred and fifty years through five generations to John Hemingway, 4th, who died July 20, 1827, leaving minor children. In 1831 the Hemingway mill property passed out of the name. Wyliss F. Colt, the guardian of one or more of these children, sold the mill property with all the mill privileges of water, milldam, water rights, land, and rights pertaining to the grant, to Truman Woodward & Company of New Haven, who erected the paper mill by the side of the gristmill. Before a sheet of paper was made there, the whole, conveying all the rights of the grant, was sold in 1834 to James Donaghee, who was a Virginian by birth and a graduate of Yale College. East Haven people were much pleased that the property had passed into the hands of a man of his standing and character, and that he was to make his residence with them. He built a house just over the line in Branford, on the first hill, but his social relations were with East Haven. The manufacture of writing paper was now commenced, giving employment to a limited number of girls and others in the town. October 30, 1840, the whole property was sold to Emanuel M. Henriques for $12,500. Mr. Donaghee moved away, and Mr. Henriques lived in the city. The business was carried on under a superintendent by the name of Loomis until 1853, when business was suspended and the mill remained idle about two years. September 26, 1855, the whole mill property was sold to George H. Townsend, with all the mill privileges, milldam, water rights, and privileges conferred by the Hemingway grant, including land occupied, together with all the machinery of every description. Mr. Townsend associated with him Mr. James Harper, an expert paper manufacturer, and a successful business was carried on for ten years. In 1856 Mr. Townsend bought Mr. Davidson's mill, formerly the old fulling mill, and ran all three of the mills until April 11, 1866, when he sold both gristmills to the Saltonstall Milling Company. Mr. Townsend had now gone very largely into the wholesale export ice business, and Mr. Harper went to Westville, where there were better manufacturing facilities; thus papermaking ceased in East Haven.

August 9, 1873, Mr. Alexander W. Forbes bought both mills of the Saltonstall Milling Company. At this time, Carrington and Fabrique established a brush factory in the former paper mill, which was continued until March, 1878, when the mill took fire and was totally destroyed, gristmill and all. During all these changes of half a century the gristmill kept grinding on, until fire put an end to all work at this point. Mr. Forbes did not rebuild the old Hemingway gristmill, but improved and enlarged the old fulling mill property, which business has been sucessfully carried on by his son, Frederick A. Forbes, to the present day.

March 7, 1882, just two hundred years since East Haven voted away its right and title to Lake Saltonstall (then called the Furnace Pond), included in the Hemingway grant, which was "ratified by New Haven," Alexander W. Forbes sold all the land which had ever been claimed or occupied by him or others, as owners of said mill, together with all the rights and privileges conferred by the grant of 1681, to the New Haven Water Company. In all probability there will be no change for an indefinite time to come. Instead of the water of the lake turning a little grist-mill, it is now carried into thousands of homes, all over East Haven and New Haven.

ICE CUTTING.

About 1840 this business was commenced in a small way by two brothers, Orlando B. and Merritt Thompson, who made it very profitable, cutting the ice and marketing it themselves. Saltonstall ice being pure and clear, had a ready sale. In 1843 George Thompson and Samuel Perry embarked in cutting ice from Lake Saltonstall. In 1848 George H. Townsend & Company, for the purpose of shipping ice, built large ice houses at the lake and at Red Rock (now Quinnipiac bridge). At one time Mr. Townsend's company had seven schooners enter the harbor in one day for ice; five of them were loaded in one day. There were no three-masters in those days, nor until after 1870. This business was continued until competition with Maine ice, which was much thicker and more dense, bearing transportation with less loss, caused it to be given up. No ice cutting is now done at the lake, although Mr. Townsend reserved the right for nine hundred and ninety-nine years, when he sold his mill privileges to the water company. The unoccupied ice houses at the lake were burned in 1896 and valuable machinery, with the engine and boiler, were ruined.

A PLEASURE RESORT.

Lake Saltonstall has always been more or less a pleasure resort. In early days it was a good fishing pond and not infrequently a fine shot of wild ducks could be made. In 1851 the New London Railroad was built across the south end of the lake. A convenient platform was made to accommodate the ice business. In 1856 and '57, when the skating craze swept over the country, the cars brought crowds of skaters to the lake, which had now been dignified by the name of "Saltonstall"; it was no longer the "mill pond." For several years the class races of Yale were rowed over a two-mile course on the lake, and attracted crowds to the contest. Many would ride out and then take a rowboat to the head of the lake. This induced Capt. G. H. Baldwin to place an electric launch on the water with a trailer, Lucy. Later he built and ran a steam launch, Cygnet. As patronage increased, Mr. Townsend made more and greater improvements, appointing Mr. Andrew J. Granniss superintendent of the adjacent ground and park. Another steam launch, the Swan, and the barge Saltonstall, capable of carrying 250 people or more, were added to accommodate picnic parties, which came from the different towns by railroad. Twenty or more fishing or rowing boats lined the shore.

Through the strenuous efforts of Hon. James M. Townsend, the New Haven Electric Railway was extended from the Four Corners to East Haven Green, and thence to Lake Saltonstall, in 1894. The following extract is from the *Morning Journal and Courier,* Saturday, June 30, 1894:

LAKE SALTONSTALL.

"The initial trip over the Lake Saltonstall branch of the New Haven Electric Railway was taken yesterday, leaving New Haven Green at 1.30 P. M. The first car was filled with invited guests of the company, and members of the press. The run to East Haven was most delightful. The appearance of the car in the center was the signal for the ringing of the church bells and the applause of the citizens, who were out in full force to welcome the visitors.

"The company also had four cars at East Haven, and two hundred citizens enjoyed the hospitality of the company. They were brought to the city and then back to East Haven."

Through the summers of 1894 and '95, this seven hundred acre park, with all its romantic names of picturesque nooks and crags, was popular as a summer resort. Ever since 1848 Mr. George H. Townsend had been adding piece after piece and lot after lot to this domain, until he owned all the land bordering the lake on the west and north, also a good share on the east side. In June, 1895, Mr. Townsend sold this large tract, together with all his interest and privileges pertaining thereto, to the New Haven Water Company.

March, 1896, Mr. Eli Whitney, president of the New Haven Water Company, made this announcement: "We will not maintain any picnic grounds on the lake hereafter, on account of the danger of polluting the water in the lake. Boats will probably be allowed on the lake, but as to the matter of picnics that has been settled."

The business soon fell off and the boats were withdrawn one after the other, and the railway company removed their tracks. Although fishing is not prohibited, the restrictions are such that few now avail themselves of the privilege.

The Indian name of Lake Saltonstall was Lo-no-to-non-ket, in their language "The tear of the Great Spirit." The Indian name of the river was Tap-am-sha-sick (Stony river). The outlet of the lake, just east of the river, they called Tap-pam-has-ie (Little stream). The river was known as Stoney river, Farm river and Muddy river. On the maps later it is called Farm river, Foxon river, and East Haven river, and locally, near the lake, Deborah's river.

The term "Deborah's" river arises from the tradition of Deborah Chidsey's geese, about which "a cruel and unnecessary war" has been related. At the time she said little, well knowing her time was to come. She assisted her husband at the fulling mill, and when occasion required could ferry one across the river at high tide. A while after, while the governor was stopping at his house, he left one morning in his official dress of red broadcloth, resplendent in gold lace, white satin long waiscoat, purple velvet knee breeches, white silk stockings, and silver knee and shoe buckles. Although only a colonial governor (as Connecticut never had any other), yet he bedecked himself with the trappings of a royal one.

He called Deborah to ferry him over. In the middle of the stream she managed to run the little boat high on a rock, fast and firm. "What shall I do?" cried the governor. "Do? Why do as I do, or stay here till the tide falls." Whereupon she jumped into the river and waded ashore, turning her head and clacking like a goose, the meaning of which he well understood, as the "geese story" had been well spread through the colony, much to his annoyance. He did not follow Deborah's example, but sat on the dry portion of the boat until the tide fell, making good sport for the neighbors, with whom he was no favorite.

MORRIS COVE SALT WORKS.

The second article to be manufactured in East Haven of which there is any record, excepting the daily family spinning and weaving, was salt. This was carried on by Capt. Amos Morris at Morris Cove, at a crescent-shaped indentation between two rocky formations on the shore, a short distance easterly from the Old Lighthouse. The Revolutionary War prevented this necessity from being brought by vessels from the West Indies, and many families on the sea coast resorted to boiling sea water, which is said to yield about a quarter of a pound to a gallon of water. The process was partly by evaporation, finished by boiling, when any quantity larger than for family use was made. Wooden vats were made 30 feet long by 20 wide and 10 inches deep. These salt pans were placed on the shore safe from wind and tide. They were filled with sea water during the March spring tides by the action of the surf beating on the shore and rocks. They were so placed as to receive the whole effect of the sun during summer evaporation.

They were covered by sliding roofs to keep off dews, rain and wind. These roofs had to be shut over at night and the whole business needed much care. When the water reached a certain point it was drawn off, and the process was hastened by boiling; for this purpose Captain Morris had five boilers. It is said that when the evaporation has reached a certain stage, the liquid assumes a reddish color and a thin crust forms on the surface, which soon breaks and sinks down. This is followed by another, and the crystallization proceeds very rapidly. The salt is then removed to sheds open at the sides, piled in heaps, and left for a few days, in order to dispel the chloride of magnesium which is quickly done as it liquefies by contact with air. The salt is then redissolved and crystallized for market.

These works were all destroyed by fire at Tryon's invasion of New Haven, July 5, 1779. Although peace was declared soon after, the works were never rebuilt, as Turk's Island salt could be imported for less cost than salt could be made here.

Near the close of the war with England in 1812, another attempt was made to manufacture salt on the East Haven side, just below Tomlinson's bridge. Owing to so much fresh water flowing down the Quinnipiac and Mill rivers it was not successful and the works were loaded on scows and moved to Merwin's Point (now Woodmont-on-the-Sound). They were destroyed by the violent gale called the *Salt Storm,* September 3, 1821.

WAX FIGURES.

In 1903 Mr. L. S. Bagley brought to light an almost forgotten industry, which he credits to East Haven as the original place of manufacture. He says: "Exhibitions of wax figures started from here, for the whole country, and there was a fortune in this for a great many." On looking up the subject it was found the business was in full blast soon after the war of the Revolution. The manufacture was carried on by Mr. Reuben Moulthrop as principal, and his

brother-in-law, Mr. Justin W. Street. Mr. Bagley
says the work was done at the "lean-to" house on
the west side of Hemingway avenue known for the
last twenty-five years as the Dillon place. Mr.
Moulthrop was by profession a portrait painter, and
probably did the modeling, moulding and painting.
These exhibitions were conducted very much as the
stereopticon views and lectures are presented at the
present time, and were quite instructive at that period.
The manager had to be a man of talent and tact, of
ease and gracefulness of manner, of refinement, and
courteous attention to all, with a certain degree of
dignity and courtliness of address. Such a man was
found in Mr. Daniel Smith of East Haven, who
traveled the country over with great success. "Whenever a man became a public character," Mr. Bagley
says, "his figure was taken in wax, boxed up and sent
off on these exhibitions." If he was married, the
statue of his wife accompanied the husband many
times. The whole business gave employment to many
in different capacities, both male and female. The
wax figures of the women were dressed with great
care and richness of material. Mr. Moulthrop brought
two expert dressmakers, sisters, from Bristol, Connecticut, by the name of Shailor, to reside in his house,
to superintend and construct the dresses. One of the
sisters was married to Mr. Daniel Hughes, April 5,
1818; she was his third wife. The exhibition carried
two ladies, a brunette and a blonde, to one of which
this placard was attached, "The beauty of this place."
If the belle of the town was a brunette, then the brunette had the card, and *vice versa,* and if there was

one of each, then both were labeled. In some places it was a source of great speculation to know who was meant.

That the business was very renumerative is proved by Mr. Moulthrop erecting what was then considered a palatial residence on Townsend avenue. Although the structure has been enlarged, built upon, and changed by its different owners, yet the original house has always been preserved, and is the basis of all the additions. For several years it was known as the "Mitchell House." It is now the the home of Mr. Frank H. Kimberly. If, as Mr. Bagley says, the business was broken up by gamblers using wax figures as an attraction to their dens, certain it is that no such proceeding would receive the countenance of Mr. Smith, its chief manager. Neither would he have anything to do with a business upon which discredit could be thrown. From boyhood he was a man of the strictest integrity, of moral purity, with a high sense of honor. In fact, the least that could be said of him is, "He was one of God's noblemen." He filled the highest offices of the town with ability and satisfaction, beloved by all.

Mr. Bagley further says: "The last phase of this wax business in East Haven was the making of shrines for the South American trade. These consisted of glass cases in which stood beautiful little figures of women in wax in front of the shrine. This trade alone mounted into the thousands, and meant a fortune to its promoters, although scarcely any one in the town knew of this part of the trade."

SHIPBUILDING.

This enterprise has been carried on at different times and places on the East Haven side since 1728, for in that year Samuel Forbes was employed in shipbuilding on the point below the mill. His son Jehiel had a shipyard south of Tomlinson's bridge, before and after the Revolution, and was succeeded in business by his son Samuel, who built the three last vessels, which were brigs, after the close of the War of 1814.

Near 1844 Lane & Jacobs, shipbuilders, removed their shipyard from New Haven to South Quinnipiac street, Fair Haven, just north of Quinnipiac bridge. This branch of industry was carried on for several years, giving employment to a large number. When Lane & Jacobs retired, they were succeeded by their foremen Gesner & Baldwin. This was a very busy place; sometimes they had three schooners on the stocks at once. They built two-masted schooners of large tonnage for coast and West India fruit trade. Three-masters were not then in use. When the general depression of shipbuilding took place all over New England, this yard was affected in common with others and the business decreased. The works were then taken by Mr. Warren O. Nettleton from Quinnipiac street to below Red Rock, now the site of the late National Wire Company; from this it went into the hands of Armstrong & Darton as a marine railway for vessel repair; finally to Capt. Wm. Wright; lastly the site was sold to the Wire Company.

HUMPHREYSVILLE COPPER COMPANY.

About 1855 ground was secured at what is now Fort Hale Park and vicinity, wharves were built, and works erected for smelting copper ore. In a very short time it was discovered that the fumes from the chimneys were so poisonous that they were killing all vegetation in the vicinity and were noticeable two miles distant. An injunction was served on the company to stop the works, and as the company had found that the business was not profitable, on June 30, 1857, the works were sold to Mr. John Dwight, through the agent of the company, Mr. T. B. Buckingham. Mr. Dwight manufactured saltpetre here until after the close of the War of the Rebellion, when he removed and passed over the works to the New Haven Chemical Company on the site now owned by the National Wire Company. The Chemical Company manufactured soda for several years and then sold the property to the New Haven Wire Company.

CHAPTER V.

HE dividing line between New Haven and Branford had not been definitely ascertained and fixed at the time New Haven sold Totoket, which left much room for uneasiness and altercation. It is a prevailing tradition, supported by collateral records, that the original line ran along the east side of Branford hills. It appears from the petition of the village to New Haven, and the grant of New Haven to the village in 1679, and the subsequent grant by Branford of the half-mile to the village, that Branford actually held in possession more land than was contained in the original purchase from New Haven in 1644, and that was not paid for. Branford claimed as far as the Furnace pond (now Lake Saltonstall). In 1656 New Haven made a grant of the Furnace farm to the Iron Company and 12 acres to the collier—both within the line claimed by Branford, though Branford was treated as having some interest in the Iron Works. About the year 1660, Branford proposed to New Haven to have the line run between them. After a long delay the business was acted upon in the following manner, as appears from the colony records, Hartford, May 14, 1674.

"This Court ordereth that the agreement between New Haven and Milford, Branford and Wallingford, about their bounds, be recorded with the records of the Court and is as followeth,

"Whereas there has been a difference between the inhabitants of New Haven and the inhabitants of Branford about the dividing bounds between each plantation, and the inhabitants of New-Haven aforesaid having chosen and empowered James Bishop, jun., Thomas Munson, William Andrews, John Mosse and John Cooper, sen., on their part, and the inhabitants of Branford aforesaid having chosen and empowered Mr. John Wilford, Thomas Blackley, Michael Tayntor, Thomas Harrison and Samuel Ward on their part, to issue the sayd difference in reference to the sayd bounds, the sayd persons above named (excepting John Cooper, in whose roome Mr. William Tuttle was desired by the authority of New Haven) being mett together this fifth day of October 1669 and a full debate and consideration of the case for the preserving of love and peace and the preventing of trouble for the future between them that have hitherto been loving neighbours, have condescended so far each to other, as to agree about the premises as followeth, viz. That from the river formerly called in an agreement Tapamshashack, (with the exception of meadows therein expressed) the great pond at the head of the Furnace shall be the bounds so far as it goes; and from the head of the said pond, that a straight line be drawn to the east end of a Hassuakque meadow out of which a brooke called Hercules brooke runnes into muddye river, and from the east end of the sayd meadowe, to runn a north lyne, with the just variation according to the country unto the end of the = bounds of Branford aforesayd, that is, ten miles from the sea according to the order of the General Assembly. In testimonie whereof we have set too our hands the day and year above written.

John Wilford	Samuel Bishop
Tho: Blackley	Thomas Munson
Michael Tayntor	William Andrews
Tho: Harrison	William Tuttell
Samuel Warde	John Mosse."

DIFFERENCES BETWEEN BRANFORD AND EAST HAVEN
VILLAGE SETTLED.

A negotiation had been carried on with Branford concerning land that lay within their bounds, which they had not yet paid for, and which New Haven had granted to the village of East Haven. Branford finally promised them land, but the execution of that promise was delayed; the village grew impatient and passed the following order: "At a formal meeting of the village, 15th Feb. 1681, it was propounded that we might choose men to treat with Branford about the land in their bounds, that was given to us and is now in contention. After same debate it was ordered and appointed, that John Potter, Samuel Heminway, John Thompson, Nathaniel Hitchcock, Alling Ball, jun. and Matthew Moulthrop, them or any four of them were empowered to treat that matter with our friends of Branford as to land or line, and finish it."

This vote was predicated on a grant from New Haven in December, 1679, as follows, viz.: "For the Quinnipiack land now within the town of Branford, and was at first bought by us, and never payed for by Branford to us, that the Towne would grant unto them our right, the better to enable them to treat with Branford for enlargement on the purchase money due, with the consideration that New Haven hath been long out of purse."

The same month that the village passed the before-mentioned vote, Branford acted on the subject thus:

"Whereas there is a difference between the Towne of Branford and the Ironworke farmers (or inhabitants of New Haven) concerning the propriety of lands in Branford bounds. At a Towne meeting in Branford, Feb. 1681, the Towne have unanimously agreed to leave the case depending to a Committee, and the Towne have made choice of and appointed Mr. William Rosewell, Mr. Edward Barker, Thomas Harrison, William Hoadley, and Eleazer Stent, a Committee for the issue of the case aforesaid; and they do give them full power, in the behalf of the Towne either by composition with the farmers (or New Haven inhabitants) or to manage the said case at General Court, either by themselves, or any other attorney, or attorneys, as they see cause, and to be at what charge they cause in the management thereof. They do also desire and appoint the said Committee to take into their custody whatsoever writings or conveyances may be had (or copies of them) that concern the Towne.—And do engage to reimburse what charges the committee shall be at in the whole case."

As this attempt to settle the controversy failed, the village proceeded to the use of some high-toned language on the subject, which was met by Branford in the annexed resolution:

"Whereas the Ironworke farmers have given us notice that if we do not grant them land, then they will run a line in our bounds. At a Towne meeting in Branford, 8th July, 1681; the inhabitants of the Towne did answer, and declare by vote that the farmers have no right to do with the running of any line or lines in our bounds, or within our Township, and, therefore, do protest against any such proceeding, as an invasion of our just rights and privileges, and further do forbid them or any of them to enter upon our Towne bounds with any such design, if they do, be it at their peril."

The case was brought before the General Court the next fall, and that body adopted some measures to promote an adjustment of their difficulties.

"At a General Court held at Hartford, 13th Oct., 1681.
"Whereas there is a difference between Branford and the farmers on the East Side, about the line between New Haven

and sayd Branford, or New Haven purchase of the Indians, this Court do request the Deputy Governor, and Mr. Andrew Leete, and Mr. Samuel Eales to take some pains to examine the case, and do endeavour an accommodation between them, and if they can not attayn an issue, they are to make report how they find it to the next Court, where both parties are to attend for issue, and the sayd towne of Branford, and the farmers, are to attend to this affayre, when they shall be appointed by the Deputy Governor; they, viz. the Committee, are also to consider whether there be any obligation that doth lie upon New-Haven, that doth hinder this people from building a Dick at the East side or South-end." (*Col. Rec.*)

This arrangement of the General Court had a happy effect. The parties came to a settlement of their difficulties and Branford gave the village a deed dated May 8, 1682, for that tract of land called the *half-mile*, in which it was stipulated, that "the line shall run and be as formerly, from the Sea to the head of the Furnace pond," etc., as is described in the bounds already mentioned.

On the 9th of May, 1682, in behalf of the village, Samuel Heminway, James Denison, John Potter, Matthew Moulthrop, John Thompson, and Nathaniel Hitchcock gave a quit claim to Branford for all lands within their bounds. The Committee appointed by the General Court reported their proceedings, which by a formal vote were accepted and ratified.

"Hartford, May, 1682. The Gentlemen of New-Haven and Branford had agreed about the purchase of their lands, which they were appoynted by the Court to issue; and Major Treat, William Leete, and Mr. Eales were desired to assist them in Oct. last." (*Col. Rec.*)

DIFFICULTY BETWEEN EAST HAVEN AND NEW HAVEN.

In the year 1678 the people of East Haven petitioned New Haven for their consent to become a distinct village, and for some other privileges. With zeal they prosecuted this object. Not succeeding this year, on the 18th of August, 1679, they renewed their application, which resulted as follows: "At a town meeting held in New-Haven, 29th Decr. 1679 a committee was appointed to examine and prepare matters against some other meeting. After the town had heard the considerations of the Committee, the request was approved and confirmed to be their order by vote." [The full text of this grant has been recorded in Chapter III, under head of Ecclesiastical Affairs.]

After the village had obtained their village grant, from the General Court, to become a society, they proceeded to transact local business, separately from the town of New Haven. They seem to have apprehended that their parish grant involved some authority for the choice of village officers, and for the laying out and disposing of land within their parish bounds. This course brought upon themselves and New Haven a long scene of confusion and trouble and not a little expense.

"At a meeting of the Village, 19th March, 1683, it is agreed by vote that in laying out the third division we will follow the method of New Haven, viz.: 20 acres for each hundred pounds in the list, and 4 acres to each child, and 20 acres to each family, tho' their heads and estates do not amount thereunto." November 26th, 1683. "It was agreed to lay out the one half of said third division upon Stoney river; and the other half where it will be most convenient, and begin the lots as to their order upon the land next to the five men's land at Foxon."

After the arrangements for the third division were made, they voted to lay out the third division "by the list of the estates we give in to the payment of the minister this present year with the addition of our persons' heads not there given in, because not rated, but here to be added, as in the list alphabetically arranged." With this small population and with this small property, they supported a minister of the Gospel about four years."

Their public expenses and some other embarrassments were so great that some began to cherish the idea that they should not be able to proceed and especially as their crops had recently failed. They therefore took a vote, March 29, 1684, "whether they should go forward in building up the Village." Nineteen men being present, they all voted to proceed.

The proceedings of the village in dividing land gave offence to New Haven, and they appointed a committee to confer with the village on the subject. The village also appointed a committee to go to New Haven and inform that committee of all their proceedings. In 1685 they appear to have relinquished their village privileges and returned to their former connection with New Haven. About this time they requested New Haven to furnish them with a further division of land, which was referred to a special committee whose report was accepted and recorded as follows:

"In answer to the inhabitants of New-Haven, the Committee appointed by the Towne to consider their proposals about the third division, order as followeth:

"1. That in laying out the remainder of the third division, not yet taken up by the said inhabitants, being approved planters, it be laid out to them in quantity according to the list of estates in 1679, by appointed sizers, and Enos Talmadge for the Towne.

"2. That the grants which have been made by the late Village Company to any of them, having a right to the third division as aforesaid, be accounted as part of such remainder of third division, except eight acres granted and laid out as appended to the Mill.

"3. That they lay out the said remainder upon and out of the half mile of lands, or addition from Branford as far as their granted bounds, provided that they lay it out as to others of the Towne, viz. one half mile in depth, and lying together, and not in particular tracts or parcels; and if there be not enough found there, then to make up their quantity elsewhere within the bounds formerly granted, provided, that the Towne commons, as formerly appointed, be stated by the now appointed sizers and surveyors, who are to view and lay out the said proportions of third division, and the remainder for commons.

"4. As to the grants of land made to the sundry particular persons by the East side inhabitants we see not cause at present to confirm; but before we so do, we expect that now, having laid down the Village designs, and being returned to their former station for power and privilege with ourselves as one plantation, that they plainly declare themselves in so doing without reservation, not to go off from us when they please, or judge themselves in a capacity for it, without the Towne's approbation in that case.

"5. We appoint Mr. Bishop, Capt. Mansfield, and Thomas Kimberly sizers, and Enos Talmadge surveyor: and at the charge of the East side inhabitants: and we desire their answer to these premises in writing under their hands." (*N. H. Rec.*)

A reply to these resolutions cannot be found, but from this time their affairs seem to have proceeded without any particular controversy until 1703, when the village moved to resume their village grant of 1680. The village bore their proportion of town and colony charges and endured great hardships and dangers in attending public worship at New Haven. After the termination of King Philip's War the Indians were frequently in a state of commotion. Some powerful tribes that were under the influence of the French in Canada frequently assumed a hostile attitude. In 1689 the town prepared a flying army, which stood ready to march at a moment's warning. A patrol of four horsemen was continually scouring the woods, and all the militia were obliged to carry their arms with them to public worship prepared for battle. The Indians near the village were sometimes employed as scouting parties and in other respects as useful auxiliaries. The following incident may be worth preserving:

A friendly Indian warrior was requested to act as sentinel in the Gap, north of Mullen hill. He consented, and for this purpose borrowed Mr. Hemingway's gun, and was assured it was well loaded. Without examination he took the gun and went to his post. He soon saw two Indians descending into the valley from Pond Rock, and advancing toward the Gap. They passed him and when he had them in range, intending to kill both at one shot, he leveled his gun to fire but it only flashed in the pan, for it was not charged. The spies, without observing it, passed on across the fresh meadows, and mingled with the friendly Indians about Grave hill. The disappointed

Indian was greatly enraged and threatened to kill Mr.
Hemingway for deceiving him in order that *he* might
be killed. Mr. Hemingway was innocent of the charge
for he had loaded the gun himself, but some
other person had discharged it without his knowledge,
and priming it, left it in the usual place in that condition. With the discovery of this fact the warrior
was finally pacified. In a day or two one of these
spies was found dead on the Indian land—supposed
to have been killed by the enraged warrior.

Nothing further appears on record of a special
nature, respecting the village, until the close of the
year 1703. The following extracts from the village
records will show the course of their affairs at that
period.

"At a Village Meeting, 23d Decr. 1703. The inhabitants
voted that they would take up their Village grant; and to
the end chose Capt. Alling Ball, Lieut. Samuel Hotchkiss,
Samuel Heminway, Sergt. John Potter, William Luddington,
Ensign John Russel and George Pardee, for a Committee to
manage the concerns of the Village in order to a settlement
according to the General Court's grant. And informed New-
Haven of their design."

"20th Nov. 1704. They voted that all the undivided land
within the Village bounds shall be equally divided unto each
of the present inhabitants, according to the heads and estates
in 1702, when we were in a Village way, according to New-
Haven grant, excepting persons that are tenants."

"The Committee appointed to search for land reported that
they judged there were yet 1200 acres of undivided lands."

"30th March, 1705, they agreed to lay out a half division
of land, according to the list in 1702, and to draw lots, who
should pitch first, and next, &c.; and none shall pitch on the
half mile gained from Branford. George Pardee was chosen
to draw lots. Samuel Thompson and Samuel Hotchkiss, jun.,
were chosen surveyors of the half division."

The town of New Haven was offended with the proceedings of the village respecting the laying out of the land and while the village petition for the renewal of parish privileges was pending before the General Assembly passed some angry resolutions, manifesting their unwillingness to admit the village to society privileges, and forbade the people south of Muddy river, and north of the village line, to pay any longer to the support of the ministry there, but to return to New Haven.

"April 24, 1705. The Townsmen moved the Towne to consider whether the Towne look on the grant formerly made by New-Haven, doth give them power to take up again a Village on the east side, and whether the right of soil in the bounds of said Village belongs to the inhabitants there. The Towne by vote declare that they look upon the said former grant for a Village on that side to have been some time since, and by sundry applications and matters of record, are superceeded and cancelled, and that those neighbours may not lawfully resume and manage a Village affairs without a new grant and allowance orderly made to them; and that the right of undivided and common land, within the former grant, in no wise is, or ever was, granted to the inhabitants of said Village, but is and must remain at the disposal of the Towne of New-Haven, as much as any other tracts of common land lying within the established boundary of New-Haven Towne, and whereas in said former grant the farmers on that side, northward of the Village bounds, were allowed to pay to the Ministry settled in said Village till further orders. The Towne likewise doth order that those inhabitants henceforward pay to the support of the Ministry in New-Haven platt, untill that matter shall be otherwise ordered by said Towne." (*N. H. Rec.*)

The right of soil in the undivided land did indeed belong to the town of New Haven. The village had no right to make a division of common land, except the half-mile that belonged to the village by a deed from Branford, predicated on a special grant of New Haven to that effect. New Haven had no right of soil in the half-mile.

The village, however, obtained from the General Assembly a renewal of the parish grant which they had received in 1680, and they proceeded to manage their religious affairs in their own way.

New Haven attempted to tax the village as before, which was resisted by the village.

April 24th, 1707, "The Village voted that 600 acres on the lower end of the half-mile should be sold to defend lawsuits against New-Haven, particularly when distressed for taxes. And that the purchasers should sue at the next County Court after New Haven had strained for taxes." William Luddington, John Russell, John Moulthrop, Joseph Tuttle, Daniel Collins and Jacob Robinson took the 600 acres on those conditions, and divided it among themselves. This tract lay between the Pond, and Bull-swamp bridge. Caleb Parmalee, Caleb Chidsey, and Isaac Penfield afterwards settled on it.

Some attempts to quiet this controversy were made, but without effect. In October of this year the village proposed to New Haven to take their whole right of lands within the village bounds and maintain their own poor. The next year, according to advice of the General Assembly, a committee of twelve was appointed by both parties and the articles of agreement proposed by the General Assembly partly consented to, i. e., to take the common lands within their bounds and support their own poor. Some of the village people, however, protested against any propositions that might infringe their old rights.

About this time also there was a difference between the village and the South End men respecting the last division of land; but this was adjusted by admitting them to a full proportion with the rest.

To accomplish their object respecting further privileges the village proceeded thus: "15th Feb. 1707. Sergt. John Potter and Joseph Tuttle were directed to attend a Town-meeting at New-Haven, and obtain their consent that this Village may be a settled distinct Towne."

The following spring the village petitioned the General Assembly for that object, which was granted.

"May, 1707. This Assembly, considering the petition of the East Village of New-Haven do see cause to order that they shall be a Village distinct from the Towne of New-Haven, and invested and priviledged with all immunities and priviledges that are proper and necessary for a village, for the upholding of the public worship of God, as also their own civil concerns; and in order thereunto doe grant them libertie of all such officers so chosen as aforesaid and sworn as the law directs, shall be inabled with power and authoritie as fully and effectually for their limits or bounds, as is already granted them, as any such officers of any Towne whatsoever: As also the said Village have libertie to have a school amongst themselves, with the priviledge of the fortie shillings upon the £100 estate, as every Towne hath by lawe, and also free their own village charge, and maintain their own poor as all towns are obliged to doe, and be fully freed from paying any taxes to the Towne of New Haven, and shall be called by the name of East-Haven." (*Col. Rec.*)

This was a very ample charter for all the common privileges and immunities and duties of a town. The right of choosing a representative is not, indeed, specified, but is implied in the "immunities and priviledges of a Towne." They were furnished with the officers and powers of a town and the specific duties of a town are imposed. So the people considered the grant and acted upon it by immediately choosing town officers, laying rates, and taking charge of their own poor. Had the village still coöperated with New Haven in dividing their common lands, instead of assuming the right of dividing them themselves, probably they would not have been molested. New Haven was displeased, as appears from the following document:

"16th Sept. 1707. The Towne taking into their consideration, that, notwithstanding all fair and friendly endeavours have been used by our Committee, for a good agreement between us and our neighbours at the Ironworkes, that they have yet given us causeless trouble and charge, in that they have four times summoned us to answer them before the General Court, and in May last, have moved the said General Court, that they may have the privileges of a separate Towne, and be freed from payment of Towne rates here, and also that they have unjustly entered upon, and granted sundry parcels of land, being our right and property, to the great prejudice of the Towne, and more particularly of some of their neighbours, do, therefore, by their vote declare, that altho' we have ever, hitherto, been willing, not only to grant them liberty, but all due encouragement to a separate society for carrying on the worship of God; yet the above proceedings being not only injurious to our right, property and privilege, secured to us by law, and our patent; but are also accompanied with great disturbance of the peace, and much disorder, which is likely to increase if not prevented, that, therefore, we may in no measure be satisfied therewith; but do order the Townsmen, with good advice in all proper methods of law, to endeavour the prevention thereof, and to secure our interest. Being informed also that the listers cannot obtain the bills of persons and estates from the aforesaid inhabitants of the Ironworkes, who refuse to deliver the same, on pretence that Towne privileges were conferred upon them separately by the General Court, in May last, that, therefore our said listers are not capable to perfect their list, and to give the sum total thereof, according to an act of the General Assembly, in October last past, the Towne considering thereof, do declare that the sum total of their list cannot be known, and desire it should not be presented, 'till it be perfected according to law."

In January, 1708, the village found themselves in debt to their minister and meetinghouse, and in order to cancel those debts they voted to sell the half-mile. "The division to begin near Mr. Pierpont's and so come down. The land to be laid out in two tiers of lots, with a six rod road thro' the middle; and the land was valued at one shilling and eight pence per acre, and proportioned at the rate of 5 acres to the £100 estate, and one acre to the poll. * * * the money was paid to Caleb Chedsey, Treasurer."

In the year 1708 Gurdon Saltonstall was elected governor. It may be pardonable here to make a little digression and give a short sketch of Governor Saltonstall.

Gurdon Saltonstall was born in Haverhill, Massachusetts, March 27, 1666; graduated at Harvard College, A.B. 1684, A.M. 1687; served as butler of the college 1684-1685; was ordained Minister of the church at New London, Connecticut, November 25, 1691. He became a celebrated preacher, and was invited to accompany Winthrop to England, to settle political difficulties in 1693. He was chosen to succeed Gov. Fitz-John Winthrop in office at the latter's death, and served by annual election from 1708 to 1724. He was a man of great influence and power. He refused to be agent to the colony, conveying the address to Queen Anne urging the conquest of Canada in 1709, but aided in raising a large force for the disastrous expedition of Sir Hovenden Walker, and in 1713 became personally responsible for the credit of the colony, which had become involved through the expenses incurred in Canada. In his ministerial teachings he was a strict disciplinarian and the "Saybrook Platform" was largely due to his urging ecclesiastical discipline, which was in some respects in harmony with the Presbyterian polity.

He was so intent that it should be printed that he bought and set up in his residence in New London, the first printing press in Connecticut, forty-five years before printing was in use in any other place in the colony. His printer was Thomas Short, who came to New London in 1709. He printed the "Saybrook Platform," which is said to be the first book printed in Connecticut.

Governor Saltonstall was very prominent in locating Yale College at New Haven instead of at Hartford, which place he strenuously opposed. He seems to have been a man of tact as well as of force and authority. The following is related of him: A strange sect called "Rogerenes" may be found in New London at present, although very sparingly. They ignored the rites of minister and doctor. One day as Governor Saltonstall was sitting in his room, smoking his pipe, a man named Gurdon came in with a woman, and addressing the governor said, "Sir, I have married this woman, and that, too, without the authority of your magistrates and ministers." The

GOVERNOR SALTONSTALL CHAIR.
(Owned by Mrs. Leverett Bagley.)

governor turned round, took the pipe out of his mouth, and in a stern voice said, "Gurdon, have you taken this woman for your wife?" Gurdon replied, "Yes, I have." Turning to the woman the governor said, "Madam, have you taken this man for your husband?" She replied, "Indeed, sir, I have." "Well, then," said the governor, "by authority of, and according to the laws of Connecticut, I pronounce you lawfully wedded husband and wife." Gurdon was astonished, and after a pause replied, "Thou art a cunning creature."

Governor Saltonstall married the only child of William Rosewell, and of course came into possession of the Furnace farm. It is not definitely known whether he ever lived there. Miss Susan Hutchinson, formerly librarian at the Blackstone Library, was the first to question the fact. The late Mr. Leverett Bagley, who was of a historical turn of mind, says, "I have searched the records of the property, but I find nothing which goes to show that the governor ever lived at this lake named after the family. Col. Roswell Saltonstall,* grandson of the governor, is the first one of the Saltonstalls to live at the lake."

* Mrs. Leverett S. Bagley has now, in her parlor, one of Governor Saltonstall's straight-back chairs, which no doubt was brought from England. After the death of the last Saltonstall, the Farm went into the hands of Lieut. Jared Bradley. Tradition among the old people has always been that this Saltonstall was not equal to the average, in mental capacity. If he was not actually incompetent, he was inactive, and preferred some one to look out for him, rather than to take care of himself, and the Farm went to Mr. Bradley for care bestowed. After the death of Mr. Bradley's wife, his niece, Mrs. Loruhamah Goodsell, kept house for him. When she left the Farm she brought this chair with her to

There was a common feeling among the people of the town that he constantly opposed their town privileges; and being a man of great influence, he had abundant opportunity to injure them. The following incident will show the spirit of the times relative to East Haven affairs:

The people of the village kept large flocks of geese; many of which found their way to the Furnace pond, and frequently passed over to the governor's farm. The governor being vexed with this invasion of his rights proclaimed a defensive war, attacked and routed the feathered army, making a great slaughter among them. The owners of the geese thought that this was a "cruel and unnecessary war," and were in turn greatly offended, and such was the effect upon the minds of the inhabitants generally, that at the next election for governor not a single East Haven vote appeared for Saltonstall. After this discovery, the singular acts were passed by the General Assembly which destroyed their charter.

Whether these representations respecting the hostility and influence of the governor are correct or not, it is certain that a most singular legislative legerdemain followed, and which whenever adopted is sufficient to ruin any charter, or fritter down any law into perfect nonsense. It is similar in effect to that exercise of power by which the Kings of England revoked charters and disannulled laws, and rendered every privilege and all property totally insecure.

her father's house in East Haven (the site of the present Bailey house), where she died. Her daughter, Mrs. Grace (Goodsell) Parmelee, gave it to her friend, Mrs. Emeline (Bradley) Bagley, the mother of the late Leverett S. Bagley.

GOVERNOR SALTONSTALL'S HOUSE.

In all probability the governor's business called him to New Haven often and he might have spent a few days at a time at the Farm. Usually such men kept a farmer on their estates, and probably he did. He was thrice married. His second wife was Elizabeth, daughter of William and Catharine (Russell) Roswell of Branford, Conn., by whom he came into possession of the Farm property. He died in New London, Connecticut, September 20, 1724.

"At a village meeting 15th Feb. 1709, agreed to sell all the undivided lands on the pond Rock to the upper end, except the parsonage land.   * * *   The rest to be sequestered for building the minister's house."

"25th Feb. 1709. Another half division of land was made at the rate of five acres on the £100 estate and one acre on the Poll." Eliphalet Pardee drew the lot.

The controversy continued, and the General Assembly undertook to explain the act containing the town charter of East Haven.

"New Haven, Oct. 1710. This Assembly taking into consideration an Act passed in the General Court held at Hartford, 8th May 1707, granting several privileges to the Village called (in the said Act) East-Haven, do declare upon the same, that there is nothing contained in the said Act that concerns property of lands, or that excludes the said Village from being within the Township of New-Haven; nor that intends to give the said Village the liberty of choosing deputies distinct from the Town of New Haven." (*Col. Rec.*)

"5th Feb. 1711. Caleb Chedsey, Sergt. John Potter, John Howe, Samuel Russell, Ab. Heminway and Samuel Thompson, were chosen to goe to New-Haven and discourse with the Committee there, about the differences they speak of between them and us, and to make return to the Village, and not to conclude anything respecting the aforesaid matters, without the approbation of the Village."

Nothing, however, was accomplished by this attempt at explanation. The commentary of the General Assembly did not even diminish the magnitude of the controversy. East Haven pursued its own course, and New Haven threatened and prosecuted the people for their taxes.

In 1716, East Haven again cited New Haven before the General Assembly in hope that they should be able to maintain their town privileges on the charter of 1707. Contrary to their expectations, this application only brought forth a commentary on the commentary last mentioned.

"New-Haven, Oct. 1716. Upon consideration of the petition of the inhabitants at the Village of East-Haven, this Assembly find upon examination, that the last act of this Assembly, dated Oct. 1710, determines them to have no other powers than those that are common to other parishes, and, therefore, are of opinion that the law does not put the care of the poor into their hands, but into the Town of New Haven." (*Col. Rec.*)

In December of the same year, New Haven "Voted to clear the inhabitants of East-Haven Village of all taxes to the Ministry or School, so long as they support the same according to the laws of this Colony." They appointed a committee to settle with them about civil matters; and if they could not settle, they were determined to prosecute. In 1713 the last division of land was made, it being now all taken up.

After the year 1716, for a long time, very little appears on record concerning the civil concerns of the village. The General Assembly having explained away all their privileges, rights and duties as a town, they had nothing to do, nor anything to enjoy, excepting the duties and privileges of a mere parish under the jurisdiction of New Haven.

Being silenced by the terror of law suits and "the powers that be," they yielded; until another generation arose that knew not a Saltonstall and which began to think again that the act of 1707 really meant something according to the natural import of words, and accordingly on the 18th of December, 1752, "Voted, that we will take up the privileges that the General Assembly and the Town of New-Haven have formerly granted for the time being; and in order to do this, do send our Memorial forthwith to the Town meeting now sitting."

"6th December 1753. We the subscribers, Selectmen of the Town of East-Haven, hereby beg leave to inform the inhabitants of the Town of New-Haven in Town meeting assembled, that whereas the General Assembly of the Colony of Connecticut, at their session at Hartford, on the 8th May, 1707, on the humble petition of the then East Village of New-Haven, were pleased to order, "That the said Village should be a Village distinct from the Town of New-Haven, and invested and priviledged with all immunities and privileges proper and necessary for a Village, for the upholding the worship of God, as also their own civil concerns," and did also grant them liberty of all such officers, as are proper and necessary for a Town, to be chosen by themselves, in order and form as all Towns by law, for each or any Town, and that all such officers so chosen as aforesaid and sworn as the law directs, should be enabled with power and authority as fully and effectually for their limits and bounds as any such officers of any Town whatsoever, and should be freed from paying taxes to the Town of New-Haven, and be called by the name of East-Haven. And whereas the Town of East-Haven, in pursuance of the said grant of the said General Assembly, did on the 6th December inst. in Town meeting regularly convened, proceed to choose the officers by law

directed in Town meetings to be chosen, and to make such
rules, orders and regulations, as were necessary for the
welfare and due regulation of said Town, and are determined
hereafter to continue to take benefit of the said grant of the
General Assembly, and therein conduct according to the laws
of this Colony, respecting the regulation and due Government
of Towns, we have thought it our duty, and accordingly do
in behalf of said Town of East-Haven, and by direction from
them, hereby notify the Town of New-Haven of such their
resolutions and conduct, in order that the said Town of New-
Haven may hereafter exempt themselves from any further
care or trouble respecting the affairs of the said Town of East-
Haven, the regulation thereof, or the appointment of officers
therein, whereof we doubt not your favourable acceptance and
approbation, and are with gratitude for your past assistance,
kindness and care:—

<blockquote>
Gentlemen, your humble servants,

ROSEWELL WOODWARD,
ISAAC BLAKESLEE,
SAMUEL HEMINWAY,
DANIEL HOLT.

Selectmen of the Town of East Haven.
</blockquote>

East-Haven, 6th Dec. 1753."

The village at the next meeting, 13th December,
"Voted to defray the expenses of the Selectmen in
defending us from the Town of New-Haven."

These proceedings, however, brought upon them
once more the broad hand of the General Assembly
as follows:

"New-Haven, October, 1754. Whereas by the law of this
Colony respecting the office and duties of listers, provision
is made for the sum total of the list of the several Towns in
this Colony, to be sent in to this Assembly, and whereas the
Village, or Society of East-Haven, in the Town of New-
Haven, have sent the sum total of their list into this Assembly,
distinct from the Town of New-Haven, which this Assembly,
judging to be contrary to the law aforesaid, for that Towns
only are to send in their list do reject the same, it not being

the list of any Town—But forasmuch as it appears to this Assembly, that the said Society in sending said list, acted through mistake and misapprehension, do thereupon order, that the sum total of the list sent in by said Society be added to the sum total of the list of the Town of New-Haven, to make one sum, and that the same be entered on the records as the list of said Town accordingly. It is also further ordered that the listers of New-Haven inspect the list of the inhabitants of said Society, with the rest of the inhabitants of said Town according to law. And the several persons who received and made up the list of said Society, as listers, are hereby ordered to deliver the several lists of the inhabitants of said Society to the listers of the Town of New-Haven, that they may make up one general list, to be delivered to the Town Clerk as the law directs; and the Secretary of the Colony is directed to deliver two copies of this act to the Sheriff of New-Haven County, one by him to be delivered to the listers of said Town of New-Haven, and the other to the person or persons who received and made up the lists of said Society, for their direction respectively in the premises." (*Col. Rec.*)

Thus another fatal blow was given to the act of 1707. The village, however, was very obstinate, and was determined not to yield. But in order to remove and prevent any further objections to what they apprehended to be their rights, on the 3d of February, 1755, "They appointed a Committee to apply to the General Court for Town privileges, according to a former Grant and to refuse to pay the two last rates of the Town; and to make an agreement with New-Haven about it, if they could."

But this plan failed. They then resumed their old ground and on the 16th June "Voted, that we will proceed further with respect to our privileges granted formerly to us by the General Assembly, and will try it in the common law with the Town of New-Haven if they strain for our Town rates." And a committee was appointed to manage this business.

They persisted in choosing officers annually and yet appear to have acted with New Haven in town business. Nothing more appears on record respecting this controversy until May, 1780, when the village "Voted to apply to the General Assembly, to ratify and confirm our Town privileges, granted to this Village in 1707, and that a Committee go to New-Haven, and let them know that we are determined to act in defence of said privileges." In December, 1781, this business was again introduced, and it was "Voted that a Committee be appointed to go to New-Haven to the next Town meeting, to petition them to give their assent and approbation to our taking up our Village grant of 1707, and to act upon the same." "January 1, 1782. Voted, that Levi Pardee go round to the people, to know whether they are willing to be a Town, or not." "3d January, Voted, that we will petition the General Assembly, that they make us a distinct town from New Haven." In the prosecution of this object they persevered. And at length after about 80 years of labor and controversy obtained their object. In 1785 New Haven consented they should become a town. They presented a petition to the General Assembly, and obtained the following grant:

"At a General Assembly holden at Hartford, on the second Tuesday of May, 1785, upon the Memorial of the inhabitants of the parish of East-Haven, in the Town of New-Haven, representing to the Assembly the many inconveniences they are subject to, by reason of their being connected with, and being a part of the Town of New-Haven, praying that they may be constituted a distinct and separate Town by themselves as per memorial,

"Resolved by this Assembly, That the said inhabitants of said parish of East-Haven be, and they are hereby constituted a Town by the name of East-Haven. And the bounds of the said Town of East-Haven shall be the same as the bounds of the said Parish now are, and the said Town of East-Haven shall be entitled to, and have and enjoy all the rights, privileges and immunities that the other Towns in this State enjoy; and shall have liberty to elect and appoint all officers necessary and proper for a Town, to lay taxes and collect them as Towns in this State are allowed by law, and to do and transact all matters necessary and proper for a Town. And the said Town of East-Haven shall be entitled to receive of the said Town of New-Haven, their part and proportion of all the Town Stock of said Town of New-Haven; and said Town of East-Haven, shall pay their part and proportion of all the debts of said Town of New-Haven already incurred, in proportion to the sum of their list, in the list of the Town of New-Haven, and shall take upon them the charge and support of their part of the Town poor of said Town of New-Haven in proportion as aforesaid. And the taxes of said Town of New-Haven already laid, shall and may be collected and applied for the payment of the debts and expenses of said Town of New-Haven, already incurred, and the same being paid and discharged, said Town of East-Haven shall be entitled to their part and proportion of the overplus, if any be, to be ascertained as aforesaid. And the said Town of East-Haven, shall bear their part and proportion of supporting the bridges and highways within the bounds of the Town of New-Haven and East-Haven, in such part and proportion, as shall be judged just and reasonable, by William S. Johnson, Jonathan Sturgis, and John Chester, Esq. who are appointed a Committee for that purpose, all the circumstances of the Town being duly considered; and said Committee shall appoint and set off, to the said Town of East-Haven, their part and proportion, of the poor of the said Town of New-Haven, and the stock and debts in proportion to their lists aforesaid.

"And the said Town of East-Haven shall hold their first Town meeting, at the meeting-house in said East-Haven, on the first Tuesday of July next, at 10 o'clock A. M. when they may choose such Town Officers as by law are required, who shall remain in office until another meeting shall be held in and for said Town, in the month of December next. And said meeting shall have power and authority to transact all matters necessary for a Town, and to adjourn, to a future period, if necessary, said inhabitants, legal voters, being warned three days before said meeting by Isaac Chedsey, Stephen Smith and Joshua Austin of said Town of East-Haven, or any of them, to meet as aforesaid, and Stephen Smith shall preside at said meeting until a moderator of said meeting shall be chosen, and shall take and count the votes of said Town for their moderator; provided nothing shall be construed to hinder the inhabitants of the Town of New-Haven from catching fish, oysters, and clams within the bounds of said Town of East-Haven, under the same restrictions, and regulations that the said inhabitants of said East-Haven shall be. Provided also that the said Town of East-Haven shall have the liberty to send one representative to the General Assembly of this State." (*State and Town Records.*)

The first town meeting under this act was held in the meetinghouse on the first Tuesday of July, 1785. The meeting was opened with prayer by the Rev. Mr. Street, and a sermon adapted to the occasion from Psalms cxxii. 3, 7, 8, 9, and the necessary town officers were appointed.

Previous to these transactions, New Haven confirmed the doings of the village respecting the divisions of land in East Haven, which had been the subject of much controversy; and the people of East Haven, on their part, relinquished their claim to all the common lands in the other parts of the town of New Haven. Thus all their controversies which had agitated the town for about eighty years were brought to a happy issue.

When we read over all the struggles, refusals and disappointments of our early settlers, in their attempts to be an independent town, we can but admire the determination, fortitude, and unrelenting fixedness of purpose which characterized all their proceedings. It is just what we should expect of men who had braved all the dangers, privations and hardships of a pioneer settlement. Yet they had the same spirit as their own with which to contend which prolonged the battle. Their contentions exhibited that strength and firmness of mind which enabled them to encounter all the dangers of the wilderness with courage and coolness, and to bear trouble and adverse circumstances without depression and without despondency. They possessed that resolution, that endurance and bravery, that never acknowledges defeat. This was the character of our Puritan fathers. Seven times they cited New Haven before the General Assembly and as many times were defeated. Nothing daunted, they persevered, until the eighth time they conquered—one hundred and six years after they had petitioned for their first privilege, and nearly eighty since their first charter had been granted, to which they clung with unflinching grip.

It is amusing to count the number of men whom they placed upon their committees. One would think such a drove of men intended to take things by storm. They believed that "in a multitude of councillors there is safety." Then their town meetings were almost as numerous as the frequent gatherings at the village store. These were their schools of parliamentary tactics. All this primitive labor was the seed sowing, of which this great nation is to-day reaping the harvest.

CHAPTER VI.

Formation of the Episcopal Society.

PISCOPACY in East Haven had its beginning March 17, 1788, when a meeting was held, and the following preamble and articles of incorporation were adopted and signed by those present:

"Whereas it is become necessary and expedient on account of the apparent increase of the Brethren in the Episcopal Church that we should Incorporate ourselves into a Religious Society for the encouragement and support of true Religion, and piety and worship God agreeable to our consciences &c. * * *

We the subscribers therefore incorporate ourselves into a Society at East Haven aforesaid. And do mutually agree to support and maintain a Clerk, Reader, or Minister, to officiate agreeable to the Rites, forms and ceremonies of the Church by law established. Witness our hands and year above established.

Henry F. Huse,	Samuel Barnes,
John Bird,	John Hunt,
Samuel Tuttle,	Stephen Thompson, jun.
James Pardee,	Dan Goodsell, jun.
Stephen Pardee,	Jehiel Forbes,
Mabel Bishop,	Levi Forbes.

"At the above meeting holden at the dwelling house of Samuel Tuttle, in said East Haven, a Moderator and Clerk being legally chosen, proceeded to business, Samuel Tuttle Moderator, John Bird Clerk. At said meeting appointed a Committee Samuel Tuttle & John Bird to transact such business as may be required by a society, and Ichabod Bishop to go to John Russell of Branford, to procure a copy of the recording of the formation of the Episcopal Society there. Adjourned to Thursday Eve next at Samuel Tuttle's at 4 P. M.

"Thursday, March 20th, 1788.

"Met according to adjournment. Finding it necessary a meeting was warned by John Hunt, by a summons, or warrant signed by Charles Chauncey, Esq. Justice of the Peace, Samuel Thompson, Samuel Tuttle, Samuel Barnes, to meet at the house of Samuel Tuttle in East Haven on Monday the 31st day of March inst at 2 o'clock P. M. Voted that the Clerk should procure a summons, to be delivered by an officer to warn the subscribers of this Society, to appear at the house of Mr. Samuel Tuttle in East Haven Monday the 31st day of March 1788, at two o'clock P. M. to choose officers &c. also to invite the Rev. Bela Hubbard to attend said meeting at the same time and place.

"Met accordingly and voted as above. To the First Society in East Haven Greeting."

Attested John Bird, Clerk.

"East-Haven, 31st March, 1788. At a meeting of the Episcopal Society of the Church of England, so called, legally warned, at the house of Mr. Samuel Tuttle, in said East-Haven, at 2 o'clock P. M. on Monday, 31st March, 1788; the subscribers, members of said Church or Society, under the kind patronage of the Rev. Bela Hubbard, Rector of Trinity Church, of New Haven, being present, who willingly and cheerfully accepted us under his care and patronage, proceeded to the usual and necessary business of choosing the needful and customary parish officers in said Society of East-Haven. Accordingly, voted John Bird to be Clerk of said Society; and being duly sworn, upon the oath of fidelity and oath of office, according to law—[By Josiah Bradley, Justice of Peace] also voted, Capt. Samuel Barnes, Moderator, John Bird, Clerk, Samuel Tuttle, James Pardee, Church Wardens;—Jehiel Forbes, Capt. Samuel Barnes, Samuel Thompson, Capt. Stephen Thompson, jun. Ichabod Bishop, Vestrymen. At the same time voted for five Vestrymen, but that only three shall be a quorum, with full power and authority, as the five by vote elected."

"Let this certify all whom it may concern, that I was present at the above-mentioned meeting, and that the above-mentioned persons were approved of in their several respective offices to which they were appointed.

Witness my hand, 31st day of March, 1788.

BELA HUBBARD,
Rector of Trinity Church, New-Haven."

When a grant of £20, additional, was made to Mr. Street's salary a few men were extremely displeased, and some having been displeased on some other account they united with a few Episcopalians then in town and formed an Episcopal society.

Probably it was not so much the rise in Mr. Street's salary as the occasion it offered to give vent to a growing unrest all over Connecticut against taxation for ministerial support. Hitherto church and state were undivided, and everyone of taxable age and condition was taxed to support the Congregational church, which was the only "approved" church recognized by law and supported by taxation. As other denominations crept into New England, the separation of church and state became a disputable point.

Of course, by reason of their superior numbers, the Congregationalists held the balance of power, and according to their puritanical ideas and teaching were loth to accede to the growing popular opinion of church and state separation. Therefore, in order to compromise the matter, "dissenters" were obliged to go through a form called "swearing off," which the following extract from the East Haven Town Records may explain:

"Mr. Edmund Bradley reported difficulty in collecting Mr. Streets rate, Some refusing to pay." Town Meeting Feb

1789 "Voted we were willing to hear some proposal that the Churchmen would wish to lay before said meeting. Voted we will appoint a Committee to treat with the Churchmen, relative to a settlement, on account of their dissenting.

Voted that Esq. Davenport, Esq. Bradley and Deacon Smith be a Committee to meet with the Churchmen, in order to try to fix something that may be likely to complete a settlement relative to ministerial matters, and to make returns to this meeting.

Whereas Mr. James Pardee and a number of the members of the Church Society in East Haven have appeared in the Town meeting, now open in the said East Haven and there agreed to make a settlement with said Town relative to their dissenting, and to settle all disputes, that have happened on account of said Pardee being taken by the Collector and committed &c. * * * upon the meeting's allowing a certificate for said members, that formed said Society, to bear date, at the time of their formation. They paying all the rates that was then laid.

Voted that Mr. James Pardee shall have his expenses, that was on account of his being committed paid to him, and that the old Churchmen should not be liable to pay the rate, that is collected by Mr. Edmund Bradley, and that upon Mr. Daniel Clark, Eli Forbes, Samuel Forbes, Capt. Charles Wedmore, Jared Thompson, Moses Thompson, Jun. & Chandler Robinson, producing certificate of their joining said Church Society in the year 1788 they shall be exempt from paying the Minister's rate in 1789. We, the subscribers, being present at the meeting, when the foregoing proposals and votes were passed and agree to the same. Certified by us.

JAMES PARDEE,
ICHABOD BISHOP,   } *Members of*
JEHIEL FORBES,   } *Church Society."*

After the independence of the country, Connecticut did not follow the example of many other states, and adopt a written constitution, because she had never, like the other states, surrendered her charter, granted by King Charles II, in 1662, thanks to daring William

Wadsworth and the hollow oak tree. After the banishment of Sir Edmond Andros, whom the English government sent over as a royal governor of New England, resplendent in red broadcloth and gold lace, the Connecticut charter was brought out from its hiding place, and the government continued under the ancient form and provisions of the old charter, amid all the changes, until 1818. In that year a convention was held at Hartford, composed of delegates from the towns of the state, elected by the people. They framed a constitution by the people for the civil government of the state, which was ratified by the people on the first Monday of October, 1818, and on the twelfth day of October the same year, Gov. Oliver Wolcott issued his proclamation, declaring the constitution was henceforth to be observed by all persons as the supreme law of the state.

The fourth section of the Declaration of rights decrees that no preference shall be given by law to any Christian sect, or mode of worship. Previous to this date, the Congregational churches were supported by a tax upon all property within the church society, and all persons who desired to escape such payment were obliged to file a sworn statement that they were attached to the worship of some other Christian denomination. It is extremely doubtful, if any of the twelve men who signed the call for the organization of the Episcopal Church in East Haven were rocked in an Episcopal cradle, excepting Henry F. Huse,* who was not of Puritan descent. He was

* Neither did he come to America by his own will. At this time it was the custom in England, sanctioned by law, to impress men into the navy, as well as by enlistment. A

THE EPISCOPAL CHURCH.

a Welsh Episcopalian, coming to America in 1748. He always attended Trinity Church, New Haven, where all his children and some of his grandchildren were baptized.

In 1789 the Episcopalians commenced to build their church, which was raised April 23, 1789. Through some mismanagement the frame fell and killed Jeremiah Bradley, aged 22 years, a son of Josiah Bradley, Esq., and very seriously injured Capt. Collins Hughes, and some others less dangerously.

The church was under the care of Rev. Bela Hubbard, most of the time, until the consecration of the church, which did not take place until July 25, 1810. Services were not held oftener than once in two weeks, and frequently only once in three or four.

The land where the church stands was given by Mr. Samuel Forbes, by a deed of gift recorded in the Church records, but the lines were not defined, till August 21, 1837, when his son, Samuel Forbes, 2d (father of the late Albert Forbes), staked off the present dimensions, three rods front by four rods rear, making twelve square rods surface. They employed a clergyman for short periods, until their

naval officer with a gang of men would seize any able-bodied young men, and there was no redress. His ship was sent to the Atlantic coast. Obtaining shore leave at Newburyport, Mass., he ran away, and made his way to New Haven, calling himself Henry Freeman, by way of self-protection. In the first deed to him in 1752 the reading is to Henry Freemanhuse, joining the true name to the assumed. H-u-s-e was the soft or Welsh pronounciation, which he retained through his life. After the independence of the country his family took the original spelling Hughes, which is very prevalent in the north of Wales.

first resident rector, Rev. Elijah G, Plumb, came in
1811. Mr. Plumb also taught a private school in his
house for advanced scholars. In 1819 he was
succeeded by Mr. Perry, who preached one-third of
the time. This arrangement ran on until 1826; then
Mr. Edward Ives came on half time to 1839, when
Rev. Henry Townsend came, also on half time. In
1843 an addition to the church was built. In 1845 Rev.
George Nichols came, and the same year another
addition to the church was made and a tower built.
December 2d, 1847, the first bell was placed in the
tower, and on February 21, 1848, this was exchanged
for the one now there. Mr. Townsend now returned
to them, but the infirmities of age were creeping upon
him, so half time was all he was able to serve. He
was greatly beloved by the people, and if his residence
had been in the town, no doubt very much good would
have resulted from his labors; as it was, the parish
was in a better condition than many times before.
The people now realized the benefit a resident minister
would be to them, and with their accustomed zeal
and energy, proceeded to buy a rectory in 1865 on
High street, and with that aid to secure a resident
rector.

June 1, 1866, Mr. O. Evans Shannon was called—
the first resident rector since 1839. He immediately
won the hearts of the people to him. He was aided
and seconded in his work by his most estimable wife,
who was a woman of rare qualities. Their efforts
were appreciated by their people, who in turn rendered
every possible aid, and for eleven years this pleasant
association of rector and people continued. On
September 20, 1877, death called the faithful servant

of the Lord to his eternal rest, much beloved, and greatly lamented.

About three months before Mr. Shannon's death, probably realizing his condition, he sent in his resignation, which his people refused to accept, expressing their hope of his recovery, and good wishes for his continuance in his ministry to them.

Rev. John Gray came in 1878, and resigned in August, 1880. Rev. Mr. Eddy was resident rector until 1885.

Since that time, there have been many changes, and rectorates of short duration. Many of the older people have died, and left no one to take their places until there is but a meager handful left.

Great credit is due the East Haven Episcopalians— they have kept the vital spark alive. Many times it would flicker and flicker, until it seemed it must cease, when some fortunate circumstance would revive the flame, and it would burn until another period of depression. No people have shown greater zeal, love and devotion to church principles than they have, and if many other church societies of far greater numbers possessed their earnestness of purpose, flourishing churches would be the result. It is astonishing how well they have preserved their church buildings and property. True they have from time to time been the recipients of small legacies, one of which was from their townsman, John Woodward Thompson (not an Episcopalian) of $250, for which a vote of thanks stands on their church records. It is not for lack of interest in church affairs, but for lack of numbers. No church can be run without people, and formerly the population of East Haven remained stationary. But a new era seems to be in sight. For the past two years regular Sunday afternoon services with Sunday School have been kept up, which is the best arrangement that could be made, without a resident rector, which it is hoped the parish will ere long be able to support.

CHAPTER VII.

The Green.

ARDLY any records can be found giving anything definite respecting the Green, which is called the "market place," or when it was laid out for a public purpose; but reference is made to it, in locating lands and places near it, as "the Green," for instance, the first meetinghouse was to be set on side of the Green. The northern boundary seems to have been more definite than any other, and the tract was much larger than at present, particularly east and west. At another place the following is found:

"It was also ordered that Matthew Moulthrop and John Potter doe set out five acres of the land upon the Green, formerly granted, the one half for the Ministry, and one half for the first Minister that shall settle with us, and they are to leave the spring clear, for a watering place for cattle."

This "watering place" is now the hollow enclosed within the Old Cemetery. This land was laid out as follows: five acres on the southeast corner of the Green, on which Mr. Hemingway's house was built (now occupied as East Lawn Cemetery). It would appear the Green extended much beyond its present limits on the west. We are dependent upon tradition for this idea, from this circumstance, viz.: "The first meeting-house should be built across the east end of the school house." "Tradition says the school house stood in the rear of the ground occupied by the residence of Geo. Talmadge and a considerable distance back from the highway. The meeting house was erected in front and adjoining it." [*Havens' Cent. Dis.*]

The last division of land was made March 28, 1715, as it is stated that the land had now all been taken up; but no mention is made of appropriating the Green for public purposes.

"At a Proprietor's Meeting held in East-Haven, 12th May, 1720, Mr. Jacob Heminway petitioned for a part of the Green west to the spring where the burying place is. Sergt. John Heminway [his brother] protested against any part of the Green being taken up or disposed of for any other use than to lye common as it now lies. Voted that Mr. Heminway shall not have any part of the land.—Voted that the Green shall not be disposed of except it be for some public use, that it may be beneficial to the whole of the Proprietors." (*E. H. and N. H. Record.*)

Probably Mr. Hemingway thought as this land had never been disposed of by a town vote, he had a right to petition for a share of it.

The next movement concerning the Green must be taken as a stroke of policy, by the town, to secure the Green absolutely and forever to the town by laying out the following roads of extraordinary width in all directions over its surface, which would more than occupy the whole space and thus establish it as town property for all time.

"We the subscribers being appointed by the proprietors of East-Haven to lay out highways in East Haven, where it may be judged needful, we have therefore, now laid out these highways upon the Green or Common in East-Haven, following, viz.: One road from the house of Gideon Potter, 10 rods wide, eastward, untill it come to the upper end of the New-Lane and Samuel Bradley's house lot. Another from that, Northward, 10 rods wide, until it comes to the country road. And another 10 rod road from the meeting-house, running about Southeast, untill it comes to the head of the said New-Lane. And another road, 10 rods wide, from the house of Abraham Chedsey, Southward, down to the swamp of John Heminway: And another road from the said Chedsey's house down to John Heminway's swamp, by John Heminway's and Moses Thompson's house lot, 10 rods wide. Also, another road from Moses Thompson's Barn, eastward down to the Spring from Thompson's home lot to the swamp of John Heminway about 8 rods." (*E. H. Rec.*)

In 1777 East Haven Green became a memorable place in the annals of the Revolution. When the army under General Sullivan in Rhode Island was transferred to New Jersey to strengthen Washington in his operations against the British under General Howe. Lafayette with his regiment encamped on the Green and river bank for a few days. Rev. Nicholas Street, the East Haven minister, a firm patriot, invited the marquis to enjoy the hospitalities of his home during his stay, which he very willingly accepted.

In consequence of a forced march across the country, the general had been obliged to leave his baggage behind. One night after he had retired, his servant came down stairs and asked for hot water, remarking, "the General has but one shirt with him, and we have to wash that while he sleeps." On learning of Lafayette's need, Mr. Street kindly supplied him from his own store. This kindness Lafayette did not forget when he made his visit to the United States nearly fifty years after.

We find nothing on record again until March 13, 1797, when a large part of the Green on the south was "voted an enlargement of the burying ground. The north line to run straight from the northwest corner of Moses Thompson's house, running westward in a straight line and course, leaving Nehemiah Smith's house 57 feet to the south of said line." Then "Voted that we do give up to the town of East-Haven all the propriety right which we now have to the common and undivided lands and highways within said Town." Of course this last vote secured to the town the Green as the town's property.

In 1799 the east district built the schoolhouse on the Green commonly known as the "Yellow School-house"—probably from the size and appearance of the old sycamore or buttonball trees as they were set out around the Green, about or before this time.

In 1824 East Haven had occasion to again display its patriotism and gratitude to Lafayette when he rode from New Haven to visit the place of his encampment. He was warmly welcomed by the townspeople. A large concourse gathered, speeches of welcome were made, and a liberty pole erected in his honor, which was the first one raised on the Green.

In his speech he stretched forth his hand and, pointing his finger in the direction of the old parsonage, said, "Yonder is the house where I stayed." The house was still standing, but the good minister had passed to his heavenly home eighteen years before, but Lafayette was able to shake hands with the sons of so noble a father. This time he was claimed as the guest of Capt. Daniel Bradley, himself a Revolutionary veteran.

THE HOUSE WHERE LAFAYETTE WAS ENTERTAINED IN 1824.

As was the custom in those days, a jolly good julep was mixed up in the three quart "sling tumbler" and passed around, each one taking a sip from it before eating. Captain Bradley's daughter, Mrs. John S. Bradley, gave this historic tumbler to her daughter-in-law, Mrs. Edwin S. Bradley, saying as she did so, "My father entertained Lafayette in this house, and he drank from this tumbler when he came to East Haven in 1824." The tumbler is now in the possession of Mrs. H. Walter Chidsey, great-granddaughter of Capt. Daniel Bradley, a highly-prized relic of bygone days and ancestors. The house of Mr. J. Ives Bradley, on Main Street, is the house where General Lafayette was last entertained.

The original pole on the East Haven Green served its purpose until the campaign of Harrison and Tyler in the fall of 1840. The night before Harrison's election, the topmast of the pole mysteriously disappeared. A sloop at Morris Cove supplied the deficiency the next day, but that fall some one sawed down the whole pole. Politics ran very high and the whole country was at fever heat for "Tippecanoe and Tyler too." This was the greatest political excitement the country had ever seen, still it furnished no excuse for such an act of vandalism as destroying the liberty pole.

East Haven was a very strong Whig town, and on the occasion of a mass convention held in New Haven, helped to swell and adorn the parade with a very handsomely decorated float, drawn by six horses, under the management of Mr. Samuel Chidsey. The float consisted of a canoe filled with little girls* not

* The writer chanced to be one of the number.

oven ten years old, one for each state, dressed in white, with red caps and blue sashes, waving banners of "log cabin and hard cider." The little girls were under the care of Mr. Daniel Smith, who never left the float but provided everything to delight his little charges. They received a great deal of attention and were loudly cheered over and over again as they passed along, to which they responded by raising their banners at arm's length over their heads. The Democrats in derision of General Harrison said he lived in a "log cabin," and drank "hard cider." No doubt he had, at some time in his pioneer life in the west. So the Whigs immediately caught up the expression and used it as an emblem of the campaign and of true American simplicity.

The subject of improving the Green began to be agitated in 1861. In special town meeting May 23, 1861,

Voted, "Rev. D. W. Havens, Samuel T. Andrews and E. Sturtevant Chidsey be appointed a committee to investigate the cost of fencing, grading and otherwise improving the Green in said town."

On June 10, 1861, it was

Voted, "To discontinue the public highways laid out around the public Green, and across said Green, for the purpose of fencing and otherwise improving said Green."

The Civil War coming on just then, the town had all its energies and funds absorbed in maintaining its war expenses, and nothing more was done at that time.

January, 1862, witnessed the burning of the "Old Yellow Schoolhouse" on the Green. East Haven had now been shorn of a liberty pole twenty-two years, and a few public-spirited men decided this should be the case no longer. Mr. Timothy Andrews and Mr. Alfred Hughes selected the spar from the Fair Haven shipyard, and uniting their teams drew it to the Green, where it was erected, April, 1862, and did good service for thirty years. After the burning of the schoolhouse the Green was no longer a common playground and as a new schoolhouse had been built in 1868 the Green would never be used again for that purpose, and the people began to realize the worth of this beautiful square and wish for improvement.

April 28th, 1869, *Voted,* "That the Green so called, belonging to the Town of East Haven, be plowed, graded and enclosed with a fense constructed of cedar posts, and rails, and that the expense be paid from the treasury of said Town. Voted that Timothy Andrews, Stephen Bradley and Leander F. Richmond be a Committee to carry out the same." (*E. H. Town Rec.*)

This was the first step taken to give prominence and protection to the public square. Hitherto it had been a common stamping ground for all sorts of purposes. In the days of the old Connecticut militia, it was the parade ground for their pranks and antics, called "Training Days," spring and fall, from which no able-bodied man between the ages of 18 and 45 could escape. This law was repealed about the forties. To show how hard it was to break up old habits, and how determined the people were to do it, the following by-law will prove:

March 3, 1876, *Voted,* "That every person who shall be found upon the public Green playing any game of Ball, shall be fined not less than ten dollars, nor more than twenty-five dollars for each offence. It shall be the duty of the acting Grand Juror to prosecute any violation of the above By-Law, which may come to his notice. Any By-Law inconsistent with the above is hereby repealed." (*E. H. Town Rec.*)

A very substantial fence was built and painted, and many elm trees set out to replace the dying old sycamores, which from their size must have been very aged. In 1886 the band stand was erected, which was done by subscription.

October 7, 1889, *Voted,* "That the hay from the Green be sold, and the benefit arising therefrom be expended for fertilizer for the Green."

October 2, 1893, a vote was taken to instruct the selectmen to mow the park three times a year at least, or when in their judgment it is necessary, leaving the grass mowed upon said park. Oct. 5, 1896, "Voted to appropriate $150 for a liberty pole on the public square as soon as possible." Town pride was aroused.

1902, On Arbor Day a Constitutional Oak was sent to the Town of East Haven, by U. S. Senator Orville H. Platt, through William H. Stevens, Delegate to the Constitutional Convention. It was planted near the north-east corner of the Green, or Public Square, on the Main St. side by Mr. John S. Tyler, first Selectman, and Henry T. Thompson, chairman of the Town School Committee, on School property. (Volume 28, page 291.)   Attest C. C. KIRKHAM,
(Town Records.)   *Town Clerk.*

The truth can not be written without saying that public sentiment has been greatly awakened and stimulated by the action and coöperation of the Woman's Club, under the leadership of Mrs. Edward F. Thompson, president, and Mrs. Leverett S. Bagley, vice president. The officers and members of the club have

done much to make history for time to come. They
have taken civic improvement for their work, and
their endeavors have been upheld and aided by their
townspeople with pleasure and gratitude, and their
achievements have been marked with unusual success.
As fast as one object is accomplished, they press on to
something greater and harder to accomplish.

EAST HAVEN TREE PLANTING.

Arbor day, 1903, was observed in an appropriate
manner on the East Haven Green, Friday afternoon,
under the supervision of the Woman's Club. Preparations for the occasion had been going on for some
time and the result was a programme carried out in a
manner reflecting great credit on those who bore the
responsibility of completing the arrangements. As
many persons know, to solicit nearly one hundred trees,
and get them planted without a hitch, is a rather large
contract, but this is what the Woman's Club of East
Haven did, and it is safe to say that there were no
better conducted services in the state.

East Haven has many beautiful trees, which were
planted by the fathers and grandfathers of the present
school children, and it is the desire to foster in the
hearts of these children such love and reverence for
the deeds of their ancestors that they will ever strive
to follow in their footsteps and be an honor to their
home and country. Among those who have presented
trees to the club are Governor Chamberlain, who gave
a thrifty young oak; Congressman N. D. Sperry, Senator Platt, Congressman George L. Lilley, County
Commissioners Walter, Thompson and Brewer, County

Treasurer Hiram Jacobs, Representative John S. Tyler, Selectmen Edmund B. Woodward and Eugene S. Thompson, Town Clerk C. C. Kirkham, who acted as master of ceremonies; the Board of Education, the chairman of which is Grove J. Tuttle, Esq., and many private citizens, but best of all, the school children, who had been saving up their pennies to buy trees. There was a splendid array of 100 young trees, which so suddenly appearing on the barren ground was a veritable illustration of a forest springing up like mushrooms in a night.

The procession of children started from the schoolhouse shortly after two o'clock, headed by the drum corps, which, in turn, was led by Mr. George Chidsey, who has won two state prizes as a drummer. A few blocks from the Green they were joined by the members of the Woman's Club. Mr. Herbert Nickerson drove Congressman Sperry in his automobile, suiting the pace of the machine to the march of the procession. The exercises opened with a speech of welcome by Mr. C. C. Kirkham, in which he commended the zeal and interest of the members of the Woman's Club and of the public, congratulating them upon their success in the arrangements, and extending his best wishes for all future undertakings.

Then followed the singing of "Columbia the Gem of the Ocean," by the school, and a prayer by Rev. D. J. Clark, pastor of the Old Stone Church. An original poem, written for the occasion by Mrs. Florence Andrews, was read by Miss Richards, and afterwards sung to the tune of "America," by the children. The lines were:

Like sentries trees shall stand,
To guard our native land
  In sun and storm.
Maple and ash we bring,
Glad let our voices ring,
On this May day of spring,
  A gladsome song.
The oak tree strong and grand,
Planted by loving hand.
  Let work be done,
And pray God's tender care
This day with us to share
And guard our trees so fair
  In years to come.

At the close of the second stanza the entire assembly joined in singing one verse of "America" with a spirit of enthusiasm which was good to hear. Congressman Sperry then addressed the children in words which they will not soon forget. Very simply and earnestly Mr. Sperry enjoined them ever to keep a guard upon their thoughts and actions, that they might always be pure and good. Although they did not realize it, he said they were now forming the character which was to last them a lifetime, and it was for them to see that that character was to be strong and good. Pointing to the beautiful elms on the Green, he said that as those trees had been planted for their benefit by their forefathers, so would the trees now planted be for the benefit of future generations, and begged that they should take an interest, not only in setting out the trees, but also in the care of them after they had been placed in the ground.

Mr. Sperry, after quoting Morris' beautiful poem, "Woodman, Spare that Tree," said that a man, woman or child who appreciates the sentiment therein expressed, is one to be trusted and endorsed, at any time, or anywhere. Those who love home, fatherland, parents and teachers, will appreciate these things fifty years from now, for the sweetest memories undoubtedly cling 'round these things. In closing, he appealed to the boys for the welfare of the birds, drawing a parallel between the feelings of parents for their children and birds for their young. Just as Mr. Sperry was about to resume his seat, he was presented with a magnificent basket of wild flowers by Miss Doris E. Thompson, on behalf of the school. Mrs. Thompson then expressed her thanks to the children for their part in the entertainment, and to the town officers and the public for their interest and assistance in furthering the work of the club, after which everyone united in singing the Doxology. After the benediction had been pronounced by the Rev. John H. Jackson, rector of the Episcopal Church, the assemblage broke up, while the drum corps played "Yankee Doodle," and rendered several other selections, which were thoroughly appreciated. One noteworthy fact was the entire absence of any appearance of restlessness on the part of the children during the entire programme, which was indicative of excellent training on the part of teachers and parents. Thus closed a very eventful and beautiful scene on the East Haven Green. It is the intention of the Woman's Club of East Haven to solicit a tree from each new incoming governor of the state—a small request in itself, but something very significant in future history. The three last governors, namely Governor Chamberlain, Governor Roberts and Governor Woodruff, are very thriftily represented.

"October 2, 1905, *Voted,* The Selectmen be instructed to remove the fence around the Green."

The following is not exactly connected with the Green, yet as the idea originated in East Haven and was successfully carried out through the energy and perseverance of the president of the Woman's Club, finally resulting in the coöperation of all like clubs of the state, it is thought best to give it place in this chapter.

The extracts following, relative to the subject, are mostly from the daily press.

MOUNTAIN LAUREL AS STATE FLOWER.

Delegation Addresses Legislative Committee.

"Whether or not the state shall have a state flower, and whether or not that flower shall be what is commonly known as the mountain laurel, were matters considered yesterday by the committee on agriculture, and a hearing of more than ordinary interest resulted.

"The principal speakers were Mrs. E. F. Thompson of East Haven and Mrs. Frank W. Gerard of South Norwalk, a special committee representing the Federation of Women's Clubs. Theoretically the room was more than filled with women; for these two were considered to represent 3,000. Mrs. Thompson in addressing the committee made several points for having a flower, and several for having the mountain laurel that flower. She showed that thirty-two states have floral emblems now, and why should not Connecticut have one? It would give a floral emblem to decorate all state and social functions, encouraging patriotism in both old and young. She favored the mountain laurel because it is ever green, indigenous to our soil, symbolic of honor and glory, rich in classical allusions, at its height at Flag day, and frequently available for use on Memorial day. Now we want a flower to encourage decoration, 'a flower the sweetest thing God ever created.'

"Mrs. Gerard spoke in support of Mrs. Thompson and said it had been endorsed by the various branches of the federation, and by the main body in convention unanimously after Mrs. Thompson had presented her arguments.   In a letter to Mrs. Thompson read before the agricultural committee, Mrs. Sara T. Kinney, state regent of the D. A. R., said: 'There is no money in your errand, and no politics, but a fine sentiment makes a whole state kin. If other states have state flowers, why should not Connecticut have hers? And if so, what more beautiful flower could be chosen, or one more suggestive of the sturdy qualities of Connecticut men and women, than our mountain laurel?' Mrs. John Holcomb of Hartford, prominent in the Colonial Dames, a member of both the St. Louis and the Jamestown exposition committees, wrote: 'I very much approve of the selection of the mountain laurel as a state flower for Connecticut.   It seems to me preëminently the one for this purpose, for it is the personification of many virtues and great beauty.' There were no other speakers and the hearing ended at this point."

"The report of the committee on agriculture, recommending the adoption of the mountain laurel as the state floral emblem, is a distinct victory for Mrs. E. F. Thompson of East Haven and Mrs. F. W. Gerard of South Norwalk, and for the State Federation of Women's Clubs, which they successfully represented before the committee for the adoption of the flower. It is confidently expected now, that as the laurel has passed the committee stage, it will run the gauntlet of the general assembly with equal success."

"At Hartford yesterday the mountain laurel—technically the Kalmia latifolia—was adopted as the official flower of the 'Constitution State.'"—"Senate-House resolution, No. 236, making the mountain laurel the state flower. Mr. Kingsbury of Coventry offered a substitute which gives correctly the name of the shrub as the Kalmia latifolia. Mr. Kingsbury explained the bill, and said the shrub is a beautiful one, and grows only in America.   The bill was favored at a large hearing, and a passage of the bill would satisfy a large number of women, and would put the state in line with thirty-two other states.   Mr. Gunn of Milford said he appreciated

STATE FLOWER
MOUNTAIN LAUREL
[*Kalmia latifoha*]

the influences which must have been brought to bear upon the committee by the large number of women. 'The Kalmia is," he said, 'one of the most beautiful products of Connecticut soil.' He advocated the passage of the bill."—"The mountain laurel has been adopted by the General Assembly as the official flower of the Constitution state; the bill having been signed by Governor Woodruff April 17, 1907."

THE LAUREL.

By Mrs. Florence R. Andrews.

The loyal oak we dearly love,
Each year brings added glory;
And still to children's listening ear,
We tell the "Charter's" story.

The fruitful vine on seal and state,
Its legend well proclaims,
That nation planted in His name,
Its root and branch sustains.

Connecticut has named her flower—
" 'Twill make the whole state kin"—
The Mountain Laurel, better type.
Not found the whole state in.

And now to tree and vine of state,
We come our Laurel bringing,
On lofty hill, and low land too,
We found its blossoms springing.

No petted child of hothouse growth,
But wild, free, rugged ever,
To heat of sun or chill of snow,
Its green leaf changeth never.

It came alike for rich and poor,
Its buds and blossoms showing.
The silent beauties of the woods
All added to its growing.

Its leaves fair crown for martyred dead
When o'er them gently falling
The stars and stripes they loved so well,
While bugle blast is calling.

'Twill beauty lend to church of God,
When bridal bells are ringing.
Its stately presence near our dead,
A requiem soft is singing.

Now He who gave both tree and vine,
His promise yet is keeping,
At morning mercies still are fresh,
And new again at evening.

Then leave our Laurel to His care
Through storm and sunshine hours,
To give new lustre to its leaves,
New beauty to its flowers.

State Seal of Connecticut.

The origin of the seal of Connecticut was told by
Governor Roger Wolcott in 1759. It is there stated
that the seal was a present from George Fenwick to the
colony. Mr. Fenwick was agent for the proprietors
of Connecticut under the Warwick patent of 1631.
The original seal had a vineyard of fifteen vines, supported and bearing fruit; above them a hand issues
from the clouds, holding a label with the motto, "Sustinet qui transtulit," meaning, "He who transplanted
still sustains." The General Assembly of 1711 ordered
a new seal, with only three vines, instead of fifteen,
and the motto read, "Qui transtulit sustinet." In the
new seal, approved by the General Assembly about
1784, the hand is omitted. The present seal was
ordered by the General Assembly in 1842. It has
three clusters of grapes on each vine; the one preced-

ing it having had four clusters on each of the upper vines, and five on the lower. The motto remains the same.

"THE CITY BEAUTIFUL."

Much has been said and recommended, by our near city neighbor, about "The City Beautiful" during the past year. But to East Haven belongs the credit that this has been energetically carried on for the past four years, in one form or another, by the Woman's Club. It may be considered a fad, as that word is now used, by those who stand aloof, more ready to criticise than to take part. If it is, it is certainly a benefit to the community, and a blessing to the rising generation.

Who does not receive a well-kept heirloom with much more joy than an old and battered relic? Therefore civic improvement is a priceless heirloom, to be handed down to coming generations—priceless not only in itself, but in the influence it exerts in all directions, stimulating a love of order, awakening a sense of the beautiful, and an appreciation of the natural beauties which surround us on all sides; a broadening of views, a stimulant to more vigorous exertion, a reaching out and grasping all those elevating purposes which time and opportunity present.

The Woman's Club added another star to its crown this year, as shown by the following extract from the New Haven *Register:*

ROOSEVELT OAK FOR EAST HAVEN.

President to Send One for Arbor Day—To Mark Lafayette Site—Where the General Camped in Wartime.

President Roosevelt has directed that a memorial oak be sent to East Haven to mark the site where General Lafayette encamped in the Revolution. Word to this effect was received to-day by Mrs. Edward F. Thompson, as president of the Woman's Club of East Haven, which organization recently petitioned the President for a tree.

The White House letter in response reads in substance as follows:

WHITE HOUSE, April 16, 1908.

"Your letter asking the President to furnish a memorial tree to be planted on the ground where General Lafayette encamped has been received. The President will be very glad to comply with this request, and has directed that the tree be forwarded. Sincerely yours,

WILLIAM LOEB, JR.

"Secretary to the President."

The credit for securing the tree is largely due to Mrs. Thompson as president of the club, and Miss Sarah E. Hughes, an honorary member, who also corresponded with the authorities at Washington. A history of East Haven by Miss Hughes, which incidentally refers to the Lafayette visits, is now in the hands of the publishers.

The Woman's Club of East Haven has been at work for some time beautifying the Green of the town, and already has memorial trees from Connecticut senators and representatives, as well as three governors. The Roosevelt oak will be planted on Arbor Day.

The exercises to mark the planting of the "Roosevelt Oak," on the historic Green of East Haven, under the auspices and direction of the Woman's Club, were very pleasantly and successfully carried out on Arbor Day, May 1, 1908. The ceremonies in behalf of the club were in charge of Mr. Henry H. Bradley, chairman of the board of education. The Green was spic and span in its walks, and circles around the trees, with large patches of flowering moss, indigenous to the soil, in full bloom scattered all over its surface.

The trees of Congressmen Sperry and Lilley, also those of the two former governors, with that of the present governor, formerly donated by them, and planted by the club, were labeled with each one's name in large letters, and a small flag floated from the label. It was a pretty sight.

The "oak," wrapped in the flag of the Union, was conveyed from Mrs. Thompson's home in an automobile, with the governor, Miss Margery E. Thompson and Mr. H. H. Bradley, the master of ceremonies.

The ceremonies commenced by raising the flag. Every eye was turned towards its waving folds, and as it rose the school children repeated their solemn promise of loyalty, which they are taught on entering the public schools of East Haven. A prayer was offered by the Rev. Daniel J. Clark of the Stone Church. The tree was now brought into the circle, and carefully unwrapped. Mr. Albrecht Dick, the caretaker of the Green, placed it in its home and held it in position while the speeches were made. Mr. Bradley, on behalf of the Woman's Club, presented to the town the "Roosevelt Oak," which the President had sent for the occasion, in a very pleasing speech. On behalf of the town, Selectman John S. Tyler accepted the tree in a speech as follows:

Fellow Citizens, Ladies and Gentlemen:
We have met to-day to take part in an interesting and significant occasion, not only because we are to plant a memorial tree, presented to the Woman's Club of East Haven by our honored and beloved President Roosevelt, upon an historic spot where General Lafayette camped over night, but for the fact that we are by these acts and these lessons bringing before our citizens the necessity of planting trees and shrubs.

It is a work in which we should all interest ourselves—the preservation of the forests. It is a glorious work in which all who understand must be interested and be teachers.

There are many things which everybody can do on Arbor day; some new trees can be planted, old ones rescued and trimmed and saved from decay. The children of our public schools can and are being taught the necessity and love for trees, and it is a duty of parents to encourage them.

The people of this country are only beginning to wake up to the necessity of legislation along this line in the matter of preservation of our forests, which have been shamelessly depleted and destroyed.

We, the citizens of East Haven, congratulate ourselves that we have with us to-day his excellency, the governor of Connecticut, and we congratulate and thank him for his great and untiring interest in tree planting and forest preservation.

A chart of this beautiful Green will be made, with the trees designated and from whom presented, filed and written upon our town clerk's records so that future generations may know the interest manifested by our Woman's Club of this town. It will also act as an incentive for those who may follow us to continue along this same line of work.

Upon behalf of the board of selectmen of East Haven, as town agent, I accept this beautiful "Roosevelt Tree." I trust it may live and be preserved, always remaining as a reminder of the good that may come from our Arbor days.

Mr. Bradley then introduced the governor.

THE GOVERNOR'S SPEECH.

Arbor day is generally believed to have originated in the mind of the late Hon. J. Sterling Morton, at one time secretary of agriculture of the United States. He came from Nebraska, the state of his adoption, and Nebraska abounds in prairies, where there are no trees. It was, no doubt, the contemplation of those vast and barren places that led him to awaken in the hearts of the school children of Nebraska and the United States a love for trees. And so Arbor day comes with the festival of spring and many a child learns its meaning. Thus the foundation, or the roots of the future forests of America, are laid and nourished in the mind of a child. And as the children of to-day are the men and women of to-morrow, the whole nation is being educated to understand the priceless value of planting trees.

Almost every state in the Union has set aside an Arbor day to encourage the growth and preservation of trees.

This important day is celebrated in Connecticut and that is our purpose here. The people of East Haven have every reason to be proud of the delightful Green. It represents a fine example of village improvement and its influence reaches every home. For many years it has been your custom to secure from some well-known person a tree which you have planted here. Many of these trees have been presented by the governors of our state. Last year it was my opportunity to add another to this beautiful spot. This year the tree came to you from President Roosevelt, the man who is inspiring us to better things, and the man who is doing more than any other man in America for the preservation of the forests. In this regard Mr. Roosevelt says, 'You must convince the people of the truth—and it is the truth—that the success of home-makers depends, in the long run, upon the wisdom with which the nation takes care of its forests.'

The people of Connecticut love to start things right and then watch and enjoy the development. There is not a place on earth where they have a larger affection for trees. We love to plant them and to watch them grow. What would the city of New Haven be without its Green and its elms? All her fame surrounds that center, and there stands one of the great universities of the world. Let us plant this tree to-day with patriotic hearts, fixing our minds upon those men and those times when this commonwealth was founded.

And may the tree show forth all the traits of endurance that made the lives and the deeds of our great ancestors sturdy and triumphant.

Some of you who gather to observe this day and this deed may never live to witness another such ceremony, but there are children here who will live on for many years. A time will come when they shall point out this tree to their children's children. It will be one of the charming and instructive incidents in their lives to tell of the observance of Arbor day in East Haven and of its significance to mankind.

At the close of the speech the school children again took an active part in the exercises, and rendered with great effect "My Own United States."

Mr. Bradley now introduced Miss Olive Andrews, the daughter of Mrs. Florence R. Andrews, postmaster of East Haven since 1892, who recited a poem written by her mother on the state flower—the mountain laurel. The exercises closed by all singing "America," and the actual planting began by the governor throwing in the first spadeful of earth. Thus ended a very pleasant and memorable occasion to all, and a very gratifying one to the club, whereby East Haven became the possessor of an oak, with the distinction of its being given to the little town by one of the greatest of Presidents, Theodore Roosevelt.

CHAPTER VIII.

THE OLD CEMETERY.

ERY little can be said of the Old Cemetery in East Haven for several years, because there was little to record; but we will trace out its history as far as possible, from the date of the sequestration of the ground.

The agreement to sequester reads thus:

13th June, 1707. "Agreed to sequester a piece of land for a burying place, on the south side of the pond on the Forthill so called, as much as may be spared from highways and watering cattle."

It seems the Quinnipiac Indians had a fort there to defend themselves from the combined attacks of the Mohawk and Mohegan tribes. This also accounts for the deep depression now existing on the east side of the ground. Naturally it was a pond, fed by a spring which no doubt was deepened and enlarged by the Indians for the twofold purpose of supplying them with water, and earth for breastworks for their defence in time of siege. Our forefathers seem to have been very economical in the use of their pasture lands, as the several extracts from the town records will show. Very little attention was given to the burying ground for many years, until people began to let their cattle feed in it. In 1777 a vote was taken that

March 13th, 1786. At an adjourned meeting Voted, "A Committee to take care of the Burying-place be Jacob Bradley, Samuel Shepherd, Joseph Hemingway, to set out the Burying-place and to provide a lock to the gate. The Burying-place not to be fed with cattle or horses, but liberty to feed it with geese, sheep and calves." (*E. H. T. Rec.*)

Jan. 1st, 1788. Voted "That Mr. Jacob Bradley should let out the Burying-yard." (*E. H. T. Rec.*)

"The burying ground should not be fed with anything but sheep and calves." (*E. H. Town Rec.*)

Jan. 3d, 1791. Voted, "Stephen Bradley, Azariah Bradley and Stephen Woodward be a Committee, for the purpose of letting out the Ferry and Burying Ground, for the year 1791. (*E. H. T. Rec.*)

1792, Voted, "That the Selectmen are authorized to let out the Burying Ground to the highest bidder to be fed with calves and sheep." Amos Thompson was to have the letting of the Burying Ground for pasturing sheep and calves, and to procure a new lock for the gate. (*E. H. T. Rec.*)

The first death recorded as belonging to East Haven was Thomas Gregson, who was the first white settler building his house at the Cove in 1644, six years after the first settlement of New Haven in 1638. He was a wealthy and influential man in the colony, and in 1647 sailed for England as agent for the colony to obtain a land patent from the English Parliament. The vessel in which he sailed was faultily built, and all were lost at sea.

Before 1707, with a few exceptions, the dead were buried in New Haven on what was called the "Upper Green," back of Center Church. From 1644, the date of the first settlement, to 1707, the time of the sequestration of the burial place, one hundred and three deaths are recorded. Thirty-eight of these were children under ten years, mostly infants a few weeks or months old. This left sixty-five persons of maturer age some of whom were fathers of families, and men of affairs in the little colony.

The first of these was Matthew Rowe, who died May 27, 1662, the father of that family and name in the country. Also the same year, William Luddington, the first of that name, died. In 1668 Francis Brown, the ancestor of that family; also Matthew Moulthrop, the founder of that family. In 1669 Matthias Hitchcock, one of the first purchasers of South End, and a signer of the plantation covenant at New Haven, June 4, 1639. In 1673 Benjamin Linge, one of the wealthy men of the colony and the first settler at Stoney river, East Haven, since known as "Bogmine" and its vicinity. He left no children, and his widow married Colonel Dixwell, one of the regicides who condemned King Charles I of England, and who lies buried back of Center Church, or is supposed to be buried there. Also in 1673 Thomas Morris, the father of the Morris family, who bought on March 16, 1671, the land since occupied by that family; he was a shipbuilder and designed to carry on that business, but two years after, death claimed him as her own. In 1674 John Thompson, father of all the East Haven Thompsons; he settled at Stoney river, and was a farmer. In 1679 Ralph Russell, who came to Stoney river as an iron worker at "Bogmine." In 1688 Deacon John Chidsey, deacon of the First Church in New Haven, now called Center Church, died after a residence of eight years in East Haven. He was the father of all the Chidsey family, a tanner and shoemaker. His home was on the north side of the Green and in the granting of lands 10 acres were set off to him on the north side of what is now Main street and Peat Meadow road, west side. The hill has always been called "Chidsey's Hill." In 1700 George Pardee, the pioneer of all the East and North Haven Pardees. In 1707 Sergeant John Potter, father of the Potter family.

Thus in sixty-three years there were sixty-five adult deaths, being a little more than one per year out of a population not exceeding 210 people, all told, in the year 1707. From this time on it is presumed most of the burials took place on the sequestered ground, known as "The Burying Ground," and they were generally south of the hill on low ground. The oldest stone found bears the date of 1712. It is doubtful if there are any earlier dates.

March 13, 1797, after a lapse of ninety years, the town voted to enlarge the Burying Ground. Thus far the northern boundary was north of Rev. Jacob Heminway's stone, about midway between that and the present Thompson monument. It was voted to run a straight line "from the northwest corner of Moses Thompson's house, running westward in a straight line, leaving Nehemiah Smith's house 57 feet to the south of said line." The ground was enlarged, but for some traditional reason the fence was not built on that line but fifty-seven feet south of it.

The ground was a free burial place, and after another period of fifty-two years it was very evident that "what was everybody's business was nobody's." It was now in a very sad state, over-run with sumach and other bushes, briars, and rank weeds of all kinds. The fences were old, broken, and in places none at all, and not infrequently cattle were seen within its precincts. Everyone deplored the situation, but no one took the initiative to remedy the state of affairs.

In the history of events, when things have reached the worst state it often happens that some unforeseen circumstance takes place which removes the evil. It was so in this case. In the winter of 1849 the Ladies Sewing Society of the Congregational Church held their annual sale, supper, etc., in the town hall. Before the close of the evening, a solicitor, with book and pen in hand, and with a winning smile and polite request to every one to "join our society," passed around asking a renewal of membership for the ensuing year.

At one side of the hall was gathered a bevy of lively, jolly, laughing, chattering girls, none of whom felt disposed to join the staid and matronly Dorcases. After the solicitor had passed, some one said, "Let us have a society." "Oh, that would be gay!" came from several voices. "Will you join our society?" "Yes, if you have one." "Well, why can't we?" It was decided then and there to form a society. Then the question arose, For what should they work? After some discussion it was decided that the Burying Ground was the most needy object. They all pledged themselves to meet the next afternoon at the home of Miss Eliza J. Barnes. Accordingly everyone was present, and some brought others with them.

While they were talking over their plans, Mr. Jeremiah B. Davidson, an uncle of Miss Barnes, drove up and came in. He was a jovial, pleasant man, and always enjoyed young people's company. He seemed surprised at the gathering and inquired, "What is up now?" They gathered around him and unfolded their plans. He listened very attentively, and said, "Go on, girls, organize, choose your officers, make your by-laws, and when I come back from the city, I will come in and see how you come on."

When he returned, they told him of their progress, whereupon he handed out a new crisp five dollar bill, saying, "Here, girls, is a starter." This was a cheering afternoon's work. The membership fee was twenty-five cents; the fine for inexcusable absence ten cents. It was decided to meet weekly at 2 o'clock on Wednesdays, and stay until 9.30 in the evening, for in the evening the young men could attend. Each member was pledged to entertain in alphabetical order; the refreshment to be "tea, biscuit and butter, and one kind of cake, nothing else allowed."

It being winter time, Miss Sarah E. Hughes proposed to organize an auxiliary branch in her part of the town, for convenience of attendance: it was to meet Thursdays and to coöperate entirely with the East Haven society. This was done with very successful results.

All worked with the enthusiasm and courage of youth, making useful and fancy articles, calculating to make a sale of something, large or small, at every meeting. Things had been progressing finely a few weeks, when Mrs. Betsy Bradley (then Miss Betsy Forbes) thought the young ladies should be aided to hasten their object by a general subscription from the townspeople. She proposed to Miss Hughes to make a house to house canvass for the purpose. Her plan was to ask for the very modest contribution of one dollar each, payable only unless enough pledged should ensure the completion of the object. Accordingly, Miss Forbes and Miss Hughes commenced at

Tomlinson's bridge and went through to Branford
line. The day after, they went to the Foxon district.
Everywhere they were most cordially received, and
good wishes expressed for their success. The next
week Miss Barnes and Miss Hughes went through
High street and Thompson avenue and the cross
streets. Two days after, they took in the Cove and
South End, so around up to the center. Miss Barnes
solicited in Fair Haven, from those who had near
friends buried here, and Miss Forbes in New Haven.
Thus within one week the whole town was canvassed
and the success of the object fully assured. The
two societies unanimously voted Miss Barnes and Miss
Hughes a committee to execute their plans.

It was now nearing April, and the first thing to
be done was to clear the ground. "Uncle Asahel
Bradley," as he was familiarly called, was recommended for the work. He was a man of some
eccentricity, but a thoroughly honest and reliable
one—his word was equal to his bond.

The committee gave him a call. At first he looked
askance at them, over his left shoulder, with his half-
shut eye, but they assured him of their purpose, and
had the money on hand to commence. They showed
him their subscription books, when he immediately
brightened, and said, "Why, girls, you have the whole
town at your back!" They saw they were making
headway, and soon a bargain was made by his own
proposition, under the following conditions: He was
to have "no boss" but to do the work in his own way,
and when it was done it would be right. Then in
order to make his spring work effective, he wanted
to again cut the ground over "in the old of the moon

in August;" and the next year at these same seasons. To this the committee readily agreed.

The next work was the fences. "Uncle Asahel" relaid the stone wall on the south side, and a contract was made with Mr. Street Chidsey, the leading master builder of the town (an uncle of the present firm of Chidsey Brothers), to build a picket fence on the east and front sides, and on the west side the division fence belonging to the ground.

On running the lines for the new fences, Mr. Chidsey proposed to bring out the fence to the present line on the front, thus giving a continuous and straight line from Hemingway avenue to the eastward. This was opposed by the town fathers, because a tradition existed somewhere in the past that the burial ground had once been a part of the Green and no more could be taken for any purpose whatever. The members of the society were so flushed with success that they would not endure any obstacle that could be reasonably removed. So a search was made of the old colonial records, which unearthed the following vote:

May 12th 1720. "Mr. Jacob Heminway," (who was the first minister in East Haven) wishing to increase his domains, "petitioned for a part of the Green next to the spring where the burying place is." This was protested against and it was "Voted that the Green shall not be disposed of except it be for some public use, that it may be beneficial to the whole of the Proprietors."

It also brought to light the vote of March 13th, 1797, which has already been mentioned. The "Proprietors" named in the vote of 1720 had now become the inhabitants under town organization, and the vote of 1797 gave the right to bring out the fence fifty-

JACOB HEMINGWAY MONUMENT.

seven feet—to the present line. Thus all objections were clearly and legally removed and all were perfectly satisfied.

The fifty-seven feet gave a fine tier of lots, besides a roadway east and west. Previous to this carriages did not go into the grounds, but were halted outside the fence, and the remains were carried on a bier to the grave by hand.

The undertaker for East Haven for a number of years was Mr. Frederick Barnes of North Haven. Living at such a distance, in order to save travel he always came with his own hearse bearing the casket, a few hours before the funeral. This custom allowed the old town hearse to disappear and the hearse-house and bier to fall to decay; standing on the northwest corner of the ground, it was swept away with all the other refuse.

The spirit of improvement seemed to be thoroughly aroused and all worked with a cordiality of interest truly pleasing. A day was appointed, and men from all parts of the town freely gave their labor and teams to plow and level driveways north and south, east and west. They also leveled off and made a driveway all around the pond, filling up several feet, and doing other work, thus enabling carriages to enter the grounds and return.

It was now the middle of May and a wonderful transformation had taken place in this ancient "God's Acre." The ground had been cleared with great thoroughness, the fallen stones reset, the leaning ones righted, and the southern wall relaid with much nicety, thus verifying "Uncle Ashael's" word, that "the work would be done right." In his early days he had served in the Navy, and he always called the committee "my officers," and as long as he lived he never met Miss Barnes or Miss Hughes, either singly or together, but he always gave the naval salute, as "my officers," very much to their amusement and that of all bystanders.

The fences were rapidly progressing, and there was nothing now to do but collect the pledges of contribution. Miss Hughes had now gone away to school, and Miss Forbes thought that, as she had set the pace, some of the younger ladies must finish the race. Miss Barnes chose Miss Ellen S. Chidsey (now Mrs. Calvin C. Kirkham) in Miss Hughes' place. Mrs. Kirkham from the first had been a very active and efficient member of the society and was well qualified to render Miss Barnes the aid she needed in making the second canvass of the town. It was driving the nail of success down to its head which was left for these two young ladies to accomplish.

It was now the second year of the late D. W. Havens' pastorate over the Congregational Church. He was a young, enthusiastic man, fully abreast of the times, keenly alive and anxious for improvement. He gave out a call from the pulpit for all the young men of the town to meet him at the town hall. Speculation was rife among them as to what was his object. They complied, however, with his request. He told them that since the young ladies had proved so energetic and successful, he proposed that the young men should crown their efforts by erecting a gateway to adorn and complete the fence. The young men with one accord acquiesced in his proposal, and supported their young pastor by appointing him as agent to carry out the plan. He employed Sidney M. Stone, then the leading architect in New Haven, to make a design, for which he paid $25. A few of the staid and steadfast ones wagged their heads, and thought the young people were "awfully extravagant," but the days of post and rail bars had gone by. For fifty-eight years the gateway has stood, a monument to Mr. Havens' interest and zeal, and his desire to share in the welfare of the people among whom he wished to be laid to rest.

A gateway of an ornamental construction was far beyond the dreams of the young ladies: they had aspired only to order and utility; but they were nothing loath to accept the pastor's "crown" which he had proposed and received it as a compliment to their work. Miss Barnes and Mrs. Kirkham had finished collecting, paid all expenses and the work of the young ladies was closed, their object accomplished, and their mission ended. They now turned over all their papers and books, with what surplus funds they had on hand, to Mr. Havens to proceed with the gateway. Mr. Chidsey followed the design, and a well-built and substantial gateway was the result, and everyone was pleased with his or her investment for the object. Thus in less than six months, what had commenced in jest among a knot of girls, ended in signal reality pleasing to everyone.

The feeling that was aroused at this time has never died out, although it has lapsed from time to time, for want of proper organization and leadership. Individually, people have given much attention to their respective plots of ground, but there are many places uncared for, which gives a very patched and uninviting appearance to the whole.

In 1866, seventeen years after the first general awakening of cemetery care, the fences needed repairing and painting, and the ground a general and thorough cleaning again. Miss Eliza J. Barnes commenced a movement to do the work again by subscription. She enlisted Miss Sarah E. Hughes, and they canvassed to some extent, but not near so generally as in 1849. They met with very ready and generous responses to their calls. Miss Hughes was so busy with her school duties that she could not devote the time to it, so the greater portion of the work was done by Miss Barnes. The fences were repaired and painted, and the south wall relaid. The action of the frost on this low ground quickly throws it out of line. The late Mr. Comfort Prout now did a great deal of renovating. The ground was cleared, the fences and gateway repaired and painted, new hitching posts set outside the fence, and things improved generally. Mr. Prout so subdued the briars and brambles by mowing the ground over two or three times each year, that he secured quite a comfortable crop of hay for his work.

In 1867 Rev. Mr. Shannon, then rector of Christ Church, proposed at the annual October town meeting to have the town take the charge and care of the cemetery. As this was not in the call for the meeting it was ruled out. The next year he had the proposition inserted in the call, and the result was as follows: "Oct. 5th, 1868, *Voted,* That the sum of $50 be appropriated from the town treasury to be used by the selectmen in paying for the removal of the brush, etc., from the cemetery, or as much of said sum as may be needed for the said purpose." But the care of the cemetery was not committed to the selectmen, only this conciliatory vote for one year.

On June 5, 1867, Mr. Samuel Forbes bought a plot of ground, with the intention of laying it out as a cemetery, which he did in 1868, under the name of "Green Lawn Cemetery." The plan of the cemetery was designed by the Rev. Mr. Shannon. This drew all those who from time to time had occasion to commence a new family plot, especially the younger families. Mr. Prout continued to do much individual work in the "Old Cemetery" as it was now called, and to mow off the grass from the neglected parts until infirmity compelled him to cease his labors. To Miss Eliza J. Barnes belongs the credit of doing more, and causing more to be done, than any other individual, for the betterment and improvement of the cemetery up to her death in 1881.

Another period of twenty-nine years had passed, up to 1895, when things again needed attention, and a movement was organized by the late Mrs. Edwin S. Bradley to improve the condition. She was a woman who always had a heart and hand to "do good as she had opportunity." She was progressive and aggressive, a very efficient and successful worker, as well as a very pleasant one, in church and state. The drinking fountain at the corner of Main street and Hemingway avenue stands as a monument to her untiring efforts in the cause of humanity and kindness to animals. Her plan was to improve the "waste places," which contrasted so strongly with the well-kept lots that they destroyed the symmetrical appearance of the whole ground. These "waste places" were the graves of former inhabitants who had no representatives living in the town, or if they had, the call of blood was not strong enough to rouse them to action, but more generally their descendants were scattered far and wide. She proposed to seek out such relatives and state the case, asking for a contribution to care for the graves of their ancestors or relatives. In this she was very successful. She wrote to all parts of the Union, usually receiving very courteous letters and substantial aid.

As always before on like occasions, her efforts were very cordially and quickly seconded by her townspeople—it only needed a leading spirit to take the introductory step. The ladies formed themselves into a "cleaning brigade," and with pails, mops, and scrub brushes scoured the old stones with a chemical mixture to remove the blackened weather stains and moss. The men from all parts of the town donated their teams and labor on May 3, 1895, to do whatever was desired. On that day 110 loads of soil were filled into the hollow, and Mrs. Bradley opened her house for a dinner to the men, the people of the town furnishing the dinner. The driveway round the hollow was regraded and set out with shrubs. Mrs. Bradley continued her supervision and labor through the years of 1895 and 1896, but in the spring of 1897 she was obliged to cease the care. She then turned over all her books and papers to Mr. Leonard R. Andrews, first selectman, and things limped along in an unsatisfactory manner, with little or nothing done, save individual efforts, till 1905, when from the annual report of the town, it was found that the town had paid to different individuals $25.05 under the head of "Cemetery." The town accounts ending September 20, 1906, show the expenditure of $124.32 under the same head, which indicates a new order of affairs.

The truth cannot be spoken without saying that the East Haven ladies have always shown their activity and ready coöperation in every good word and work. This is no reflection on the men, for they have ever proved themselves ready to aid and further the wishes of the ladies. In fact there is no acting independently of each other; if any good is accomplished, there must, and always should be, unity of purpose.

According to the present custom of the day, the East Haven ladies are active in club life. There are several clubs, the Mothers' Club, the Woman's Club and the Radium Club being the leading ones. All are under very able leadership, and doing excellent work in their respective lines. The Woman's Club, Mrs. Edward F. Thompson president, for several years has taken up its line of action in the direction of "Village Improvement." Mrs. Thompson is an incessant and tireless worker, for improvement in any and every line where her quick discernment and discriminating judgment sees the need. Through the efforts of the Woman's Club, Arbor day of 1903 witnessed a very interesting and memorable event, beneficial for all time to come.

Since so much had been accomplished on the Green, and the work practically ended with the biennial planting of a tree donated by each governor, the Woman's Club turned its eyes towards its nearest neighbor, the Old Cemetery opposite. With commendable zeal, it

has brought about a new order of things, interesting
and seeking the aid of others within and without the
club. The movement had been under discussion for
some time, but took definite shape in the spring of
1906. At the annual town meeting October 1, 1906,
the town appointed Mrs. Edward F. Thompson, Mrs.
Leverette S. Bagley, Mrs. Frederick Forbes, Miss
Charlotte A. Hemingway, and Miss Ida M. Fonda as
trustees of the Old Cemetery. Their plan is to take
yearly care, and raise a "Perpetual Fund" to care
for it in all time to come. This of course does away
with the occasional spasmodic, individual reforms
which have taken place in the past and puts matters on
a firm basis, giving power to collect and pay out in
regular form. This brings us down to June, 1907,
the bicentennial of the sequestration of this ancient
ground, where we have one more noble act to record.

On Memorial day, 1907, the Old Cemetery and
town were presented with a beautiful stone gateway,
through the munificence of Mr. Edmund Brainard
Cowles, now of Boston, but who spent several years
of his early life in East Haven, and who has a long
line of ancestors on the maternal side entombed within
its grounds.

To the credit of East Haven it must be said, she
far surpasses many towns of much larger size in her
yearly memorial exercises; and it is safe to say, that
for the size of the town there are no better conducted
exercises in the state. For thirty years Town Clerk
Calvin C. Kirkham, himself a veteran, has been marshal of the day and arranged the order of exercises, placing the wreaths on the graves, and leaving
a large bouquet for the unknown dead.

THE COWLES MEMORIAL GATEWAY.

This year when the decoration was completed, the whole procession halted at the entrance to the Old Cemetery to witness the impressive ceremony of unveiling the arch. The presentation was made in Mr. Cowles' name by Mr. Edward Foote Thompson. Mr. Thompson spoke briefly, in presenting the structure to the township, recalling the respect and love with which the father and mother of Mr. Cowles, whose memory was thus honored, were held by all who knew them personally or by repute. He spoke of the fact that the occasion was the bicentennial of the cemetery, and dwelt somewhat upon the history of the beautiful little spot. He told of the fact that it was once an Indian fort, and then told of those who were buried there, mentioning by name many who had been prominent in the town and state. He commended the spirit of the women of the town, who had been energetic in keeping up the plots, and who have now commenced a perpetual fund for the maintenance of the Old Cemetery as it is affectionally called.

John Tyler, first selectman of the town of East Haven, responded to Mr. Thompson's words, in behalf of the town; his speech in detail follows:

"*Mr. Chairman, Ladies and Gentlemen:* This beautiful memorial gateway, which has been presented to us by Mr. Cowles of Boston, is greatly appreciated, and the grand old town of East Haven should congratulate herself upon having such good friends to aid us in beautifying her surroundings.

"To-day being Memorial day, is a fitting occasion to dedicate this gateway. We have just honored the brave boys of '61 to '65, who lie buried in this cemetery, by strewing their graves with flowers. This memorial gateway will always be to our citizens a reminder of the donor and a monument to

the Cowles family, who no doubt are ever proud of their
Connecticut ancestry.

"East Haven is further to be congratulated to-day, upon
her selection of ladies who comprise the board of trustees
for our cemetery, who have been so enthusiastic in their work
for this memorial, under the leadership of Mrs. Edward F.
Thompson. I desire to take this occasion to thank them,
and as a member of the board of selectmen, I have the
honor, as agent, on behalf of the town of East Haven, to
accept this beautiful memorial gateway, and to assure the
donor that it will be carefully guarded with pride and consecration.

"While such a gift as this must surely be appreciated for
the great beauty which it adds to our town, it is most pleasing to us all in a higher and broader sense; showing that
those who have gone out from this place to fields of greater
activity still have a warm and kindly remembrance of their
native town, and such gifts will surely act as an incentive to
all our residents, to emulate the example of those who have
gone from us, to aid heartily in making and keeping this
town in all respects one worthy to be remembered."

Following Mr. Tyler's speech of acceptance, Rev.
George A. Alcott, the Episcopal clergyman, pronounced the benediction and the procession proceeded
to the town hall, where a luncheon was served.

The gateway is a beautiful structure, of Westerly
granite, the pink of its columns making a striking and
pleasing contrast to the green of the hedges and lawns
about the cemetery. The lines of the gateway are
simple, though massive and impressive, and though
the monument is magnificent it is felt that the appro-
priateness of the memorial to Mr. and Mrs. Cowles
cannot be overestimated.

The present generation will be pleased and very
proud of this new and enduring monument, but when
all now earthly shall have passed away, the finger of

praise will not only be pointed to this lasting structure, but also to him who delighted to honor his ancestors. This is a growing feeling in all parts of .the "Old Colonial States." Old cemeteries are looked after and provision made for their future care. Being of East Haven parentage and birth, I am happy and proud to say that East Haven is in line. The Daughters of the American Revolution (of whom there is a goodly sprinkling in this ancient town) are doing much in this work. Even the all powerful and gilded hand of business can not wrest from some of our largest cities these sacred grounds, which would be literally paved with gold, if the removal of the dead could be accomplished. Public sentiment will long preserve "Old Trinity Churchyard" in New York City, and the "Old Granary Burying Ground," "King's Chapel" and "Copp's Hill" in Boston, whose value in dollars can never be estimated.

A notable fact is connected with this venerable ground: it contains the remains of all the ministers who have ever been settled over the Congregational Church in East Haven, who have passed away—five in number.

The first minister was Rev. Jacob Hemingway, whom his native townsmen called November 20, 1704, "to give them a taste of his gifts in preaching the word." His probationary call continued two years, which seems to have satisfied their "taste," and he was engaged permanently, but was not ordained until October 8, 1711. His pastorate continued fifty years. He died October 7, 1754. It has often been said he was the first graduate of Yale College; but according to President Stiles' "Notes of Yale," he was not the *first graduate,* but he was the *first student,* and for several months, perhaps the first year, the only one. He studied for two years, but for some reason was absent two years, and others graduated ahead of him.

Singular as it may seem, none of the five pastors buried here, with the exception of Mr. Nicholas Street, have descendants living in East Haven. There are four other Congregational ministers buried here, viz.: Rev. Samuel Street, Rev. John Davenport of Stamford, Rev. John Woodward, who assisted in the Council that compiled the Saybrook Platform in 1708. These three ceased from ministerial labor after coming to East Haven to reside. Rev. Lucas Hart died while in active labor in Wolcott, Connecticut, in the 29th year of his age. His married connection was with the Street family.

In most old cemeteries there are many quaint and striking epitaphs and stones, and East Haven is no exception. One which has attracted much attention is that of Mr. Edmund Bradley with its seven outlined faces representing three pairs of twins and the eldest born.

> "See death removes the eldest son
> Just as the family's begun
> And three pair of twins in a short space
> To quicken them in the christian race."

> "Children of Edmund & Mrs. Lydia Bradley."

Another stone which has received considerable comment is that of Rev. Nicholas Street, erected to his "Dear Desire."

> "Here my dear Desire lies,
> Obscured in the dust,
> Thus all but virtue dies,
> Whose memory cannot rust."

No doubt he had a fatherly as well as a husband's affection for her, as she was his bride at thirteen years of age. As time passes on, generations to come probably will see quaint and unseemly things of the present day, for the face of all things changeth, and the fashion thereof passeth away.

"Our buried friends can we forget,
Although they've passed death's gloomy river?
They live within our memory yet,
And in our love must live forever,
And though they're gone awhile before,
To join the ransomed host in heaven,
Our hearts will love them more and more,
Till earthly chains at last be riven."

CHAPTER IX.

NATURAL HISTORY.

HE town of East Haven contains about nine thousand acres of land.* The soil is generally light and sandy; but capable of yielding good crops when properly cultivated. It is congenial to Indian corn and barley. In favorable seasons potatoes do well. In some parts of the town rye succeeds, but it is very subject to blast and rust. By good husbandry the lands may be made more productive; though unhappily there is very little good pasturage in the town. There is very little clay, and some parts of the town are encumbered and disfigured with rocks and ragged barren hills.

About the first spring, or the head of Bloomary brook and the head of Claypit brook, and along the intervals of Stoney river, good brick clay may be obtained. Some of the best land lies in the fresh meadows and Cove swamp, which are now uncultivated and unproductive. Were these low lands drained, as they will be at some future period, they would be the most productive lands in the town.

Along the seashore, there is a range of granite rock, of the purest kind, but it is not found in any other part of the town. Pond Rock and the ridge west

* That was until 1882, when about one-third of its surface was annexed to New Haven.

of it are green or whinstone. The same kind of rock appears in detached eminences and ridges, in some other parts of the town. Sandstone of the secondary formation commences on the Indian land northeast from the Cove and running north spreads through Fair Haven woods, and terminates on the Davenport farm. Another mass lies on the east side of the fresh meadows, and runs in a northeast direction to the north line of the town on the half-mile. The greenstone, generally, on the surface is in such a state of fracture as to be nearly useless, except the smaller fragments, which make excellent gravel for the roads. In some places the sandstone is in a state of decomposition. In the ridge north of Mullen Hill agates are found in abundance.

The plains appear to be composed of sand, coarse and fine, washed from the lands and valleys on the north, and accumulating gradually by some powerful operating cause. The salt marshes are founded upon a bottom of sand, like that of the plains adjacent.

The town is well supplied with water of an excellent quality. There are numerous springs and some fine rivulets, while Stoney river and Furnace pond [now Lake Saltonstall] afford an inexhaustible supply of water of the best kind.

The pond is about three miles long, and from one hundred yards to three hundred yards broad, and very deep.

The fisheries in the waters of East Haven are excellent and valuable. In Quinnipiac river, oysters are taken in vast quantities and those of a superior quality are taken in the Cove and Stoney river.

Clams, blackfish and whitefish abound in their season. Whitefish are used in vast quantities for fertilizer.

The trade in oysters is carried to a great extent. From sixty to one hundred thousand bushels are annually imported; these are opened, put into kegs of small size, and dispersed all over the northern and western country, quite into Canada. The amount of sales for this town and vicinity is estimated at twenty-five thousand dollars during the fall and winter season. And it probably sometimes exceeded that sum.*

A considerable number of men are employed in the coasting, packet and oyster trade: but this town has suffered exceedingly by the loss of active men at sea. Farming occupies the attention of the principal part of the male population.

On October 8, 1797, great damage was done by a tornado, which passed over the center of the town. The same week, the following account of it was published in a New Haven paper:

"On Sunday evening last, between six and seven o'clock, we experienced a violent gale of wind from the westward, attended with heavy rain and thunder. The damage done in this town was not great, compared with that done at East-Haven and Branford."

"The roofs of some buildings were injured, the tops of chimneys blown off, and windows blown in, some trees and fences blown down, and a barn in the New Township removed from its foundation. At East-Haven the steeple of the meeting-house was blown down, which falling on the roof, broke through the side, where it fell, leaving only one rafter standing, and penetrating the floor, greatly damaged the seats."

* This was correct in 1824. In 1907 it reached the million point.

A large new house was removed from its foundations; several dwelling houses were partly, and others entirely unroofed. A number of barns met the same fate. Three large barns were entirely demolished; the materials of which they were built were scattered in every direction. The town of Branford experienced nearly the same fate. Part of the roof of the meeting-house was blown off, and all the windows on the western side destroyed; six or seven houses, a new store, and several barns were unroofed, other barns blown down, the trees in several fine orchards laid prostrate. The height of the tornado continued but a few minutes."

The same tornado is described in Dwight's Travels, with the addition of several particulars to the above account.

"On Lord's day, October 8, 1797, in the afternoon, a Tornado, the commencement of which, so far as I was able to learn, was at Upper Salem in the County of Westchester, and State of New-York, passed over Ridgefield, in Connecticut, and thence over Redding, Newtown, Huntington, Derby, Woodbridge, New-Haven, East-Haven, Branford, Guilford, and Killingworth; whence it directed its course over the Sound. At times it rose from the earth, and held its most furious career in a higher region of the atmosphere. Such was the fact at New-Haven, where, although its force was great, it did not blow with sufficient strength to do any material damage. At Upper Salem it destroyed orchards, groves, and buildings. At East-Haven it blew down the steeple of the Presbyterian Church, and ruined several other buildings. It left many marks of its· violence also at Branford, and some other places; while in others it did little or no mischief. This alternate rise and fall of a Tornado I have not seen mentioned; nor do I remember a storm of this kind, at so late a season, in any other instance."

Another violent gale, called the Salt Storm, occurred September 3, 1821. Light showers passed in the morning; it was somewhat misty through the day,

with a light rain about 5 P. M., the wind rising about
that hour, it having been all day south and southeast.
At six o'clock it became a gale, still increasing and
blowing with dreadful violence until eleven o'clock,
when it broke, and a calm succeeded. In this town
very little rain fell; but in the region of New York
a vast quantity poured down. The sand and gravel,
however, were scooped from the earth and dashed
against every opposing object. A salt spray covered
everything within its reach, and mingling with the
dirt then afloat, rendered the glass windows quite
opaque, and formed a coat so firm that it was not
easily washed off.

The morning light disclosed a scene of mournful
devastation in the vegetable kingdom. Trees of every
kind were stripped of their foliage, and also of their
fruit. The small limbs upon the windward side were
killed and still exhibit the deadly properties of the
storm, and along the coast the fruit trees are rendered
barren. Many small trees were destroyed. The shrubbery and vegetation of the garden and the field
appeared as is common after a severe and early frost.
The atmosphere was loaded with a very nauseous
fetor. The buckwheat was completely destroyed: the
corn lay prostrate, the leaves of which were whipped
into strings. The weather afterwards being very
warm, the trees and living shrubbery put forth new
leaves, and the fruit trees and the lilac were adorned
with flowers.

The deadly effects of the salt on vegetation might
be traced twelve or fifteen miles inland; but gradually
diminishing according to the distance from the shore.
It having been a very dry season in this town, and the

ground being very hard, but few trees were over-
turned, compared with what took place a few miles
north, where the ground was softer, for there great
havoc was made among the tall timber.

A singular phenomenon of frequent occurrence is
noticeable in this town respecting the motion of
thunder clouds, proceeding from the west. The cloud
advances over the harbor and approaches Fort Hill
[now Beacon Hill] presenting a great and, in a dry
season, a hopeful appearance of a refreshing rain.
But presently it breaks* and then separates to the right
and left; one part passing to the north of the village,
and the other part passing down the harbor and across
the south end of the town, pours down its refreshing
streams upon the Sound. Sometimes no rain at all
falls upon the plains east of the hill and at other times
only a sprinkling from the skirts of the cloud.
Whether the hill possesses a repulsive, or the water
an attractive, quality that operates upon the cloud, is
a question left to the wisdom of the reader to solve.

The town affords a few curiosities. On an island in
Stoney river there is a regular cavity cut into the
granite rock, called the Indian Well. It is from
twenty-six to thirty-three inches in diameter, and very
smooth, especially the bottom of it. It is now about
five feet deep, but formerly was deeper. When the
dam below was built, some part of the rock was
removed and much injured its natural appearance.
The water on both sides of the island passes through

* Old people who were not much in love with the pranks
of the college boys, used to say the clouds parted over Yale
College, because there was so much witchcraft carried on
there.

a narrow channel of granite rock. I have seen similar excavations in the beds of the Mohawk river below the Cohoes falls, which were evidently formed by sand and pebbles set in motion by the rotary action of the water. Such cavities are common near the falls of rivers. The Indian Well was, doubtless, produced by the attrition of the sand and pebbles, which passed over
. this rock, it being then in the bed of the river. The bottom of the river was then from eight to twelve feet above the present high-water mark, the valley on the north being once a considerable lake and connected with Furnace pond [now Lake Saltonstall]. A great change has evidently passed over the land and marsh in that vicinity. Stumps and fragments of trees lie in the bed and on the banks of the river. The marsh has but a small depth, and lies on a bed of sand. Some fragments of Indian manufacture and other articles have been thrown up in ditching the marsh.

On the land of William Woodward [now the house yard of Mr. Fred B. Hinckley] and a few rods west of his barn, is a rock of greenstone resting in a few places over a cavity upon a ridge of sandstone. The under side of the rock is very smooth. Its mean height is about five feet and a half, and its length and breadth about eight feet. The top of it is flat. There is no other rock of the kind in that neighborhood. Is this rock of Celtic origin? Its size and peculiar position resembles that of other rocks in this country which have been the subject of scientific speculation.

Another rock of sandstone somewhat similar to the other, not so high, but having a longer table, is on a hill of considerable elevation, west of Bridge swamp. It originally rested on the apex, like an inverted cone,

EAST HAVEN RIVER AND DARROW ISLAND.

but now reclines towards the south. From this situation there is a charming view of the Sound and the surrounding country.

The great burying place of the Indian tribes in this town and vicinity is on the north end of the hill on which the fort stands which anciently, in allusion to this place, was called Grave Hill. [Now much of it is Fort Wooster Park.] Some of the graves have been levelled by the plow, but many of them are yet visible. In the year 1822 I examined three of these graves. At the depth of about three feet and a half, the sandstone appears, on which the bodies were laid, without any appearance of a wrapper or enclosure. They all lay in the direction of southwest and northeast, the head towards the west. Of two of them the arms lay by the side; the other had the arms across the body, after the manner of the white people. The large bones and teeth were in a sound state. The thigh bones of one measured 19 inches in length, the leg bone 18, and the arm from the elbow to the shoulder 13. By measuring the skeleton as it lay, it was concluded to be that of a man six and a half feet high. No article of any description appeared with the bones. It is said that about 50 or 60 years ago some of these graves were opened, and a number of Indian implements of the kitchen and of war were found in them. Few Indians have been buried there within a century past.

The Indians had a fort on the hill in the burying ground, and from that circumstance it was called Fort Hill. It is also a tradition that they had another on the hill north of Mr. Daniel Hughes' house, and near the old ferry road [now Fairmont avenue]. The appearance of shells shows that they had a village on that spot. The same indications appear in the woods of South End Neck, west of the sluice. Great quantities of oyster shells are collected among the rocks, and in the little valleys, and on the banks of the river, showing the places where their wigwams stood. It was stated in the first chapter of this history that Thomas Gregson, who settled at Solitary cove, and several others on a voyage to England were lost at sea. That affair is noticed by Dr. Mather in his "Magnalia," and the story of the apparition of a ship is given in connection with the biography of Thomas Gregson, in the first chapter, and is therefore omitted in this place.

INDIANS.

There is nothing to sustain the tradition that the Indians had a fort "north of Mr. Daniel Hughes' house," excepting the make of the land and the ease with which one could have been built. That they had wigwams there, is undisputably true; not only there, but all over the flats south to the harbor through which Forbes avenue now runs. This was the ground reserved to them by the English when they bought the land. Also all of Townsend avenue down to the harbor, and so on to South End. In laying out streets, and excavating for cellars, numberless relics of Indian make have been unearthed. Mr. George G. Hitchcock, in building his houses on Fairmont avenue, made quite a collection of Indian implements, which he gave to Capt. Charles H. Townsend. As late as 1828, in digging the cellar for the·residence of the late Mr. Aaron A. Hughes, about a foot and half underground was found a large space paved with flat stones, all laid very evenly together. Mr. Hughes thought he was disturbing an Indian burial ground; but his father said they were Indian hearths where the wigwams had stood. About 1840 Mr. Alfred Hughes unearthed a similar place northwest of his house. His grandfather, Mr. Daniel Hughes, gave the same explanation, saying they were where the Indians had their summer villages when they came to fish. In winter they went into the woods to hunt and for the convenience of fuel, and when they left, they covered the hearths with earth, so that no other Indians might find them and profit by their labor. In the summer they scraped the earth to one side, and erected their huts.

All the flat lands near the shore are plentifully flecked with broken shells, especially all around and west of the old stone house, now the site of the Chapel of the Epiphany. The Hughes family have given away to curiosity hunters, from time to time, many relics found on their grounds. One, a very curious old spoon, still in the possession of the family, some experts think was one of the "twelve alchemy spoons" given to the Indians by Rev. John Davenport and Theophilus Eaton, when they bought the land of Momauguin. It is not copper, or brass or iron; yet it seems to be a composite of metals, hence called alchemy.

The Passing of the Indians.

The statement has often been made that the white man has greatly wronged the Indians. This may have been the case in many places, but after a candid and careful search of town and Indian records, the facts stand out in bold relief that this charge cannot be sustained against the Connecticut and New Haven colonies; particularly the New Haven Colony, which in their first purchase of Momauguin, rights of land, and protection from other hostile tribes, were secured to them by the Davenport and Eaton treaty. The Indian reservation seems to have been kept intact, as originally laid out.

In 1679 a proposition was made to purchase some land of the Indians near Mr. Gregson's farm, "if the Indians were willing to sell it." Due caution was advised, as the Quinnipiacs at that date (1680) numbered about 100 men, it was thought best not to sell their lands. In 1638 they numbered 46 fighting men and with squaws and children about 150 in all; but by living a peaceful life under the protection of the English they had increased now to over 300 all told. Between the years of 1680 and 1750 this Quinnipiac tribe was greatly reduced in numbers, occasioned by King Philip's War in 1675, the Canadian War in 1690, the Cuban Expedition in 1740, and the siege of Louisburg in 1745. In all these wars the Quinnipiac Indians helped to fill the quota of Connecticut. Some went as sailors, but most of them as soldiers. Disease and battle had thinned their ranks. In 1695 the General Court of Connecticut granted the town of New Haven the right to sell Indian lands. Nayhassatt, alias George Sagamore, sold to John Morris and others 18 acres in the old "Indian Field" near the old ferry. President Stiles says, "In 1720 there were between the ferry and Mr. Woodward's house twenty wigwams (old Indian village)." This section extended from Farren avenue south to Forbes avenue and the harbor.

The Indians in 1725 living on the East side numbered about 20 in all.

"In 1727 John, alias George Sagamore, son and heir to George, late sachem of New Haven, and James, Tom, Indians, sons of James, Indian, deceased, and Nimrod, Indian, and Jacob, Indian, being all the men of our tribe (1727 five only) belonging to New Haven, sold to John Morris several pieces of land amounting in all to 58 acres. In 1760 the Indian land in East Haven was occupied by only one Indian and three squaws. In 1745 James Meekyeuh, sachem of the East Haven Indians, died in Cheshire. His son James Mennau-yush died in Derby in 1758. Dr. Ruggles says in 1760 'there died in Guilford the only remaining man Indian between Saybrook and New Haven Ferry.' " The same year, Dr. Stiles says, "there was but one wigwam on the East Haven reservation, and that was occupied by a squaw, and her son 16 years old."

In 1769, the memorial of one Adam, an Indian, of a New Haven tribe of Indians, who had lived in Farmington some time, requested of the Assembly of Connecticut that the planting land reserved for said tribe in the parish of East Haven, which contained about 30 acres, might be sold, and the money received by the sale of such land be laid out in Farmington, for the benefit of said tribe; whereupon said Adam was empowered to make the sale; but he soon after died. In 1770 the last sachem of the Quinnipiacs, Charles, was frozen to death, near a spring about a mile north of East Haven meetinghouse. In 1770 Samuel Adam, an Indian belonging to Farmington, one of said tribe, was empowered to sell the East Haven land to Capt. Timothy Tuttle, June 2, 1773.

This Samuel Adam was the last one of the tribe remaining, who was at this time living with the Farmington Indians. The money for the land was expended in Farmington for Samuel Adam's benefit, which he had the Farmington authorities sell for his benefit, according to law, when he removed with his family into the Mohawk country. From the above we see that the rights and property of the Quinnipiacs were strictly preserved, and extended to them to the last man, by the New Haven Colony and parish of East Haven.

SLAVES.

East Haven is not without its taint of slavery. In common with many New England towns, slaves were owned in many families, as slavery existed in all the early colonies of the United States. There was a great difference of opinion on the subject in those primitive times, as well as in more recent years. Connecticut passed a law of total emancipation in 1794, thus doing away with the evil forever in the "Constitution State."

The first record of slave ownership in East Haven was in the early part of the eighteenth century. We find in a will of Joseph Tuttle, 1761, that he bequeaths "the house, shop and negro rooms at East Haven." He also mentions four negro men, "Richard, Bethuel, Cambridge and Reuben," and four women, "Dinah, Lucy, Statira and Axsee." Doubtless these were parents of children which are not named. These slaves ranged in value from £20 to £75.

The families owning the greatest number of slaves were John Woodward, Sr., Capt. Amos Morris, Jehiel Forbes, the Hemingways, Thompsons, Pardees,

Chidseys and Smiths. Even the saintly Mr. Street owned his Tom, who used to sometimes come to him and say, "Master, I wish I could be free!" Mr. Street always replied, "Well, Tom, you shall be free any day that you will sign a paper that I need not take care of you when you are old and can do nothing." Whereupon Tom would roll his eyes, and whistle, going off grinning and shaking. He died in servitude in 1791, in the 57th year of his age. That Mr. Street had some qualms of conscience on the subject of slavery is very evident, from an extract from one of his sermons when he says, "While we abhor oppression as it comes upon us from the mother country, we may be harboring it in our own bosoms." Furthermore, he exhorts all to "a careful search and examination of all that has been written on the subject, in an impartial and disinterested way." Pink and her daughter Chloe, slaves of Isaac Forbes, were the last remnants of slavery dying in East Haven. Pink was a town charge for some time, dying after 1850. Below are a few names of slaves which have been gathered, showing their owners, their own names, ages and deaths.

Owner.		Age.	Died.	
John Woodward	Guido	65	1781	
John Woodward	Abigail	65	1781	
John Heminway	Nancy	75	1794	
Samuel Thompson	Chloe	35	1773	
Amos Morris	Tony	27	1778	
Amos Morris	Cajoe	45	1773	drowned
Dea. Stephen Smith	Cato	11	1783	
Widow Mary Pardee	Peggy	30	1783	
Widow Mary Pardee	Titus	18	1797	
Capt. Isaac Chidsey	Andrew	28	1789	

Owner.		Age.	Died.
Capt. Woodward	Thate	70	1795
James Chidsey	Flora	15	1805

Jehiel Forbes (Cork and wife, Sybil), Will, Cæsar and others.

It has always been currently reported that Sybil declared her master's son, Dr. David Forbes, ate up her boy Cæsar! The latter was sold to pay David's board bill while in college, hence her construction, which might have been true. Charles Bishop and Nathaniel Barnes owned Harry.

WITCHCRAFT IN EAST HAVEN.

As John W. Barber in his "Historical Collections of Connecticut" thought best to give this subject space in his work, it may not be amiss to transcribe into this work the following, which he says is "a fair sample of witch stories, which were generally believed in ancient times."

"An old gentlemen was riding, one bright moonlight evening, through a very lonely place called Dark Hollow (a by-road which leads from East Haven to Fair Haven), when he saw two females at the head of his horse, very earnestly (apparently) engaged in conversation, and keeping pace with his horse. He was considerably excited and his feelings of fear aroused, as he had no doubt, that these were the famous hags, who were disturbing the peace of the land. He had, however, courage enough to speak to them in these words: 'In the name of God, I beseech you tell me who you are.' When, wonderful to behold, they immediately vanished. He got off his horse to look for them, but could find nothing but a riding hood, which lay where they disappeared."

"A short time after this event, the same gentleman was riding past one of his orchards, when there appeared to him to be someone shaking one of his apple trees, and a considerable quantity was falling to the ground. He went up to the tree, and the ground was covered with apples, which had just fallen, but there was no one to be seen, all was still as the grave."

"The following is still more mysterious: There was an old woman who lived not far from the neighborhood of this old gentleman, who was suspected by the neighbors of being one of these tormentors of mankind. Their hogs would run about on their hind legs, and squeal as though they were possessed by legions of unclean spirits. Their children would be taken sick and cry out 'that some one was sticking pins into them.' A member of one of the families would roll about the floor with great rapidity as though urged forward by some invisible power, and the members of the family had to keep an eagle's eye on the rolling gentleman, lest he should roll into the fire. When the neighbors made their bread, it was full of hairs, and their soap would run over their kettles, and fly about the floor like burning lava from the crater of Mount Etna. In the night large stones would tumble down their chimneys and break their cooking utensils, setting the whole family in an uproar. It appeared as though the powers of darkness had been let loose from Pandemonium to torment these neighbors. But not long after, these difficulties all ceased in a singular manner, i. e., one of the neighbor's pigs was running about on its hind legs as described, when a man who was noticing it jumped into the pen, and cut off one of its ears. The old woman mentioned always after-

wards had one of her ears muffled. The neighbors
were now satisfied that this woman was the cause of
all their troubles. However, they thought they would
say nothing or do nothing for the present but see how
these things continued."

"A short time after this, one of the neighbors was
making potash beside the river, and it began to fly
out, and run about so they could do nothing with it.
They held a consultation, and concluded they would
shoot into it with a rifle, which they did, and immediately there was a calm, and they were enabled to go on
with their work and finish it. In the morning the
neighbors went to the place where this woman resided,
where they found her dead and thus their troubles
ended. But it appears this woman was not the only
suspected witch in the place. In an old lonely house
which stood on the road leading to New Haven, lights
were seen in the night; the sound of the violin and
the noise of persons dancing, were heard by the inhabitants of the place around it, until they went to work
day after day, pulling its clapboards off, until the house
was completely destroyed to the joy of the inhabitants
of the town. Nothing more of any consequence was
heard of witches from that time."

CHAPTER X.

LOSSES BY WAR.

 N the French War of 1755, a number of men were drafted from East Haven for the English army near the lakes, and the greater part of them were lost by sickness and battle. Of these I have obtained the following names, viz.: Jacob Moulthrop, David Moulthrop, Adonijah Moulthrop, Jacob Robinson, Benjamin Robinson, Thomas Robinson, Jr., David Potter, John Mallory, Abraham Jocelin, Samuel Hotchkiss, James Smith, Samuel Russell and Stephen Russell, brothers, and Asa Luddington. Benjamin Russell was captured at sea.

In the War of Independence, which began April 19, 1775, the following persons were lost. In 1776, Elijah Smith was killed in battle on Long Island; Thomas Smith conducted a fire ship to the enemy, but was badly burned, and the attending boat having left him too soon, he had to swim ashore, where he was found three days after in a helpless state; he was brought over to Rye, and there he died. Nathan Andrews died a prisoner. In 1777 Isaac Potter perished in the prison ship. July 5, 1779, Isaac Pardee was killed on Grave or Fort Hill, by a cannon shot. In October, on board a privateer, Zabulon Bradley was killed. Richard Paul, Jacob Pardee, Jr., Asa Bradley, Abijah Bradley, and Elijah Bradley, were made prisoners and all, except the last, perished in the prison ship at New

York the following winter. In 1780 Medad Slaughter died in the prison ship. In 1781 John Howe was killed by the tories, when they surprised Fort Hale. John Walker was killed upon Long Island.

Thus twelve young men were lost, and several men returned from captivity so injured by hard usage that they pined away and died—particularly Edward Goodsell, Isaac Luddington and Jared Hemingway.

On July 4, 1779, the enemy intending to capture New Haven, landed a covering force on Morris Neck and South End, and marched directly to Tuttle's Hill, where they encamped that night, and the next day reëmbarked. They were led by the tories. In this invasion they burnt most of the dwellings within their reach, and made the rebel whigs feel the effects of royal British vengeance.

To meet these losses and those of other towns of a similar nature, in May, 1792, the General Assembly of Connecticut passed an act appropriating "500,000 acres of land west of Pennsylvania, for the relief of the sufferers by fire." The damage in each town was assessed, and the amount of each person's loss in East Haven was as follows:

Amos Morris,	£1235	15	4
John Woodward,	838	17	3
John Woodward, jun.,	740	19	11
Elam Luddington,	408	6	7
Joseph Tuttle,	79	9	5
Jacob and Abijah Pardee,	402	8	2
Jehiel Forbes,	173	13	1
Mary Pardee,	134	14	0
Mary and Lydia Pardee,	40	8	4
Noah Tucker,	99	17	4
	£4154	9	5

Equal to $13,848.24.

FORT WOOSTER TABLET.

They burnt eleven dwelling houses, nine barns, and some other out-buildings. Gurdon Bradley lost £66, in a sloop that was burnt. The enemy and the militia plundered the inhabitants of all they could carry off. The whole of this loss was collected by the commissioners appointed for this purpose, and the amount was £421 1s. 4d. The entire loss of East Haven by this invasion in property was $15,251.79.

Since 1824 a very great change has taken place in the sentiment, interest and pride of ancestry of the Revolutionary patriots. As East Haven was one of the historic places of the Revolution, and one whose inhabitants suffered more, in proportion to their numbers, than almost ony other place, as the British burned nearly every building on their line of march, besides destroying crops, slaughtering cattle and spreading ruin everywhere, it is thought advisable to give the occurrences a place in history. Besides, East Haven was one of the first places in Connecticut to be marked with a tablet erected on Beacon Hill in 1895 by the Sons of the American Revolution. In fact, if the ladies of East Haven were so disposed, they could form a very respectable sized chapter of the D. A. R.'s within the limits of the little town with a fine record to each one. So, for the benefit of those who may succeed the present generation, and who may take pride in their noble ancestry, a more detailed account has been written. There may be some omissions of facts, which could not be gathered, but which might be of much interest. It is the regret of the writer that such may be the case.

BRITISH INVASION OF NEW HAVEN.

July 4, 1779, occurred on Sunday, and as has always been the custom, the people proposed celebrating it on the following Monday. It is within the memory of the older inhabitants that all New England observed Saturday night with great religious precision; but Sunday night was of a holiday nature. It was now the third anniversary of American Independence, and as New Haven had never celebrated this great event to any extent, it was decided that this year it should be fittingly observed; accordingly at "sundown Sunday" the people assembled in the middle brick church to make arrangements. Everything was decided about 9 o'clock, and the inhabitants were quietly retiring for their night's rest, when the booming of a signal gun announced the approach of the enemy, and instead of its being a day of celebration, it proved to be a day of defence.

It had been reported in the town, that a fleet was preparing for the eastward, from New York. Commodore Sir George Collier was commander-in-chief of all the British naval forces in American waters, rendezvousing in New York. It was supposed this fleet was destined for either Newport or New London, until they had passed Stratford and nearly rounded into New Haven harbor, which was late in the evening of July 4th. About midnight the whole fleet was at anchor, the large ships about a mile from Southwest Ledge Lighthouse. The smaller vessels came into the mouth of the harbor about 5 A. M., July 5th, which was then about high tide. The first division of 1,500 men and four field pieces landed at Savin Rock (West

Haven) under Brigader-General Garth. As soon as the boats, which had landed the men on the west shore, returned to the transports, they were filled with British troops, and were rowing to the East shore, under command of General Tryon.

Morris Cove or Point had long been a coveted and objective place to the tories and British. Long Island Sound was full of foraging and marauding parties, from the war ships generally commanded by a British officer, led by tories, who were well acquainted with the localities. Cattle, sheep, and poultry were killed or driven off, houses broken into and robbed, and not infrequently heads of families captured and imprisoned. Just before the invasion of New Haven, Capt. Amos Morris, of Morris Point, was one of the victims of a raid made on his place. "He and his son were awakened, and captured, taken to a boat in waiting, and conveyed to the British with little clothing to protect them from the night air, and finally lodged in one of the far-famed prison-ships, at that time the terror of all captured Americans.

"While on their passage across the sound, as daylight appeared, Captain Morris recognized one of his captors as a man who had lived in the town of East Haven, and had been for a time in his employ. Turning to him with the same commanding air and tone of authority that he was wont to assume when occasion demanded it and which few men ever wielded with more effect, he exclaimed, 'And is it you, J! What do you mean, sir, by this treatment?' The tory, cowering at the captain's rebuke, replied, 'You shan't be hurt, Squire, you shan't be hurt.' 'Hurt,' retorted the squire, 'What do you call such treatment as this?

Dragging a man from his bed, in the dead of the night, tearing him from his family, plundering his house, exposing him, half-clad, to the air of the cold night, in an open boat, is this no hurt, sir?' His son, taking courage from this bold tone, and seeing its effect, cast his eye upon the plunder, and discovered among it his father's coat, and threw it to him in the other end of the boat. It was a time of more than ordinary solicitude on the part of the son for his family, his wife being in delicate health, and profiting by the lesson of his captors, he availed himself of a dark night to effect his escape. The effort cost him many perils and hardships, but was in the end successful. Captain Morris was subsequently liberated on his parole." [*Morris Gen.*]

The British now pulling oar for the shore were about 1,500 men, composed of the 23d Regiment, the Hessian, Landgrave, and King's American regiments and two pieces of cannon. As soon as the boats were within range, the fieldpiece, which a company of East Haven patriots had hauled to the beach at Morris Point and was masked, opened fire. When half a mile from shore, the line of boats divided, one division putting into Morris Cove. On account of the well-served battery of three guns on Black Rock Fort (now Fort Hale) they were compelled to land near where the Grove House wharf is now built. General Tryon it appears landed here, and from the top of the Palisades directed the storming of the Rock Fort. The other line of boats landed on the beach east of the outer rocky point, and as it landed, an officer hailed the shore, shouting, "Disperse, ye rebels!" and the next moment fell back into the boat dead, from the fire of this detachment, who were armed with rifles. This was the first enemy killed on the East shore; he was Adjutant Watkins of the King's American regiment. As soon as life was extinct, they buried him near the Old Lighthouse. In fact that is what they did with all those killed on the East shore. It seemed to be their object to conceal their loss from the patriots as soon as possible, and their dead were buried along their line of march. The main body after forming on the beach and throwing out skirmishers, one party going along the Fowler Creek meadows, east side, and the other along the beach, protected by a section of marines and sailors in Morris Cove, took up its march. As the advance guard of this division approached the Morris mansion, they were frequently fired upon, and this grand old manor house, built of stone, was the first to be consigned to the flames, together with the barns and all other buildings.

When the alarm guns called to arms, great fear and consternation seized all, as it was evident that rapine and murder would mark every step. The first thing to be done was to send the women and children, with what valuables could be best collected and transported, to a place of safety. Those who possessed horses quickly saddled and loaded them with bags of household goods, while others filled oxcarts with the same, driven by the mothers or older children, while the fathers and older sons seized their guns, to go forth to harass and annoy the enemy.

The time of preparation was so short that many heard the whistling of bullets from the guns of the enemy. The experience of one family is nearly the same of all those fleeing to some place of supposed safety. "Captain Morris and his men made every effort to secure such loose or movable property as could be conveyed to secret places in the short time allowed for such work. Some were hidden in ditches, some in a bushy swale, and some were carried to the woods whither the stock had been driven, excepting the swine, which took fright at the discharge of muskets, and breaking out of the sty took shelter in a field of rye. They remained at the house as long as prudence would permit, securing the property. His last act before leaving was to spread a table with refreshments and luxuries for their entertainment, with the hope of rendering them more favorably disposed toward himself, and thus saving his buildings.

"Being now about to leave he cast a glance out of the door, and saw a company of redcoats, within a stone's throw, advancing towards the houses. 'They are upon us,' he exclaimed; and with his hired men made their retreat under cover of the house, until they gained a stone wall. By this time the house was no longer between them and the enemy and a rapid fire was immediately opened upon them. The stone wall protected them, until they reached a pair of bars in the wall; as they passed this, they were greeted with a shower of bullets, but escaped all injury. One of the balls struck a rail just above Mr. Morris' head and grooved out its center. The rail remained in its place on the farm till 1845, when that portion showing the mark of the ball was placed with the Connecticut Historical Society of Hartford. He now escaped into the woods just beyond, and finally joined his family. His house, barns, and buildings for the manufacture of salt and cider, and for storing goods, were burned, inflicting a loss of more than £1,235.

"A short time after the war, Captain Morris had occasion to visit the state prison, and to his surprise discovered among the prisoners the man who betrayed him at the time of his capture by the British. 'What! is it you, J?' he exclaimed, 'and have you come to this?' Not another word was spoken; but calling to mind the noble revenge prescribed in the gospel, he drew from his pocket a golden coin, and saw the tory brush away a tear as he received it." [*Morris Gen.*] This same fellow was engaged in a raid on the house of Capt. Ebenezer Dayton, in Bethany, Connecticut, with five others, headed by a British officer, five of whom were caught, tried, convicted and sentenced to Newgate prison.

The march from the Point to the Palisades was rapid and destructive. The Pardee houses, and one belonging to the brother of Captain Morris were fired, and destroyed; Jacob Pardee's house was held for a short time as Tryon's headquarters. The Pardees had barely time to throw into an oxcart their valuables, which they buried in Bridge swamp, a few rods northeast of Jeddy Andrews' house. The enemy destroyed everything in their wake; but several of them had fallen and were hastily buried in the thick woods just off the road. The earthworks on Beacon Hill and at Black Rock Fort were the only obstacles that this powerful land and sea force had to oppose them. The enemy did not get possession of the Rock Fort until its brave defenders had expended all their ammunition. The fort was stormed by Tryon's land force, and at the same time their shipping drew up and attacked it from the harbor. The fort had only 19 men, under the command of Lieutenant Bishop, and three pieces of artillery, yet was defended as long as reason or valor dictated, and then the patriots spiked and dismounted the guns, and retreated northward, but were outnumbered and captured, when not far distant. Everything in the Cove was now in .blazing or smoking ruins, and the advance guard of the main body was marching up what is now Townsend avenue, a road of only two rods width thickly set on each side with bushes, stone, and in some places a Virginia rail fence, forming an excellent covert, from which the patriots were firing on the enemy with much execution.

The next house after leaving the Cove was Mr. Joseph Tuttle's, standing opposite the present Townsend homestead. Mr. Tuttle owned the farm extending from Black Rock to Beacon Hill, which he sold to the Townsends in 1709. Mr. Tuttle and his eldest son, Josiah, a lad not yet seventeen, were in the fort defending it; both were now prisoners of war. His son was a regularly enlisted soldier, having joined Captain Phineas Bradley's company when only sixteen years and four months old. The British on both sides of the harbor were led by Joshua Chandler's sons. William led those on the West side, and Tom, those on the East side. Chandler was acquainted with Mr. Tuttle and knew the ground well, having hunted it over, often, with the boys on the East side. On coming to his house, Chandler told the officer this was Tuttle's house, and pointed him out. The officer told Mr. Tuttle they would burn his house and everything surrounding it, if he would not lay down his arms, and promise he would not take them up again. He replied, "Not for

all the gold in the British kingdom." A shout rang
out, "Run the rebel through." He raised his right
hand high above his head and said, "By all the laws
of civilized warfare you are bound to protect your
prisoners." The officer then asked, "What are you
fighting for, any way?" "God and my right," was
his reply. The same shout rang out the second time.
The officer, waving his sword, said, "No, you cannot
do that; that is the King's motto, and you cannot do
it, but he will get his rights in the old hulk Jersey."

Our troops were forced back step by step. Some of
the East Haven patriots had fallen back on the road
east of Prospect Hill; others remained with the main
body, fighting and disputing every inch of the way,
and keeping up a galling fire upon the British from
bushes and hedges in front and flank; and from this
point there was continual slaughter until the earthworks on Beacon Hill were carried. The patriot forces
were about equally divided, some in the road, and some
in the fields, keeping back the skirmishers and sending
an occasional volley into the advance guard, always
with effect. There were two fieldpieces, under the
gallant Lieutenant Pierpont; these would open a rak-
ing fire, and then be rapidly hauled back by the brave
patriots, and then moved to a new position, each shot
making a swath through the ranks of the invaders.

The Tuttle house, barns, outhouses and fields of
ripened grain were now in a fierce blaze. On the site
of the present residence of Mr. Asa L. Fabrique, the
British met with a severe check. At this point was a
clump of bushes and towards the road a brush hedge.
About 40 of the patriots masked themselves behind
this hedge. Below, our troops were hard pressed, as

the enemy's cannon were better served, and it was
decided to make one more stand, fire, and fall back
up the road to the intrenchment on Beacon Hill, where
they had sent their cannon. As the enemy followed,
the party behind the fence were to welcome them with
a shower of leaden hail, and then fall back to the
hill. The stand was made when the enemy were midway between the Mitchell and Townsend houses. The
order was given to fire, which they did with considerable effect. A general stampede took place as agreed
upon; but Adam Thorp of North Haven said "he
would not run another step for all Great Britain." He
loaded and fired his piece and the next instant fell,
pierced with many bullets. He was the first one of
the patriots killed from the East side, of whom we
have any record. Afterwards the spot was marked
with a stone thus inscribed: "Here fell Adam Thorp,
July 5th, 1779." His great-grandson, Sheldon Thorp,
says he was buried in North Haven.

This check brought the whole division to a halt, and
after the smoke had cleared away, the patriots were
seen retreating toward the hill, and the division
advanced at double quick. The advance guards had
passed the patriots in the bushes, when Captain
Bradley said, "Wait till you see their eyes, then fire
and run." This was done with great effect. The
street was strewn with killed and wounded. The
patriots, who fell back to the hill, were pursued by the
British in hot haste; they lost one of their field pieces,
but the other now opened upon the enemy, causing
them to halt under the depression of the hill, out of
range, a few rods north of Mr. E. J. Upson's resi-

dence. There lying flat on the ground, out of harm's way, they rested, till reinforcements came up; the hill was stormed, the patriots falling back, some northwards towards the ferry, others to the heights, and to Saltonstall. The fighting on the East side was now practically over, but the burning and devastation by the British continued to the water's edge. The dead were many, buried in the rye lands on the west side of the road, north of the Tuttle home; the spot being burned over, the locality of the graves was not discovered. Many wounded soldiers were seen being taken to the boats, and carried on board the fleet, and it was supposed that the dead were removed, in order to hide their great loss.

The next house north of the Tuttle house was that of John Woodward, Sr., which they burned, with all the out-buildings; the site was where the old Woodward mansion stands, now owned by C. Edward Woodward. General Tryon made Beacon Hill his headquarters, sending one detachment north to Tuttle's Hill (now the site of the reservoir of the New Haven Water Company) and another to the lower ferry, now called Tomlinson's bridge.

The next house on the line of march was that of John Woodward, Jr. (the site of the present residence of Collis B. Granniss), which they also burned. After pillaging and burning this house, their march was towards the lower ferry, kept by Henry Freeman Hughes. His house was directly opposite the brick residence of the late Samuel Forbes, on what is now Forbes avenue. It happened at this time that two of Mr. Hughes' sons, John and Daniel, had gone into the country to Simsbury, to visit their brother, who had removed thither a year previous. Their object was to see the country with the intent to each buy a farm if sufficiently pleased. On the alarm of the approach of the British, his only daughter, Abigail, and John's wife filled bags of the valuables of the house, and placing them on a horse, fled to the woods, where they remained over night. This took the remaining horse, and left nothing to propel the scow ferry boat. The enemy came rushing on to the ferry. Mr. Hughes was alone with his invalid wife, who was a cripple, and had not walked a step for years. She was greatly alarmed, and fearing she would be taken and killed persuaded him to desist from his purpose of fleeing.

The advance guard rushed into his fields of grain and corn, trampling and destroying both. They broke open and scattered his flour and sugar, pitched his pork about with their bayonets, and let out his molasses and rum till his cellar was shoe deep with the mixture. They also abused him, one soldier piercing his ear with a bayonet. When the officers came up, while the blood was still trickling down on his shoulder, he went out and asked protection. They said: "Are you a friend to King George?" He replied, "I am." Then they told him no further violence would be done, and placed a guard around his house. From this circumstance, his brother-in-law, Joseph Tuttle, before mentioned, called him a tory, which the family justly resented and denied.

Mr. Hughes did not keep a store, but like many other men in the maritime towns of Connecticut was interested in West India shipping, and he kept staple groceries and provisions on hand, for his own use, and the accommodation of those who did not wish to cross the ferry to New Haven. His house always afforded accommodation for those who desired it, when prevented from crossing by adverse winds or tides; or, having spent the day in travel, wayfarers would pass the night with him before entering the city.

Mr. Jehiel Forbes' stone mansion was the next place upon which the British wreaked their vengeance. After breaking and destroying everything possible, they burned out the interior, leaving only the blackened walls of this beautiful home. The next house to be destroyed was Mr. Elam Luddington's—a new house just completed, standing on the site nearest the water's edge on the north side of the road. Mr. Luddington was the fourth heaviest loser by this invasion. The next and last house to be destroyed was Capt. Timothy Tuttle's, standing on the shore south of Forbes avenue where a small stone house now stands. The walls of this house were stone, so it was not entirely destroyed. Captain Tuttle was a brother of Joseph Tuttle. Gurdon Bradley of East Haven had a sloop lying at a wharf in front of Captain Tuttle's house, which they also burned. They had now reached the water's edge, and there was nothing more they could burn and destroy. Every house and building from Morris Point to Tomlinson's bridge had been swept by the flames, excepting the Hughes house, which they now made officers' quarters.

General Tryon sent a detachment to occupy the village of East Haven, but the enemy's advance only reached the "Stone Meetinghouse," which they ransacked for plate, and then fell back to the hill, near the present residence of L. F. Richmond, Esq.

Several shots were exchanged between the patriots and British, for when the old Bradley house (the site of the present Levi Bradley home) was taken down, many bullet holes were found in the timbers.

When the patriots retreated from Beacon Hill they were pursued in hot haste by some British skirmishers, and Chandler Pardee, a son of Mr. Jacob Pardee, was shot on the fresh meadows, a ball entering one lung, and he was left on the field for dead. Soon after he was taken to the Governor Saltonstall house, where Dr. Hubbard extracted the ball, and he recovered to tell the story while a prisoner in New York, to the same party of soldiers who had left him dying, as they supposed, on the field.

Not far from the place where Pardee fell lived Mr. Samuel Tuttle, who with his neighbors had marched to meet the foe. Satisfied the day was lost, he returned home and started with a cart load of household effects to conceal in a quarry, east of the Pardee's or upper ferry, near the home of William Day. While Tuttle and Day were storing away their goods, the Chandler Pardee pursuers passed Mr. Tuttle's house, which they set on fire. Mrs. Tuttle rushed out with her children into the tall grass. She saw the regulars aiming their muskets, when she called to her children "to lie down in the grass, and say their prayers, as they had but one minute to live." The next instant the whole volley went over their heads. The pursuers passed on, and the neighbors put out the fire with water from the brook. This party made a circuit of the peat meadows and, coming back, found Day and Tuttle, and made them prisoners. They slaughtered Tuttle's cattle; Day being an Englishman, they permitted him to escape, after he had shown them a spring of water, in the rear of Mr. G. E. Lancraft's house, saying, "When I am drinking, I can't see all that passes." Tuttle was carried to New York, where he was paroled after six months.

The detachment sent to what is now Reservoir Hill found the fieldpiece used on Beacon Hill; this the patriots had hauled there on their retreat, fired a number of times, but finally spiked and rolled down the hill into the bushes near Mr. Roswell Lancraft's house, now called Burwell street. This was sent on board the fleet. This detachment busied themselves with roasting an ox on the hill in the evening, which was distributed among the different corps. On the site of the present N. W. Kendall mansion, forty different animals were slaughtered, with pigs and poultry in great abundance, all of which were sent on board the fleet. After the enemy had left, Mr. Isaac Pardee took from this hill the sheep and cattle skins and had them tanned. The detachment sent to Ferry Hill, now near Quinnipiac bridge, seemed to destroy little, as there was only one house on the line of their march; and for some reason they did not burn that which is still standing, on South Quinnipiac street, No. 332, for the last sixty years known as the Goodyear house.

The condition of affairs in the harbor at a little after two o'clock in the afternoon when General Tryon reached Beacon Hill was about this: A line of British ships lay anchored the whole length of the bay, with springs on their cables, and guns run out on both sides, ready to belch forth fire and destruction as soon as the expected order should be given to fire the town. General Tryon kept chiefly on the East side; but

crossed over to New Haven before sunset, holding
a council of war with General Garth and Commodore
Collier. The council now found their losses in officers
and men had been heavy, and the patriots, better
armed than they expected, had made a stubborn resist-
ance; that the country around New Haven being hilly,
it was not safe to go any farther inland for forage;
that large reinforcements, with heavy cannon, were
actually occupying high ground about the north part
of the city and that the militia were coming in from
all directions. The harbor was shoal, and many of
the vessels at this time, 8 P. M., were touching bottom,
and one large vessel did actually lie on her broadside
guns, just out of water. It was decided to hold the
north and west part of the town over night, with the
balance of the tired and drunken soldiers, who were
collected on the Green, having been commanded to lie
on their arms all night. General Garth fearing his
men would become too drunk to remain safe on shore,
proposed to Tryon to go on board that night, but
Tryon refused.

Affairs at 9 P. M. July 5th were in the worst possible
condition, as the British soldiers were mostly all
drunk and lying in the open air on the Green, surrounded by a few sober ones, who stood guard to
keep them from getting more rum. The officers were
at a banquet at the house of Joshua Chandler, the
father of William and Tom, who acted as pilots for
the British. At one o'clock in the morning of July
6th the troops were ordered to parade, and the tories
were notified of the departure. About forty people
left with the British, the Chandlers among the number.
It is well they did, for had they remained not one of

the three would have lived to see the setting sun. The enemy was in a constant state of alarm, and were all concentrated within a hollow square of sentinels for the night. It has since been believed, that had the patriot militia known the state of things they could have come into town about midnight and made the whole division prisoners. The withdrawal of the British from the town has been described as partaking of the ridiculous—the drunken, reeling soldiers trying to keep in line, carts and wagons and even wheelbarrows being used to get them to the boats. Drunkenness has not been ascribed to the enemy on the East side, and certainly they did not appreciate, or appropriate, Mr. Hughes' rum, which they let out in his cellar with his molasses.

On the morning of the 6th of July they called in their outposts and the march of the main body began before sunrise. Some of the troops went directly to the shipping, others who were sober enough crossed the ferry and joined General Tryon's division on Beacon Hill, and the whole body left the hill about noon Tuesday. As the last boat shoved off from the East Haven shore, the Pardee house at Morris Cove, in which officers had been posted, was standing. This boat was ordered back to fire the house, and every house from Morris Cove to lower ferry, except one in which officers had been quartered, was burned. It seems that when the last ship left the pier, she fired several shots at the town, as a parting salute, while sailing down the bay, and as she was passing Black Rock Fort, which had been re-occupied by the patriots, as well as the earthworks on Beacon Hill, she rounded to and fired a whole broadside at the fort. Many balls bounded as far as Beacon Hill, one of which struck Isaac Pardee, aged twenty-two, severing his head clear from the body. He was just ascending the hill, on the street side, with Mr. Smith of South End, having gone to a spring to bring water. Smith says they heard the report of the firing; he turned with Pardee to look, saw the ball and dodged it but it carried away Pardee's head. Pardee and Thorp are the only ones of those who were killed of whom any record is given. Chandler Pardee of the East side was wounded but recovered. If there were any wounded or killed at Black Rock Fort, no record has been made of it, so far as is known. The estimate made of the enemy's losses during the invasion sums up two hundred in killed, wounded and missing. As to the missing, it is an established fact that many Hessians deserted and remained in New Haven, choosing honorable trades and becoming good citizens. There were certainly several of the British killed and wounded while landing, also others in the woods north of Morris Cove and back of Prospect Hill, where they were quickly buried. East Haven patriots said the loss was heavy after Thorp fell.

While widening Townsend avenue in June, 1870, this tradition of the slaughter was well sustained by the discovery of human bones. These remains were proved not to be Indians by Dr. T. Beers Townsend, who was on the spot when the graves were opened, and who made a most careful examination. While the doctor was making a critical study of the bones, Capt. Charles H. Townshend thoroughly searched the graves with a spade, and was rewarded by finding a number of German silver buttons, about the size of a dime. A

copper coin was also found, about the size of an
English half-penny, known as a stiver. It had a hole
in the circumference, and was probably worn on a
string around the neck. On the face side is the motto,
"Dominus Auxit Nomen" ("The Lord increased our
glory"), in its center a man with a mantle about his
loins, left hand on his hip, in his right hand a sword,
drawn over his head, as if to strike. On the opposite
side is a laurel wreath, with the word in the center
HOLLANLIA. Dr. J. Edwards of Yale University,
an expert, and the best authority, says this coin was
struck off in Holland, a province of the Nether-
lands, between the years 1648 and 1795. A pompon
socket of brass, bell-shaped, was also found. It had
upon it No. 8 or 5, with these letters, D. M. A. U. X.
The captain says, "These relics satisfy me that these
were the graves of soldiers, of Tryon's division." He
further verified this idea by subsequently "obtaining
in an old print store in Paris, some colored engravings
of the uniforms worn by the Hessian Land-
graves, a regiment of which was a part of
the second division of Tryon's army, which par-
ticipated in the engagement on the East Haven
Shore." March 22, 1879, the captain made a visit to
Europe, and in London made an exhaustive search of
the records in the colonial office; obtaining much
valuable information, and many copies of events and
war correspondence, which had never been published
in America. To Capt. Charles H. Townshend the
whole community is indebted for rescuing from
oblivion the account of New Haven's invasion, historical as well as traditional, the latter supported and
confirmed by records, from which copious extracts

have been made, in this work, and to whom the thanks of the compiler are gratefully due.

The enemy's loss on the East Haven side was perhaps greater in proportion to the patriots killed and wounded than on the New Haven side. The East Haven men were most excellent marksmen from long practice of hunting, and everyone carried his own often-tried Queen Anne musket. They knew every inch of advantage ground and, with their long range guns, could keep out of the enemy's fire and do good execution, as they were fighting for their own hearthstone and families. On the other hand, they were greater sufferers than those of New Haven; every thing but the soil was destroyed; homes burned, crops destroyed, animals of all kinds killed, and destruction everywhere. Who can describe the feelings of those mothers who fled for safety with their children, when they returned? Not a shingle left for shelter, or a mouthful of food, save the little they took with them! Everything in ashes, excepting the few household effects in the returning oxcart! Fortunately the weather was warm, and the devastation did not extend over the whole town, but a clean sweep was made as far as the enemy marched. The present line of the street railway is mainly the same route that the British took from Morris Point to Pardee's ferry (now Quinnipiac bridge), through Ferry street to Neck bridge, at the head of State street, New Haven. At that time this was the only bridge between New Haven and East Haven.

The earthworks on Beacon Hill and Black Rock Fort were quickly occupied, even before Tryon's forces reached the water, and a lively fire was kept

up between Beacon Hill and the galleys as they passed
out of the harbor. This accounts for the numerous
cannon balls and shot formerly plowed out in the fields
on the East side. A garrison was still kept at the
fort. April 18, 1781, a very thick foggy night, the
British, led by tories who were acquainted with the
locality, came in with muffled oars, surprised the
garrison, killed the sentry, John Howe, and made
the men prisoners. They then turned the guns towards
the magazine, and setting a slow match, rowed off
to an awaiting vessel. Mr. Joseph Tuttle had always
done coast guard duty at night at the fort, but this
night he had a very sick child at home, who was
not expected to live until morning, so he sent his
second eldest boy, a lad about thirteen, in his place.
He went out at daybreak, and glancing towards the
fort, saw a small blue stream of smoke issuing from
it; losing no time, as he reached the place the
fuse had only a foot more to burn, when the whole
magazine would have exploded and wrecked the fort.
Seizing the fuse, he threw it into the water and thus
saved the structure. This time he had two sons
captured, one eighteen, an enlisted soldier, and one
thirteen. He immediately went to New York with
a flag of truce, and with the aid of some English
captains, whom he knew, succeeded in releasing his
younger son. His older one, on account of his youth,
was taken out of the prison ship and placed as a
waiter to an officer, when he made good his chance,
and escaped. He fled up Long Island, until he thought
he was about opposite New Haven, where he hired
out at 9d. per day. He worked until he earned enough
to buy cloth for a coat, which he cut out with a jack-

knife, and made it in a barn. Thus equipped he took
a boat and rowed across the Sound, landing at the
Lighthouse.

A garrison was kept at the fort until the close of
the war. On October 19, 1781, General Cornwallis
surrendered his whole army to Washington, which
practically ended the struggle, although there was
still some fighting, but nothing of note occurred.
The British held for two years or more the cities of
New York, Charleston and Savannah. September 3,
1783, a treaty of peace was signed at Paris, which
conceded all that the Declaration of Independence had
proclaimed; and the new nation, now called "The
United States of America," took its place among the
nations of the earth.

No doubt there are many interesting incidents connected with the fleeing women and children if they
could be collected, and yet the experience of one is
typical of all. In the writer's family, at the present
time, is a silver tablespoon, which was buried on
what is now the Townsend farm by Mrs. Joseph
Tuttle, in a large iron kettle, used to boil sea water
to make salt, which had become scarce during the
late years of the war. She took the money of the
house in one hand and her silverware in the other,
saying, "I will bury one and take the other, maybe
I can save one"; as it happened she saved both. They
packed this great kettle full of valuables of the household, and buried it among the currant bushes. They
then drove off in the oxcart, with her six children,
one a babe in arms, to the woods in the north part of
the town, where they all passed the night. Here they
stayed until the departure of the British, who took

with them her husband and son as prisoners from Black Rock Fort. No mention has ever been made of robbing and abusing women on the East side, because they all fled out of the way.

The British had stationed a signal corps on Prospect Hill, directly back of the Townsend home, out of which the next day the commander and two of his men were picked off by Capt. Jedediah Andrews and some of his neighbors. The morning of the 6th a very dense fog hung over the land, and Mr. Andrews and others crept along under cover of the bushes, and picked off each his man, while they were roasting a sheep for their breakfast. Their remains were buried at the foot of the hill, and for a long time a large red boulder marked the place.

The following story has often been told, among other reminiscences, of an East Haven Bradley, and Captain Townshend gives it as coming from an old Mr. Pinto who saw it. "While sitting in his door, a finely-dressed officer in red uniform came riding down Elm street, and turned up State, toward Grove. Just then a Mr. Bradley, from East Haven, came from a direction which is now Grand avenue, on horseback, with loaded musket, all primed. Seeing the officer, he levelled his piece and fired. The officer dropped off his horse and Bradley rode up to him, took the officer's sword, and gave him several cuts over the head. He then took the officer's horse, and on his own rode out of town." The officer crawled into a yard, where some of his comrades found him.

Very little, if anything, has been related about tories in East Haven and it is doubtful if there were any; if there were, they were in no way active. Mr. Henry

F. Hughes' second son was a tory. He was a merchant, residing in New Haven, and persisted in selling
tea. Complaint was entered against William Glen and
Freeman Hughes, Jr., and both were cited to appear
before the committee of the Continental Association.
Glen pleaded guilty and begged to be restored to favor;
but Hughes would not appear to make his defense,
whereupon the evidence was called and sworn:—

"On motion voted that the evidence is sufficient to convict
Freeman Hughes jun. of a breach of the association, by buying and selling Tea:—and ordered that he being advertised,
that no person have any further dealing or intercourse with
him."

Joh'th Fitch, *Chairman,*
Test, Peter Colt, *Clerk.*

When the British left New Haven, he with his wife
and two children went with them. So bitter was the
feeling of the family that they never afterwards would
hold any communication with him or his family. And
so strongly did his brother, Daniel Hughes, feel on the
subject that he would never allow a dust of tea in his
house. Although he lived to be 83 years old, dying
in 1842, and was married three times, yet none of
his wives ever enjoyed a cup of tea at his table.
Being a man of means, and a very hospitable one, he
set an abundant table, to which everyone was welcome,
but tea was conspicuous by its absence. "Had disgrace
and trouble enough with the stuff," he always said.
Chocolate was his substitute at the evening meal. Mr.
Hughes' store of goods was either destroyed or
removed to the vessels in the harbor, probably the
latter. His real estate was confiscated, and the whole
transaction brought much financial trouble upon the
family.

FORT HALE.

It has often been asserted that rum saved the city of New Haven from the flames. No doubt it was quite a factor in the matter, but the real savior was Col. Edmund Fanning, who was a son-in-law of General Tryon, and commanded the King's American regiment. He was a graduate of Yale, having spent four years in New Haven, and was well acquainted with tory and patriot. Then too, perhaps, he possessed the "Yale spirit," which could not see his *Alma Mater* destroyed. His influence, coupled with that of some influential tories, saved the city.

FORT HALE.

The first mention of this site, which was a bold trap rock of basaltic formation, was in 1657. It was then thought to be useful for defensive purposes, and the records show it was made a coast guard station in 1659, mounted with "great guns." The Black Rock Fort of the Revolution was constructed early in the year of 1775 on this site, and manned with cannon made in Salisbury, Connecticut.

Although the site is considered of no defensive use at the present time, yet in the Revolution it did good work in keeping off plundering and foraging parties from the warships constantly moving up and down the Sound. Its capture in 1779, and subsequent history, has been related in the invasion of that date. After the close of the Revolution in 1783, these fortifications were dismantled, save a gun or two, and allowed to go to ruin. At the beginning of the nineteenth century, when the war cloud was threatening Europe, the idea was originated, in our own land, of fortifying the whole Atlantic coast of the United

States, and money was voted in 1808 by Congress to erect a new fort on this ancient site for the defence of New Haven Harbor.

In 1808, the United States government ordered a battery to be built on the site of the old Black Rock Fort at New Haven, as the channels had deepened there. The fort was to hold six guns, the barracks forty men; $6,295 was paid by Congress for the fortification in 1809. Reported in December, 1811, as an elliptic enclosure battery of masonry, mounting six guns, brick magazines, brick barracks for fifty men, and officers in a field outside the fort. At the commencement of the War of 1812, the fort was garrisoned with seventy-eight artillerymen and named Fort Hale. The garrison at this fort was at no time in a regular engagement, yet on several occasions it opened fire on British ships in the offing, and forced them to "haul off." During the time from 1812-1814, Commodore Hardy's British fleet of twenty sail were kept at bay by the guns of this fort. On receipt of the news of the Treaty of Ghent the guns of Forts Hale and Wooster proclaimed the glad tidings. They were the last guns ever fired from either place.

After the war, Capt. John A. Thomas was appointed custodian, residing with his family in the barracks and dying there in 1840. The barracks accidentally took fire and were burned in 1850. About 1855 Mr. J. A. Stock rebuilt the brick barracks, which he and his employees occupied while manufacturing was carried on in the vicinity. When the War of the Rebellion broke out, government took possession of the property, demolished the old fort and rocky promontory, cut a ditch through the rocks from the moat, and built a new earthworks fort, armed with Dahlgren guns, costing $125,000. This was built under the direction of Lieutenant Mansfield, United States Engineer, superintended by P. Ferguson and Hemingway Smith, the latter of East Haven. It was completed about the close of the war, but was never garrisoned. In 1867 the public property and tools were sold. The Farrel works of Ansonia, Connecticut, bought the guns, to be melted up for other purposes. The wooden barracks and buildings were shipped in sections to Newport, Rhode Island, and the whole reservation, later on, was imparked, by the consent of the United States, into Fort Hale Park.

PENSIONERS.

There was no general pension law passed by Congress until March 18, 1818, when those who had served nine months in army or navy could, under the conditions of that act, become pensioners. These conditions were such that few could take advantage of the law. A few special cases were pensioned before 1818. But one pensioner under the act of 1818 is found credited to East Haven, viz.: Daniel Bradley.

Under the head of "Individual Records" is found that of Thomas Shepard, East Haven, Douglass' regiment, wounded by cannon shot at Kips Bay, New York, Sep. 15, 1776.

"Invalid Pensions" granted under the act of 1833-4 were given to Chandler Pardee, East Haven, Russell's regiment militia, and Thomas Shepard, East Haven, Douglass' regiment.

A serious difficulty in locating East Haven pensioners has been that all names were registered under counties, instead of towns. As two or more surnames would be the same it could not be positively stated which one belonged to East Haven. In that way some names may have been omitted. Application was made to the Bureau of Pensions, Washington, D. C., and the answer received was:

"This department has no other record of pensioners than those contained in the list of New Haven County."

A request was then made to the adjutant-general at Hartford, Connecticut, when the same answer was returned.

From "Connecticut Men in the War of the Revolution," the following statistics are copied. In 1832 a new pension act was passed, removing most of the restrictions of 1818, and the following names are from East Haven, viz.:

Elijah Bradley,	Enos Hemingway,
Elisha Andrews,	Jacob Mallory,
Eli Forbes,	Elle Granniss,
Jesse Luddington,	Chandler Pardee,
Jared Granniss,	John Tyler.

Elijah Bradley was the only one out of seven confined in the prison ships that lived through that terrible ordeal.

In 1840 another pension act was passed removing all restrictions, and the following names are placed in a list as belonging to East Haven, viz.:

Elijah Bradley,	80 yrs.	
Sylvia Brown,	76 yrs.	
Hannah Chidsey,	83 yrs.	Widow of Abraham, Jun.
Abigail Goodsell,	94 yrs.	" " John.
Phoebe Davenport,	81 yrs.	" " John.

Temperance Hotchkiss,	79 yrs.	Widow of Joseph.
Rosanna Pardee,	78 yrs.	" " Abijah.
Mabel Tyler,	74 yrs.	" " John.
Abraham W. Johnson,	89 yrs.	
Eli Forbes,	80 yrs.	
Anna Smith,	88 yrs.	Widow of Thomas.
John A. Thomas,	70 yrs.	
John Rowe,	86 yrs.	
Enos Hemingway,	85 yrs.	
Lucinda Miles,	77 yrs.	
Sarah Smith,	81 yrs.	
Jared Granniss,	85 yrs.	
Jesse Luddington,	84 yrs.	

The above list is all that could be gathered from the work "Connecticut Men in the Revolution." No doubt there were many more entitled to pensions, belonging in East Haven, who, with their wives, passed away before 1840, therefore no mention is made of them, although their record of service is to be found in the volume referred to above. Neither does this list contain all who received pensions under the several pension acts. The widow of Josiah Tuttle received a pension under the act of 1832, dying in 1838. The widow of Hezekiah Woodward, who died in 1854, received a pension under some of the acts, but no mention is made of either. Two in this list were not Revolutionary soldiers, but were in the War of 1812, viz.: John A. Thomas of the 25th United States Infantry, and the husband of Sylvia Brown, who were entitled to pensions under some other of the acts. So it is seen that the information which can be gathered at the present time does not include all of those entitled to honorable mention, but it is the best which the records afford.

Thanks are due to Dr. Bela Farnham, who through the kindness of his nature, so firm and so gentle and just, was very much interested; and who through his official capacity of town clerk for forty years was enabled to render much aid in securing pensions for these aged, infirm, and beloved townspeople of his time. Otherwise these pensions might never have been secured.

Many of the East Haven men belonged either to Capt. Phineas Bradley's company of Matrosses Artillery, which was raised for the defence of New Haven, and was stationed partly in the town at one of the forts, and partly in New Haven and West Haven, or were members of Captain VanDeusen's company, State Guards, stationed at New Haven. No doubt many were scattered through all the different branches of the army. Their war record will be found in the "Connecticut Men of the Revolution," a copy of which is lodged in every town clerk's office in the state, as also a copy of the "Connecticut Men in the Rebellion."

WAR OF 1812 WITH ENGLAND.

The second war with Great Britain was declared by the United States Congress June 18, 1812. It was brought about by this government denying the right of search of American vessels, and the restrictions laid upon American commerce.

This was principally a naval war; although the British troops took and plundered many towns on the southern coast, finally burning the Capitol and President's house—a dastardly act censured by all nations. At this time a new beacon on Beacon Hill, and new earthworks were made by volunteer work of New Haven, East Haven and surrounding towns. Cheshire sent 100 men and teams for two days; North Haven 100 men; Hamden, Meriden and Wallingford the same. At first it was called Fort Treadwell after Governor Treadwell of Connecticut, but a short time later, Fort Wooster, after Major General David Wooster whose home was in New Haven. A musket ball from a tory's gun broke his spine, just after he had called, "Come on, boys, never mind such random shots!" He lived six days. He died in Danbury, May 2, 1777.

At this time the government rebuilt Black Rock Fort, naming it Fort Hale, after the martyr spy of the Revolution, whose expiring words were, "I only regret that I have but one life to lose for my country."

Mention is made of the Fourth Connecticut Militia being garrisoned at these two forts. These men were members of the state militia and were generally drafted, although there were some volunteers. Most of these men received pensions, granted many years after the war. The war lasted two years and six months.

PENSIONERS OF WAR OF 1812.

It is very much regretted that no official list of pensioners of the War of 1812 can be obtained. Application was made to the adjutant-general, at Hartford, who referred the writer to the Bureau of Pensions, Washington, D. C., whench the following answer was received, viz.:

"You are advised, the pension records of the war of 1812 are arranged alphabetically according to names of soldiers, not according to residence. This Bureau is unable to furnish you with a list of pensioners of the war of 1812, belonging to East Haven, Connecticut."

WAR OF THE REBELLION.

No one not in the midst of it can imagine the excitement that arose in all the northern states when the news came that Fort Sumter had been attacked.

Up to that moment, there had been a great division of feeling at the North; and there were many who thought that by patient efforts, those who wished to secede from the Union could be brought back again. Few really believed there was to be any serious fighting; but the fact showed that the whole South had been preparing for war eight years before it came. All through President Pierce's administration it was, in theory, preparing the minds of the people. President Buchanan's inauguration took place on March 4, 1857. Although he was a Pennsylvania man, yet his sympathies were with the South. At this time the writer was living South, and the remark was made by one of the leading men, "that it was only an armistice of four years," and that "Virginia would be the battleground," which subsequently proved but too true.

While the white population of the South had been actually preparing for war, the northern people had gone about their usual employments and when the attack came they were taken by surprise.

Mr. Buchanan's secretary of war was himself a firm secessionist, and had sent several hundred thousand muskets to southern arsenals, ammunition and other army supplies also, leaving the northern arsenals almost bare. The regular army was very small, and that also had been sent to widely scattered posts. Cannon and ammunition were mostly in the southern states. The navy of the United States was very small;

at the outset there were but four ships available for
service at home, with less than three hundred sailors.
At the present time it is amazing that such a state of
things should have been allowed. The consequence
was that a great war was on hand with no ready facilities to meet the situation. President Lincoln was
inaugurated March 4, 1861, which was the signal gun
for the South to open the war. On April 12, Fort
Sumter was attacked. The 15th of April, President
Lincoln issued a call for seventy-five thousand volunteers for three months only, which order was very
quickly filled. One year from that time the Union
army amounted to more than five hundred thousand
men, all volunteers—a thing never before known in
civilized warfare. Before the close of the four years'
war over a million men had been connected with the
Union army—mostly volunteers.

In some of the severest battles fought, one hundred
thousand men were engaged on a side, each losing
more than fifteen thousand.

On both sides the self-devotion of the women at
home equalled that of the soldiers on the field; and
in the northern states, the multitude of women who
worked for the "Sanitary Commission" rendered
very valuable services to their country. The sacrifices
made during the Civil War can never be computed
on either side, although they were greater on the
confederate than the unionist, because their country
was the one overrun. There were few families, North
or South, which did not suffer some bereavement during the long contest, and if not actual loss, the daily
anxiety and apprehension of what the next day's news
might bring. At the close of the war, the United

States debt was more than two billion seven hundred thousand dollars, besides more than a half million lives lost, including both sides.

The South had lost that for which they fought and slavery was abolished. The North had won that for which they contended, that the United States must be regarded as a nation, one and indivisible, and not a mere alliance of independent states. The Civil War has proved that the people of the United States are strong enough for self-protection against any foreign powers, and that those who founded the American colonies left to their descendants the rich legacy of noble lives and unselfish purposes, which will be carried out with the same high motive and religious self-devotion.

To Capt. Jason Dickerman Thompson belongs the honor of being the first man from East Haven to enlist as a soldier in the War of the Rebellion in 1861, which he did just ten days after Fort Sumter was attacked. He enlisted in the 2d Regiment Infantry, Company G, April 22, 1861, for three months' service. He is credited to New Haven in this enlistment, probably because his business was there. In October, Capt. Thompson again enlisted, this time in the cavalry, where he won his spurs and title.

Henry C. Burr of Forbes avenue was the second man from East Haven to shoulder his gun in defence of his country. The night before he enlisted, he and his wife were spending the evening at a neighbor's, when he remarked, "You, I, and every other Republican have voted Lincoln into this trouble, and it is our business to see him out of it, and I for one am going to do it." The next day, April 25, 1861, he enlisted in the 3d Regiment, Company B. He is reported from Meriden, as his business was there, and this whole company, without exception, were from that place. These were the only three-months' men from East Haven. September 18, 1861, Mr. Burr enlisted in the 8th Regiment. He lost a limb at Antietam, September 17, 1862.

The official records of the adjutant-general in Washington, D. C., credits East Haven with one hundred and twenty-four tried and true men who volunteered and served during the war. Of this number, there were many who were not native born, who gave East Haven as their place of residence. At that time, forty-six years ago, farming was carried on far more extensively than at present, and every farmer employed more or less young men on the farm. Probably East Haven was as much home to them as any other place. They gave honorable service to the country, and reflected credit upon the town. All true soldiers are of one brotherhood.

East Haven was afflicted with the genus "tramp" who are ever keen of scent where there is "bounty." No mention is made of these "jumpers," although a few served several months. The ban of desertion casts them out altogether; they have no part with the men who sealed their service with their lives, and many others with their blood. The East Haven soldiers were distributed among the regiments of the state as follows:

	Men.		Men.
First Reg. C. V. Cavalry	5	Second Heavy Artillery	4
First Light Battery	6	Fifth Reg. Infantry	6
First Heavy Artillery	17	Seventh Reg. Infantry	5

Men.		Men.
Eighth Reg. Infantry	2	Thirteenth Bat. Infantry 1
Tenth Reg. Infantry	13	Fifteenth Reg. Infantry 31
Eleventh Reg. Infantry	4	Twentieth Reg. Infantry 2
Twelfth Reg. Infantry	4	Twenty-seventh Reg. Inf. 25

Total   125

First Regiment C. V. Cavalry.

Jason D. Thompson, East Haven, Co. B, Oct. 29, '61. Mustered in corporal; promoted sergeant Feb. 17, '62; first sergeant Sept. 10, '62; first lieutenant Co. E, May 28, '63; captain Co. M, Jan. 29, '64. Mustered out Aug. 2, '65.

Charles Redfield Dayton, East Haven, Co. B, Aug. 4, '62. Mustered in private; promoted March 1, '63; captured June 28, '64, Ream's Station, Va.; released Nov. 19, '64. Discharged June 3, 1865.

Giles W. Clark, East Haven, Co. B. Mustered in private, Oct. 15, '61; captured July 29, '62, Madison Court House, Va.; released Sept. 14, '62; promoted from private Co. B to corporal Co. E March 1, '63; sergeant Sept. 1, '63; promoted quartermaster-sergeant Nov. 1. '63. Discharged Nov. 2, '64, term expired.

Michael Gagan, East Haven, Co. E, Nov. 14, '64. Mustered out Aug. 2, '65.

John Forress, East Haven, Co. H, Dec. 10, '63. Captured June 28, '64, Stony Creek, Va.; released Nov. 19, '64. Discharged July 8, '65.

First C. V. Light Battery.

Frederick Besley, East Haven, Feb. 1, '64. Wounded May 14, '64, Proctor's Creek, Va. Mustered out June 11, '65.

James Burns, East Haven, Dec. 2, '64. Mustered out June 11, '65.

William Johnson, East Haven, Dec. 2, '64. Mustered out June 11, '65.

Frank La Billa, East Haven, Dec. 9, '64. Discharged June 11, '65.

Edward McCormic, East Haven, Dec. 2, '64. Mustered out June 11, '65.

Henry L. Wilmot, East Haven, Jan. 18, '64. Killed May 14, '64, Proctor's Creek.

First Regiment C. V. Heavy Artillery.

George W. Potter, East Haven, Co. A, Aug. 8, '64. Mustered out Sept. 25, '65.

Charles Boissier, East Haven, Co. B, Nov. 5, '64. Mustered out Sept. 25, '65.

John Burns, East Haven, Co. C, Aug. 16, '64. Discharged disabled June 23, '65.

Hiram Jehiel Forbes, East Haven, Co. C, March 17, '62. Discharged March 18, '65, term expired.

James H. Casey, East Haven, Co. E, Jan. 4, '64. Mustered in private; promoted corporal March 10, '64; sergeant May 24, '64; second lieutenant Co. K, Nov. 10, '64; brevetted first lieutenant March 28, '65. Mustered out Sept. 25, '65.

Gilbert VanSickles, East Haven, Co. E, Jan. 4, '64. Mustered in private; promoted May 5, '64. Discharged disabled June 20, '65.

Thomas Honan, East Haven, Co. F, Dec. 7, '64. Mustered out Sept. 25, '65.

Frank Quinn, East Haven, Co. H, Jan. 18, '64. Mustered out Sept. 25, '65.

Aner W. Brown, East Haven, Co. L, Nov. 30, '63. He first enlisted in Co. F, 6th Regiment Infantry, Aug. 26, '61. Discharged disabled Feb. 9, '63. Reënlisted as corporal; promoted May 25, '64. Mustered out Sept. 25, '65.

Wilbur F. Brockett, East Haven, Co. L, Nov. 30, '63. Mustered out Sept. 25, '65.

Edward J. Dailey, East Haven, Co. L, Feb. 1, '64. Mustered out Sept. 25, '65.

Alfred D. Fuller, East Haven, Co. L, Dec. 10, '63. Mustered out Sept. 25, '65.

George O. Higby, East Haven, Co. L, Nov. 30, '63. Mustered out Sept. 25, '65.

Michael Killoy, East Haven, Co. L, Feb. 2, '64. Mustered out Sept. 25, '65.

Jesse W. Perkins, East Haven, Co. L, July 26, '64. Mustered out Sept. 25, '65.

Samuel R. Rose, East Haven, Co. L. Dec. 15, '64. Died March 1, '65.

Charles E. Goodale, East Haven, Co. L, Feb. 24, '62. Reëntered veteran Feb. 15, '64; promoted Apr. 21, '65. Mustered out Sept. 25, '65.

Second Regiment C. V. Heavy Artillery.

John Keefe, East Haven, Co. D, Dec. 20, '64. Transferred to Co. D from Co. M, July 20, '65. Mustered out Aug. 18, '65.

John H. Bradley, East Haven, Co. G, Jan. 4, '64. Died March 18, '64.

George Parker, East Haven, Co. L. Sergeant Feb. 1, '64. Discharged disabled Sept. 24, '64.

James Bishop, East Haven, Co. L, Feb. 1, '64. Captured Oct. 19, '64, Middletown, Va.; paroled Feb. 5, '65; furloughed Feb. 17, '65; failed to return. No further record, adjutant-general's office, Washington, D. C.

Fifth Regiment C. V. Infantry.

Andrew Brown, East Haven, Co. A, Aug. 17, '63. Mustered out July 19, '65.

George Carr, East Haven, Co. A, Aug. 1, '63. Reported on muster out as absent, sick in hospital since Apr. 30, '64. No further record adjutant-general's office.

Henry T. Baldwin, East Haven, Co. E, June 22, '61. Reënlisted veteran Dec. 21, '63. Mustered out July 19, '65.

Brayton Ives, East Haven, Co. F, June 21, '61. Mustered in as adjutant; promoted to Co. F, captain, Sept. 25, '61; appointed assistant adjutant-general U. S. Volunteers May 14, '62; commissioned lieutenant-colonel June 10, '63; declined Aug. 8, '63; resigned Aug. 5, '63. Reënlisted First Conn. Cavalry Feb. 4, '64; mustered in major; promoted lieutenant-colonel Nov. 1, '64; colonel Jan. 17, '65; brigadier-general by brevet March 13, '65. Mustered out Aug. 2, '65.

John Lewis, East Haven, Co. I, Aug. 1, '63. Transferred from Co. H, 20th Connecticut Volunteers, June 13, '65. Mustered out July 19, '65.

John Spinks, East Haven, Co. H, Nov. 30, '64. Mustered out July 19, '65.

Seventh Regiment C. V. Infantry.

William L. Knapp, East Haven, Co. E, Aug. 26, '61. Discharged disabled June 3, '64.

William Brown, East Haven, Co. E, Nov. 8, '64. Mustered out July 20, '65.

Arza Riggs, East Haven, Co. F, Feb. 2, '64. Mustered out July 20, '65.

Samuel Bennet, East Haven, Co. I, Dec. 21, '64. Mustered out July 20, '65.

Augustus R. Robinson, East Haven, Co. K, Aug. 27, '64. Mustered out July 20, '65.

Eighth Regiment C. V. Infantry.

Warren M. Parsons, East Haven, Co. K, Sept. 18, '61. Promoted March 15, '62. Discharged disabled Dec. 24, '62.

Henry C. Burr, East Haven, Co. K, Sept. 18, '61. Wounded Sept. 17, '62, Antietam, Md. Discharged disabled April 14, '63. (First service, see Private Rifle Co. B, 3d Connecticut Volunteers.)

Tenth Regiment C. V. Infantry.

Hendrick H. Bradley, East Haven, Co. K. Sergeant Sept. 25, '61; wounded Feb. 8, '62, Roanoke Island, N. C. Reënlisted veteran Jan. 1, '64; promoted corporal Jan. 23, '64. Mustered out Aug. 25, '65.

George Thompson, East Haven, Co. K, Sept. 26, '61. Reëntered veteran Jan. 1, '64; wounded Oct. 27, '64, Darbytown Road, Va.; promoted corporal Nov. 1, '64; sergeant Jan. 1, '65. Mustered out Aug. 25, '65.

Charles L. Talmadge, East Haven, Co. K, Sept. 27, '61. Promoted Dec. 15, '61. Discharged Oct. 7, '64, term expired.

Samuel C. Thompson, East Haven, corporal Co. K, Sept. 23, '61. Discharged disabled May 9, '63.

Walter J. French, East Haven, Co. K, Dec. 2, '61. Reëntered veteran Jan. 1, '64. Mustered out Aug. 25, '65.

George L. Beach, East Haven, Co. K, Nov. 16, '63. Wounded May 16, '64, Fort Darling, Va. Mustered out Aug. 25, '65.

Edwin A. Brooks, East Haven, Co. K, Sept. 26, '61. Wounded. Discharged disabled May 9, '63.

John W. Grant, East Haven, Co. K, Oct. 30, '61. Wounded Dec. 14, '62, Kinston, N. C. Discharged Oct. 7, '64, term expired.

Theron B. Hotchkiss, East Haven, Co. K, Sept. 23, '61. Discharged disabled March 5, '62. Reënlisted 15th Regiment, Co. B, Aug. 6, '62. Discharged March 13, '65.

Willis B. Perkins, East Haven, Co. K, Oct. 3, '61. Reëntered veteran Jan. 1, '64; transferred to Co. G, 18th Regiment Veteran Reserve Corps, April 23, '65. Discharged Aug. 28, '65.

Morton Rood, East Haven, Co. K, Sept. 23, '61. Died Apr. 6, '62.

John M. Tucker, East Haven, Co. K, Oct. 1, '61. Discharged disabled March 27, '63.

George R. Woodward, East Haven, Co. K, Sept. 5, '61. Discharged Oct. 7, '64, term expired.

CONNECTICUT TENTH REGIMENT.

Principal Engagements.

Roanoke Island, N. C., Feb. 8, 1862.
Newbern, N. C., March 4, 1862.
Kinston, N. C., Dec. 14, 1862.
Whitehall, N. C., Dec. 16, 1862.
Goldsboro, N. C., Dec. 18, 1862.
Seabrook Island, S. C., March 28, 1863.
Siege of Charleston, S. C., from July 28th to Oct. 25, 1863.
St. Augustine, Fla., Dec. 30, 1863.
Walthall Junction, Va., May 7, 1864.
Drewry's Bluff, Va., May 13 to 17, inclusive, 1864.
Bermuda Hundred, Va., June 16, 1864.
Deep Bottom, Va., June 20, 1864.
Strawberry Plains, Va., July 26 and 27, 1864.
Deep Bottom, Va., Aug. 1, 1864.
Deep Bottom, Va., Aug. 14 and 16, 1864.
Deep Run, Va., Aug. 16, 1864.
Deep Gully, Fuzzell's Mills, Va., Aug. 28, 1864.
Siege of Petersburg, Va., Aug. 28 to Sept. 29, 1864.
Fort Harrison, Va., Sept. 27, 1864.
Laurel Hill Church, Va., Oct. 1, 1864.
New Market Road, Va., Oct. 7, 1864.

Darbytown Road, Va., Oct. 13, 1864.
Darbytown Road, Va., Oct. 27, 1864.
Johnson's Plantation, Va., Oct. 29, 1864.
Hatcher's Run, Va., March 29 and 30, and April 1, 1865.
Fort Gregg, Va., April 2, 1865.
Appomattox Court House, Va, April 9, 1865.

Charles Walter Benedict enlisted in the 10th Regiment from New Haven, Co. A, Sept. 12, '61. Wounded May 14, '64, Drewry's Bluff. Discharged Oct. 7, '64, term expired. After the war always resided in Fair Haven East side until his death on April 24, 1907.

Eleventh Regiment C. V. Infantry.

Charles Benoit, East Haven, Co. C, Feb. 1, '64. Wounded and captured May 16, '64, Drewry's Bluff, Va. Died July — '64, Andersonville, Ga.

James Murphy, East Haven, Co. D, March 24, '64. Captured May 16, '64, Drewry's Bluff, Va.; transferred from Richmond, Va., to Andersonville, Ga. Reported died — '64, Florence, S. C.

Claudius Zemioz, East Haven, Feb. 1, '64. Killed Drewry's Bluff, Va., May 16, '64.

Edward Allen, Sept. 18, '61. Musician in the 9th Regiment. Discharged Sept. 17, '62. Reëntered in the 11th Regiment. Mustered out May 26, '65.

Twelfth Regiment C. V. Infantry.

Edwin N. Crouch, East Haven, Co. B, Nov. 20, '61. Promoted Sept. 2, '62. Killed June 11, '63, Port Hudson, La.

Charles R. Burns, East Haven, Co. B, Apr. 7, '64. Captured Oct. 19, '64, Cedar Creek, Va.; transferred to Co. B, 12th Battalion, Connecticut Volunteers, Nov. 26, '64; paroled Feb. 22, '65. Mustered out Aug. 12, '65.

Henry E. Johnson, East Haven, Co. B, April 7, '64. Transferred to Co. B, 12th Battalion, Connecticut Volunteers, Nov. 26, '64. Mustered out Aug. 12, '65.

George E. Smith, East Haven, Co. F, Oct. 20, '61. Died Feb. 26, '63.

Thirteenth Battalion Infantry.

John H. Norman, East Haven, Co. C, Aug. 27, '64. Transferred from Co. K, 13th Connecticut Volunteers, Dec. 29, '64. Mustered out April 25, '66.

Fifteenth Regiment C. V. Infantry.

Henry J. H. Thompson, East Haven, Co. B, Aug. 9, '62. Mustered out June 27, '65.

William A. Allen, East Haven, Co. B, July 30, '62. Captured March 8, '65, Kinston, N. C.; paroled March 26, '65. Mustered out June 27, '65.

John L. Bradley, East Haven, Co. B, Aug. 9, '62. Captured March 8, '65, Kinston, N. C.; paroled March 26, '65. Mustered out June 27, '65.

William Brockett, East Haven, Co. B, Aug. 5, '62. Mustered out June 27, '65.

Justus Brockett, East Haven, Co. B, July 28, '62. Discharged May 23, '65.

Leverett P. Clark, East Haven, Co. B, Aug. 6, '62. Mustered out June 27, '65.

Ebenezer R. Davis, East Haven, Co. B, July 22, '62. Mustered out June 27, '65.

Samuel H. Doolittle, East Haven, Co. B, Aug. 1, '62. Mustered out June 27, '65.

George B. Hills, East Haven, Co. B. Transferred to Co. A, 14th Regiment Veteran Reserve Corps, June 9, '63. Discharged Jan. 22, '65.

Egbert Jacobs, East Haven, Co. B, Aug. 4, '62. Mustered out June 27, '65.

John O'Brien, East Haven, Co. B, Dec. 6, '64. Captured March 8, '65, Kinston, N. C.; paroled March 26, '65. Discharged June 21, '65.

Willard F. Pardee, East Haven, Co. B, Aug. 6, '62. Wounded Dec. 17, '62, Fredericksburg, Va. Mustered out June 27, '65.

Arza Riggs, East Haven, Co. B, July 28, '62. Discharged March 10, '63. (See Private Co. F, 7th Conn. Vol.)

Benjamin Street, East Haven, Co. B, Aug. 1, '62. Transferred to 159th Co. Second Battalion Veteran Reserve Corps, Sept. 14, '64. Discharged July 31, '65.

Isaac B. Thompson, Co. B, Aug. 8, '62. Wounded Dec. 12, '62, Fredericksburg, Va. Died Dec. 15, '62.

Albert James, East Haven, Co. C, Sept. 1, '64. Transferred to Co. C, 7th Regiment Connecticut Volunteers, June 23, '65. Mustered out July 20, '65.

Morris Lehan, East Haven, Co. C, Aug. 31, '64. Captured March 8, '65, Kinston, N. C.; paroled March 26, '65; transferred to Co. C, 7th Regiment, June 23, '65. Mustered out July 20, '65.

John C. Mansfield, East Haven, Co. C, Sept. 1, '64. Captured March 8, '65, Kinston, N. C.; paroled March 26, '65. Discharged disabled July 15, '65.

Martin Allen, East Haven, Co. D, Aug. 11, '62. Mustered out June 27, '65.

George W Bunnell, East Haven, Co. D, Aug. 9, '62. Promoted first lieutenant Co. C, 124th Regiment, U. S. Colored Infantry, Jan. 23, '65. Discharged Oct. 24, '65.

Samuel Dickenson, East Haven, Co. D, Aug. 11, '62. Transferred to Co. F, Veteran Reserve Corps, Aug. 13, '63. Discharged July 6, '65.

Henry E. Doolittle, East Haven, Co. D, Aug. 12, '62. Died April 2, '63.

George H. Grannis, East Haven, Co. D, Aug. 12, '62. Mustered out June 27, '65.

Daniel H. Granniss, East Haven, Co. D, Aug. 12, '62. Transferred to Co. B, 7th Regiment Veteran Reserve Corps, Dec. 30, '64. Discharged June 29, '65.

Zadoc R. Morse, East Haven, Co. D, Aug. 9, '62. Discharged May 22, '63.

Orrin Potter, East Haven, Co. E, Aug. 16, '62. Captured March 8, '65, Kinston, N. C.; paroled March 26, '65. Mustered out June 27, '65.

Frank Cardnell, East Haven, Co. G, Dec. 8, '64. Missing in action March 8, '65, at Kinston, N. C., probably killed. No further record at adjutant-general's office.

Samuel J. Pierce, East Haven, Co. G, Aug. 20, '62. Captured March 8, '65, Kinston, N. C.; paroled March 26, '65. Mustered out June 27, '65.

Lyman W. Button, East Haven, Co. K, Aug. 11, '62. Discharged April 27, '63.

Augustus R. Robinson, East Haven, Co. K, Aug. 27, '64.
Transferred to Co. K, 7th Regiment Connecticut Volunteers,
June 23, '65.

Henry T. Thompson, East Haven, Co. D, Aug. 13, '62.
Mustered out June 27, '65.

Twentieth Regiment C. V. Infantry.

Baptiste Fallio, East Haven, Co. A, Aug. 1, '63. Transferred
to Co. H, Fifth Connecticut Volunteers, June 14, '62. Mustered out July 19, '65.

John J. Dayton, East Haven, Co. G, Aug. 5, '62. Discharged
disabled Jan. 28, '63.

Twenty-seventh Regiment C. V. Infantry.

Augustus B. Fairchild, East Haven, Co. A, Sept. 9, '62.
Killed Dec. 13, '62, Fredericksburg, Va.

Joseph R. Bradley, East Haven, captain of Co. F, Aug. 18,
'62. Wounded July 2, '63, Gettysburg, Penn. Mustered out
July 27, '63.

Charles P. Prince, East Haven, second lieutenant Co. F,
Aug. 18, '62. Promoted first lieutenant May 17, '63; wounded
July 2, '63, Gettysburg, Penn. Mustered out July 27, '63.

Henry D. Russell, East Haven, Co. F, Aug. 25, '62.
Wounded Fredericksburg, Va., Dec. 13, '62. Died Jan. 4, '63.

Charles A. Tuttle, East Haven, sergeant Co. F. Reduced
to rank, sick, June —. Mustered out July 27, '63.

Albert Bradley, East Haven, corporal Co. F, Aug. 20, '62.
Mustered out July 27, '63.

Alvin B. Rose, East Haven, corporal Co. F, Aug. 20, '62.
Mustered out July 27, '63.

Charles M. Barnes, East Haven, musician Co. F, Aug. 25,
'62. Mustered out July 27, '63.

Charles L. Rowe, East Haven, wagoner Co. F, Aug. 25,
'62. Mustered out July 27, '63.

John Allen, East Haven, Co. F, Aug. 23, '62. Mustered out
July 27, '63.

Rodney Bradley, East Haven, Co. F, Aug. 22, '62. Mustered
out July 27, '63.

Lewis Brockett, East Haven, Co. F, Aug. 21, '62. Mustered
out July 27, '63.

David Burrell, East Haven, Co. F, Aug. 19, '62. Mustered out July 27, '63.

Ai K. Burwell, East Haven, Co. F, Aug, 25, '62. Mustered out July 27, '63.

Calvin Deming, East Haven, Co. F, Aug. 31, '62. Mustered out July 27, '63.

Edward B. Fowler, East Haven, Co. F, Sept. 29, '62. Wounded July 2, '63, Gettysburg, Penn. Mustered out July 27, '63.

Willis Edgar Hemingway, East Haven, Co. F, Aug. 25, '62. Mustered out July 27, '63.

Charles Higgins, East Haven, Co. F, Aug. 20, '62. Wounded Dec. 13, '62, Fredericksburg, Va. Mustered out July 27, '63.

William A. Kelly, East Haven, Co. F, Aug. 23, '62. Wounded Dec. 13, '62, Fredericksburg, Va. Mustered out July 27, '63.

Lina Mallory, East Haven, Co. F, Aug. 18, '62. Mustered out July 27, '63.

Lyman A. Mallory, East Haven, Co. F, Aug. 22, '62. Mustered out July 27, '63.

Leverett Potter, East Haven, Co. F, Aug. 25, '62. Mustered out July 27, '63.

Charles E. Potter, East Haven, Co. F, Aug. 25, '62. Mustered out July 27, '63.

William Prout, East Haven, Co. F, Aug. 25, '62. Mustered out July 27, '63.

Leonard Russell, East Haven, Co. F, Aug. 21, '62. Wounded Dec. 13, '62, Fredericksburg, Va. Mustered out July 27, '63.

Out of this number, seventy-seven were mustered out; twenty-seven discharged for disability from wounds or sickness; nine died; five were killed; four term expired, and three died in Andersonville, Georgia. Whole number, one hundred and twenty-five.

The three infantry regiments which had the greatest number of East Haven men were the "old fighting Tenth," with thirteen; the Fifteenth with thirty-one,

and the Twenty-seventh with twenty-five. The First
Regiment Heavy Artillery had seventeen men. The
Connecticut regiments which fought in the greatest
number of engagements were: the Seventh in nineteen,
the Eighteenth in twenty—all but one in 1864; the
Fifth in twenty-three; the Fourteenth in twenty-four;
the sixth in twenty-five, and the Tenth in twenty-seven.
Five of the Tenth were fought in '62, three in '63, sixteen in the "battle summer" of '64, and three in '65 ending the war at Appomattox Court House, Virginia,
April 9, '65. Brigader-General Otis says this of the
Connecticut 10th Regiment: "For steady and soldiery
behavior, under the most trying circumstances, they
may have been equaled, but never surpassed." The
Fifteenth Regiment did not do as much fighting as the
Tenth, yet it was a greater loser in killed, wounded,
and by fever and disability. It was first sent
to guard Long Bridge, on the Potomac, below Washington, and in that low, damp, foggy ground they
suffered fearfully with malaria. Then its strength
was exhausted by long fruitless marches in the hot
July weather, which accomplished nothing in a military sense. All along during the whole term of service, at intervals, it did much camp duty, also, guard,
picket and provost duty. Then while on provost
duty at Newbern, North Carolina, that terrible
scourge, yellow fever, broke out, and nearly a hundred men died, and more than half the regiment were
down with it; before the frost in November put an
end to the disease, there were few who had not
suffered from its effects. The principal engagements
were Fredericksburg, Virginia, December 13, 1862;
Edenton Road, Virginia, April 24, 1863; Providence

Church Road, Virginia, May 3, 1863; siege of
Suffolk, Virginia, April 12 to May 4, 1863; Kinston,
North Carolina, March 8, 1865. Mustered out June
27, 1865. The Twenty-seventh Regiment was composed
of nine-months' men, but they were engaged in as
severe battles as any of the war, viz.: Fredericksburg,
Virginia, December 13, 1862; Chancellorsville, Virginia, May 8, 1863, and Gettysburg, Pennsylvania,
July 2 and 3, 1863.

The morning after the last battle, Colonel Brooke,
commander of the brigade, called General Hancock's
notice to the gallant action of the Twenty-seventh in
the Wheat Field charge; he had said, turning to the
men: "Stand well to your duty now, and in a few days
you will carry with you, to your homes, all the honors
of this the greatest battle ever fought on this conti-
nent." When the regiment severed its connection with
the Army of the Potomac, Colonel Brooke, brigade
commander, said: "You have won an enviable name
and reputation, which may well in future years cause
all who belong to it to feel a pardonable pride in saying they served in the Twenty-seventh Connecticut."

To the First Connecticut Cavalry belongs the palm
of being in eighty-eight engagements. "On its muster
out, it was allowed to return to its state *mounted,* a
privilege granted to no other regiment in the whole
service! It was detailed to escort General Grant when
he went to receive Lee's surrender. A battalion of it
was sent to Gettysburg at the laying of the corner stone
for the soldiers' monument there, July 4th, 1865. It
was discharged at New Haven, August 18th, 1865,
almost three years and ten months from the date of its
first encampment at West Meriden. Its record is a

noble one, an honor to itself and to the State that sent it." The same can be said with truth of every regiment which went from the "Constitution State." They did not all see the same amount of fighting, but each discharged its duty wherever it was assigned.

CONNECTICUT MEN IN THE NAVY.

The descriptive lists of the naval records in the navy department are very incomplete. Inasmuch as the residence of the recruit is not given at the time of enlistment, by which he could be identified, as in the army records, "Connecticut" is placed against his name. Only in a few individual cases is the residence given. On this account there may be many more from East Haven than it is possible to locate.

OFFICERS.

Connecticut Men in the U. S. Navy.

Edward M. Baldwin. Acting master, Connecticut, Oct. 1, '61; acting master's mate '61; acting master May 24, '62. Honorably discharged March 12, '66.

Theodore E. Baldwin, Connecticut. Acting master's mate Jan. 19, '62. Honorably discharged Dec. 27, '66.

Calvin C. Kirkham, East Haven. Enlisted Sept. 6, '61, at Brooklyn, N. Y., as landsman, was immediately promoted to paymaster's steward, in charge of paymaster's department on board U. S. S. "Satellite," under fleet paymaster Edward Foster, of U. S. S. "Wyandotte," was appointed master's mate Oct. 31, '62, by Gideon Wells, secretary of navy. Discharged Nov. 7, '62.

Marine Corps.

Clinton Rood. Private March 22, '61, East Haven. Discharged May 9, '65.

Lee's Army surrendered April 10, 1865. War ended.

RECORD OF EAST HAVEN MEN IN THE WAR OF THE REBELLION.

Army—One hundred and twenty-five........... 125
Navy—Four 4
                                          ____
Total 129

SPANISH WAR OF 1898.

There may have been some volunteers from East Haven in this war; if so, it is left for the next chronicler to record.

CHAPTER XI.

AST HAVEN had now obtained the long contested and much coveted desire to be a separate town, and it now settled down to its industries and pursued the even tenor of its way, dispensing its routine business of town affairs without friction or controversy. The water bounds between New Haven and East Haven were settled in 1789. The line is in the middle of Quinnipiac river and along the channel of the harbor to the sea. In 1789 the town granted the owners of the salt meadows the privilege of building a dam across the Stoney river at the lower narrows.

BRIDGES.

The first account of any bridge building is in the year 1644, which was the first in East Haven. In 1644 a bridge was built over Stoney river, on the road to Totoket, by William Andrews, for which he charged the town of New Haven £3 8s. 9d.

GRAND STREET BRIDGE.

The first improvement to present itself in connection with New Haven after the separation was a bridge over the Quinnipiac river at some convenient point for both towns. A committee was appointed to oppose it, but without effect. The people considered the days of ferries were numbered. After due deliberation and an agreement with New Haven, the two towns decided to locate the bridge where one has ever since been maintained, at the corner of Quinnipiac street and Grand avenue, now known as Grand street bridge. The bridge was built in 1790-1.

August 29, 1791, the town surveyed a road leading to the new bridge from what is now the Four Corners to North Haven line, now known as North and South Quinnipiac streets. In order to reach New Haven before this, by team, they left Main street at Peat Meadow road, and followed round to the East side, where the reservoir now is, through present Burwell street to Russell street, thence through that rough, crooked road to Fair Haven. Probably this was an old Indian trail, which formed the basis of many of the winding roads in New England. The bridge was opened as a toll bridge. This was very distasteful to the people of the neighboring towns, and others, who absolutely refused to pay toll. Samuel Davenport was appointed to show cause why the people of East Haven should not pay toll to the bridge; after much altercation the remonstrance came to nothing.

A little time after, one very dark rainy night, the toll gates disappeared and were nevermore found. The public benefactor who carted off the gates was generally believed to be a daring young farmer in the neighborhood; no inquiry was made, however, by either town, and the bridge was forever free. The ferries were now abandoned.

TOMLINSON'S BRIDGE.

In 1796 a grant was made by the General Assembly for a bridge at the new or lower ferry, to Enos

Hemingway, Stephen Woodward and others. This
has always been known as Tomlinson's bridge, named
from the man who contracted to build it.

"16th Feb. 1797. At a Proprietors' meeting, granted to Enos
Hemingway, Stephen Woodward and company, of the bridge,
the flats, 187 feet in width, from the landing where the lower
Ferry hath lately been kept, running westward to the channel,
on which a bridge of 27 feet in width is to be built on the
centre, and the remainder for the perpetual use of the company for wharves, stores, &c. so long as the said bridge
shall be built and be kept in good repair."

This bridge was built by shareholders and kept as
a toll bridge until 1889. Through the strenuous and
long-continued efforts of Mr. Alfred Hughes, commencing in 1872, it became free January 1, 1889.

SECOND GRAND STREET BRIDGE.

About 1855 the Grand street bridge needed so much
repairing it was considered best to contemplate and
prepare to erect a new bridge. No definite action was
taken until November 24, 1858, when a special town
meeting was held and it was voted

"To appoint a Committee to confer with a Committee
appointed by the Town of New Haven relative to building a
new bridge in Fair Haven. George Hultz, James C. Woodward and Samuel T. Andrews were appointed that committee."
After viewing different bridges, and obtaining much information on the subject, they made a lengthy report in favor of
Whipple's iron bridge.

May 3, 1860, Special Town-meeting. *Voted,* "We will build
a new bridge in Fair Haven, over Quinnipiac River, to cor-
respond with that portion of the bridge to be built by New
Haven. *Voted,* William H. Shipman, Wyllis Hemingway, and
Charles A. Bray be and they are hereby authorized a com-

mittee with full power and authority to contract for, and in the name of the Town of East Haven in connection with New Haven, one of 'Whipple's Iron Bridges.'" *(E. H. Town Rec.)*

QUINNIPIAC DRAW BRIDGE.

In 1871 agitation commenced respecting building another bridge over Quinnipiac river. May, 1872, the legislature passed an act to build a bridge over Quinnipiac river.

Dec. 5th, 1872. *Voted,* "That the three Bridge Commissioners required by the act of the General Assembly of the State of Connecticut, passed at its May session 1872, are hereby appointed by ballot, viz: Edward A. Mitchell 1st Commissioner, E. Edwin Hall 2nd, and Edwin Granniss 3rd Comm.

Sept. 11th, 1873. The Commissioners appointed reported concurrent action with the City of New Haven, in locating said bridge, and have prepared plans &c. for the building of the same, so that the City of New Haven and Town of East Haven can enter contracts for building said Bridge. Therefore resolved that Edward A. Mitchell, E. Edwin Hall and Edwin Granniss are appointed a Committee on the part of the Town of East Haven to jointly contract with the City of New Haven for the construction of said Bridge." *(E. H. Town Rec.)*

Proceedings were not rapid, but the work was commenced, and October 4, 1875, the selectmen were authorized and empowered to borrow money on the credit of the town, such sums to complete the new Quinnipiac bridge and approaches. The bridge was completed in 1876, and bonds issued.

DYKE BRIDGE, FARM RIVER.

March 18th, 1876. *Voted,* "That the sum of $2,250 be appropriated to pay for East Haven's portion of said bridge, and approaches. The Selectmen are instructed and authorized to lay out and work the highway leading from the plains road to said bridge, and assess benefits and damages. Voted to pay E. Ellsworth Thompson $200 to satisfy his claim of damages." (*E. H. Town Rec.*)

Stone Arch Bridge.

July 25, 1876. At a special town meeting the condition of the stone arch bridge was taken into consideration, and a committee appointed by the chair, consisting of Alfred Hughes, Willet Hemingway and Timothy Andrews, to consider what was best to be done.

July 31, 1876, Alfred Hughes, chairman of the committee, reported that it was the unanimous opinion, that there was no other way but to rebuild the bridge. It was in a very dangerous condition, the sand had washed out five feet under the abutment, and that it hung shelving with danger of falling any day.

Voted, "The Selectmen be authorized and instructed to build a bridge, with 28 ft. in the clear, the foundation to go down to solid rock. The work to be done as soon as possible, also given power to contract and receive proposals for the same." (*E. H. Town Rec.*)

Lewis Bridge.

Oct. 7th, 1878. *Voted,* "The Selectmen coöperate with New Haven in building a new bridge at Lewis Bridge, and a sum not to exceed $2000. be appropriated." (*E. H. Town Rec.*)

East Haven River Draw Bridge.

May 23rd, 1904. *Voted,* "The Selectmen to coöperate with the Selectmen of Branford in building the bridge at East Haven River."

As this bridge was ordered by the United States Government, there was no other way than to comply with the demand.

The village of Fair Haven grew very fast after the bridge was built, and within a few years had a large trade with the surrounding towns, and was a very busy place. Horace R. Hotchkiss had one of the largest and best stores for dry goods and groceries in the county, and carried on an extensive trade. The town had shared its municipal offices and honors with the village equally. It was the custom to alternate the representative to the legislature with each part of the town, and village, but the seat of government was at the center of the town.

About the year 1840, the daughter, like many another precocious one, concluded it was time for the mother to resign the reins of government into the hands of the daughter. Accordingly a town meeting was called to remove the seat to Fair Haven. This caused a tremendous buzzing in the hive, and everyone was at white heat with spread wings. So sure were the Fair Haveners of success, that they brought with them a set of colors and a band of music, concealed in a wagon. The old town arose, and shaking her locks, roared forth a healthy No! So the Fair Haveners went home a sadder but a wiser people and thus saved their colors and music for a better occasion. This experiment was never tried again. In 1857 the town was divided into two voting districts: East Haven was First District and Fair Haven was Second District. This was for general elections, but all business and special town meetings were held in East Haven.

TOWN HALLS.

Until 1841 East Haven had no place for miscellaneous public gatherings. The first town meeting was held in the Stone Church, but that was an extra occasion, and dignified with a sermon by its pastor. There is no account that this was repeated. According to Episcopal rules, their churches being consecrated can only be opened for religious purposes.

Previous to 1841, town meetings were held at private houses. While Josiah Bradley was the "Squire of the town" they were held in his house, in a very large old room, said to have been used as a meeting place before the first meetinghouse was built in 1706. The site of the house is where the Bailey house now stands. Afterwards, town meetings were held in the unused bar room of the old Gurdon Bradley tavern, in the center of the town, subsequently the home of Mr. Ruel Andrews. He was a man much in public affairs and so opened his house for the good of the public. The town did not see its way to aid in the matter, so a few public-spirited men concluded to remedy the want by building a town hall by stockholders at $15 per share. Not that they expected it to be a paying investment, but for a public convenience, as some of the younger men declared they would not vote in "Aunt Molly Gurdon's kitchen" any longer. It was a proud day for East Haven when the first town meeting was held in the town hall in 1842.

Jan. 10th, 1866. *Voted,* "That Bradley Pardee and Charles A. Bray be and are hereby appointed as a Committee to purchase in the name and behalf of the Town of East Haven the Town Hall property, so called. Provided it can be secured on reasonable and judicious terms." (*E. H. Town Rec.*)

The property was secured to the town.

April 30, 1864, Deacon Ruel Andrews passed away, in the 18th year of his town clerkship. He was a man

MAIN STREET.

of unusual enterprise, industry and integrity, holding the higher offices of church and town. East Haven had only two town clerks in the 58 preceding years. At the next annual town meeting, Charles A. Bray was chosen town clerk. Mr. Bray's residence and business were in Fair Haven, so of course the town records had to be removed there. This caused a twinge of regret to the older men of the center, but as it was a square deal, and Mr. Bray was popular in both sections of the town, the ripple on the surface soon smoothed out, and all went harmoniously along to the end. East Haven still held the supremacy. The next most important event was the annexation of the western part of the town to New Haven, in 1882, when the ancient and more modern archives of the town were carted back to the center for all time.

CIRCUMSTANCES LEADING TO ANNEXATION.

We have now seen that between the years of 1860 and 1880 East Haven had built, either in part or wholly, five bridges; some were very expensive, particularly Quinnipiac draw bridge.

During the Civil War, East Haven kept up her quota of men to the full, and was liberal to her soldiers. The extra war debt and extensive bridge building brought the town very heavily in debt. Some parts of the town desired more improvements than the town felt justified in making under the existing circumstances. After much deliberation between the two towns, a decision was reached, whereby New Haven would assume and pay East Haven's debt* provided the western portion was annexed to New Haven,

* The whole indebtedness was over $200,000.

thereby giving New Haven the control of the harbor, and waterfront (of which East Haven owned the lion's share), also other considerations favorable to East Haven residents in the western part. ,

At this time, Dwight W. Tuttle, afterwards state senator, was East Haven's representative in the legislature. He introduced this bill in the House of Representatives, and it was referred to the Committee on Cities and Boroughs, which reported adversely. Whereupon the town of East Haven immediately called a special town meeting, April 11, 1881. An overwhelming number was present, so much so that a motion was made to adjourn to the street for lack of room. The house was divided, resulting in 286 votes in the affirmative and one in the negative.

Voted, "The proceedings of the meeting signed by the Chairman, and certified to by the Clerk of the Town, with the seal of the Town affixed, and that one copy be transmitted to the President of the Senate, and one to the Speaker of the House of Representatives, and one each, to the Chairman on the part of the Senate and House, of the Committee on Cities and Boroughs. *Voted,* A Committee of five be appointed to report the result of this meeting to the Legislature now in session, viz: Hiram Jacobs, George H. Townsend, Leander F. Richmond, H. H. Strong and A. L. Chamberlain, also Dr. H. E. Stone be added." (*E. H. Town Rec.*)

ANNEXATION OF THE WESTERN PART OF EAST HAVEN
TO THE CITY OF NEW HAVEN.

A special Town Meeting of the Electors of the Town of East Haven was held first Monday of May, 1881, for the purpose of voting upon the acceptance of an act of the General Assembly of this State passed at the January session of 1881, providing for the annexing of the Western part of the Town of East Haven to the Town of New Haven, and for the division of the property of said Town, and the payment of its indebtedness, and certain other matters, more particularly referred to in said act, and reference is here made to said act for more particular description of its provisions.

By the terms of said act, before its takes effect, it must be approved by the Electors of the Town of East Haven, in the manner therein provided.

The Electors of the Town of East Haven, living in that part to be annexed to the Town of New Haven, by the provisions of said act, will meet and vote in the Engine House of the Borough of Fair Haven, East. Those living in the remaining portion of said East Haven will meet in the Town Hall, in East Haven Center. The meeting will be open at each place at 6 o'clock in the morning; the vote will be by ballot, the polls will be open at six o'clock A. M. and close at one o'clock P. M. Ballots with the word "Yes" will be counted in favor of the acceptance of said act; those with the word "No" against the acceptance of said act.

The part proposed to be annexed to the Town of New Haven is described as follows. All that part of the Town of East Haven, lying westerly of a line commencing on the dividing line between the Town of North Haven and East Haven, at a point 1600 feet east of the East side of North Quinnipiac Street, where said street crosses said dividing line, thence running southerly in a straight line to a point three hundred feet due East of the south side of Hill St., where said Hill Street intersects with East Street, thence running Southerly in a straight line to a point on the main road running East and West from New Haven through East Haven Center, 400 ft. East of the East side of a road running North and Sotuh where said North and South road intersects said East and West road near the house of Dana A. Bradley, thence in a Southerly direction to the junction of Mile Creek with Morris Creek, thence Southerly following the center of Morris Creek to its mouth, thence in a due Southerly line to the Southern boundary of the State.

HUDSON B. FORBES   ) *Selectmen*
SAMUEL CHIDSEY   } *of the Town of*
JOHN CHESTER BRADLEY) *East Haven.*

Dated at East Haven
Apr. 25th, 1881.

"Pursuant to the above call, a special Town Meeting of the Electors of the Town of East Haven was held on Monday May 2nd 1881, for the purpose of deciding by Ballot, the ratification, or rejection of House Bill No. 334 passed at the session of the General Assembly, January term 1881, to which reference is made for particulars, the result of the meetings named in the two other places specified in said bill, is as follows:

Whole number of votes cast in that portion of the Town, not to be annexed to the Town of New Haven...........132

 Vote in favor of Annexation 123
 Opposed to Annexation.................... 9

Report of the result certified to by
       JONATHAN DUDLEY *(Moderator).*

Vote in that portion of the Town to be annexed to the Town of New Haven:

 Whole number of votes cast...................... 386
 Vote in favor of Annexation................ 301
 Opposed to Annexation.................... 85

Report of result certified to by
       MARTIN ALLEN *(Moderator).*

Received and recorded
May 2nd, 1881   By A. L. CHAMBERLAIN,
           Town Clerk.
  (*E. H. Town Rec.*)

East Haven was now free from debt, with no costly bridges to maintain and many long and expensive roads taken off her hands. There was no annoying rivalry of any part of the town, as Foxon and South End were always loyal to the old town. True she had lost about one-third of her territory, but that was the most expensive part to manage, and she still had the full use of all the roads and bridges without expense. There was nothing now for her to do but

settle down to the march of improvement, and keep
abreast of the times, which the foregoing history
proves she has done with a will.

In 1889 a water tank was located at the northwest
corner of the public square.

June 1, 1892, the whole center of the town was
stirred as it never was before, when the store of C. C.
Kirkham and the town hall were burned to the ground
by an incendiary. Fortunately the safes with the
records were saved. An occasional barn in different
localities had been burned before, with greater or
smaller loss.

June 25, 1892, a special town meeting was held in
the basement of the Congregational chapel.

Voted, "To appropriate from the Town Treasury a sufficient
sum of money for the purpose of building the Town Hall."
Voted, "If desirable to build said building of suitable size for
use as a Public School building, as well as Town Hall."
"To appoint a Committee composed of taxpayers and property
owners to superintend building the same." *Voted,* "To lay
a tax to cover the expense of the same." Adjourned to July
16th, 1892.

"The report of the Committee appointed, accepted and Committee discharged with thanks." *Voted,* "The Selectmen procure estimates and plans of a building, to be used as Town
Hall. Dimension 35 x 50 ft." Adjourned to July 30, 1892.

Voted, "The Selectmen procure plans and specifications and
bids, and cause to be erected a building to be used as a
Town Hall, without basement, on the same foundation as the
old one. Cost not to exceed $2000."

August 13th, 1892, a special town meeting was held
and former vote of $2,000 was rescinded, and a vote
of $3,000 was passed. Same dimensions. After
several special town meetings, *pro* and *con,* were held,

it was definitely decided at a meeting held October 3, 1892, that a town hall should be built.

Voted, "That a committee of three be appointed to superintend the erection of a Town Hall." *Voted,* "That Henry T. Thompson, Albert Forbes, and H. Walter Chidsey, be appointed that Committee." *Voted,* "That the Committee be instructed not to exceed the sum of $3000 in building said Town Hall. To give the contract to lowest bidder." *Voted,* "That that person to whom the contract is awarded be instructed by said Committee to proceed immediately and finish the Building as soon as possible. *Voted,* "That the Selectmen are hereby instructed to borrow, on the credit of the Town the amount sufficient to complete the Town Hall."

Thus the second town hall was erected and finished.

EAST HAVEN FIRE DEPARTMENT.

The burning of the town hall was a very convincing argument that the town needed some protection in case of such disasters. Therefore in the first call for a special town meeting the following was inserted, viz.: "To locate one or more hydrants for fire purposes." This was the foundation and first step taken for a fire department in East Haven. The people realized the situation, and acted with promptness.

June 25th, 1892. *Voted,* "A Committee of three citizens be appointed to inquire the cost of one or more hydrants, to be located in the center of the Town, also ascertain the cost of 500 feet of hose, and a hose carriage. The Committee were Wm. H. Robinson, Frank M. Sperry and H. Walter Chidsey." July 26th,1892. Adjourned town meeting. *Voted,* "To accept the report of the Committee appointed." *Voted,* "The Selectmen be authorized and instructed to locate hydrants, and to procure 500 ft. hose and a hose carriage within 30 days."

The people did not propose to be caught napping again, for November 26, 1893, "The Selectmen bought 200 ft. additional hose." October 2, 1899, "The Selectmen were to purchase two extension ladders for fire purposes." There was no regular organized fire department but a kind of mutual agreement and Mr. Isaac Hagaman was made the chief and Charles Gerrish foreman. Things proceeded under this arrangement for several years when the young men decided to form a regular organization, and place themselves under the regulations of the State Firemen's Association. Previous to this time, the fire apparatus had been kept in an addition to the town hall, built for the purpose. March 1, 1901, a special town meeting was held when it was voted,

"That the Selectmen be authorized to buy a suitable lot, for a Hose House." *Voted,* "That the Selectmen borrow money necessary to pay for said lot." *Voted,* "That they are authorized to provide means for the erection of a suitable building on said lot, when purchased." *Voted,* "That the Selectmen borrow $2000 to build a suitable house."

March 14, 1901, at an adjourned special town meeting "A motion was made that the vote authorizing the Selectmen to purchase a lot for Hose Co. Building be reconsidered." *Voted,* "The vote to be taken by ballot, which resulted as follows: Yes 27. No 57. Motion to reconsider lost." Motion "to reconsider vote authorizing the Selectmen to borrow $2000 to erect a building for the Hose Co. ballot taken, result: Yes 31. No 50. Motion lost." (*E. H. Town Rec.*)

Oct. 6th, 1902. *Voted,* "The Selectmen be instructed to purchase 250 ft. additional Hose for use of Fire Department."

The lot was purchased and house erected—a two-story building and finished basement, cost nearly $3,000. It is a volunteer company belonging to the

Connecticut State Firemen's Association, and has between 35 and 40 members.

As matters now stand the town owns the land and building, with 950 feet of hose, two extension ladders and hose carriage. The volunteers are called the C. C. Kirkham Fire Hose Company. They have provided themselves with the hook and ladder and chemical apparatus, at a cost of about $750. They have furnished the basement with some gymnastic implements, and the second story as a club room, for social purposes. The first story is occupied with the fire property of town and company. The first chief under the organization was Frank W. Willoughby. The present chief is Harry B. Page [1907]. The town is very favorably situated for a comparatively inexpensive fire equipment, as the force of the water from the lake will throw a stream, one and one-half inch pipe diameter, from 80 to 90 feet, no engine being needed. The chief expense of the fire department is the water rate to the water company, which is by no means a charitable institution. Hydrants have been located all over the center and radiating streets, until protection seems ample. Certainly there is no organization of men more entitled to the gratitude and hearty appreciation of the community than the volunteer firemen. No class of men give evidence of greater disinterested benevolence, kindness, sympathy and willing coöperation, in times of distress, than they. When the cry of fire is heard, all else is forgotten but the one idea of help and rescue, save the consciousness of doing one's best, without reward, like a brave true man to his brother in distress. Besides, there is no greater defence against incendiarism, than an effective fire department.

TELEPHONE COMPANY.

In 1899 the people of the town, realizing the convenience of the telephone system, organized a town telephone company, with a substantial working capital; at the present time it has about seventy-five subscribers. Some, however, had previously availed themselves of the service of the Southern New England Telephone Company, and did not change to the town company. The local line commenced in quite a novel way, by the Kirkham brothers establishing a line between their respective residences. The idea was readily taken up by others and a company was formed, with George C. Kirkham president and Herbert C. Nickerson secretary and treasurer.

FIVE CENT FARE OBTAINED.

After Saltonstall Park was closed in 1896, the electric company took up their track and ran their cars to the Green only. They then wished to extend their road to Momauguin. Connecticut law gives the selectmen considerable power in the location of street railways. Mr. John S. Tyler, who has been selectman continuously since 1886, and most of that time town agent, while guarding the interests of the town in every particular, displayed his usual good judgment in locating the road, and his readiness to do justice to all parties concerned. So the road was extended in 1898.

The fare from East Haven to New Haven was ten cents, which the people thought unjust, since the distance from New Haven Green to Westville and Fair

Haven was about the same as to East Haven, and the former had only a five-cent fare. They brought several petitions before the company, but to no avail. Finally they appealed to the legislature in 1897 but were unsuccessful. In 1899 the electric company wished to extend their tracks to Branford center by way of Short Beach and the seashore resorts. It was now Mr. Tyler's turn to give the deaf ear to the company's entreaties. He could not see any benefit to East Haven arising from the extension, and it was useless to extend franchises where no advantage was to be derived. The company now saw that they wanted quite as much of East Haven as the people did of them; so they compromised by giving the people a five-cent fare all over their lines where that fare was given to others, for the right to lay their tracks over less than an eighth of a mile on the outskirts of East Haven soil. The road was extended in August, 1900.

Grateful Recognition of Services.

Oct. 2nd, 1893. *Voted,* "That it is the desire of this annual meeting to recognize the fact, that our former representative, Dwight W. Tuttle, first called the attention of the Legislature of Connecticut at the Jan. session A. D. 1891 to the injustice done this Town, relative to the expense occasioned by eliminating the grade crossings near the Shore Line R. R. Depot, and whereas at the recent session of the General Assembly our present representative, Grove J. Tuttle, by a persistent and fearless advocacy of house bill No. 7, succeeded in having said bill become a law, resulting in the state recently paying the Town of East Haven the large sum of $2280, it is therefore the sincere desire of this meeting to thank our representative and his immediate predecessor, and the same is hereby tendered, for their efforts and successful labor in this particular, and also in other important matters affecting the interests of this town."

Voted: That the above vote be entered at length upon the Town records.

Attest. CHARLES T. HEMINGWAY.

Town Clerk.

CUSTOMS.

It is a noticeable fact in the history of East Haven people, from the earliest days to the present time, that they are an argumentative community but by no means a quarrelsome one. Let a question arise which is to be decided by the voice of the people, they will agree to disagree, then disagree to agree. This sounds paradoxical, but it is true. A meeting will be called, and a vote will be taken favorable to the object. This is wherein they agree. Within a few days another meeting will be called to rescind the first vote. This is wherein they agree to disagree. After the question has been tossed to and fro, through a series of meetings, with prolonged debate, and sometimes heated discussion, the vote of the first meeting will be sustained, and they now all settle down to harmony as before. This is where they disagree to agree. They are strictly a peace-loving and law-abiding people. They may have their petty animosities and neighborhood jealousies, but they never have quarrels which end in litigation like many of the neighboring towns. Law suits between the native born are very rare, a thing almost unknown. True, in settling estates and in various other technicalities of the law, counsel is necessary, generally, to settle points of law involved. In 1866, when the present senior resident lawyer was admitted to the bar, and decided to make East Haven his residence, one of the sages of the town deplored the event seriously; remarking, "Now the peace of the town will be gone, for no greater calamity could befall a country town than to have a lawyer settle in it." But the good man lived to see four of his townsmen full-fledged lawyers, residing in the town at the same time, all in practice, and the whole town as calm and unruffled as a mill pond in a May morning.

The subject of temperance has always received its share of support from the people. Various temperance societies have arisen and flourished in their day and generation. The town has often voted "No license," and were it not for the various seashore resorts, would be a "dry town"; as it is, license is only voted by a very small margin. Even cider, which was so very prevalent and abundant at one time, is scarcely seen in the homes of the people to-day.

East Haven has always been called, socially, a very democratic town, which in a sense is true; but at the same time many family clans have felt their distinctive superiority, arising from one cause or another, yet they all met on the same general plane. The social customs of the town have kept pace with the changing times. In the days of spinning spells, quilting bees, and singing schools, they generally ended in a dance—particularly the two former. It may be a query how the sons and daughters of such strict puritanical parentage ever learned to dance. Youth will have its pleasures and amusements, whether by tacit consent, or more direct opposition. In the first quarter of the last century, there were very few young people but well knew the stately minuet and the Scotch reel, to say nothing of the more familiar "money musk," "felicity," and a score of other dances. There was no "calling off" in those days; each one knew his or her part and kept step and time with the music. Every old hostelry had its spacious ball room, with spring floor, and balls were very common through the winter months. Eli Whitney's invention of the cotton gin relegated the flax spinning wheel to the garret about 1830, but the great or wool wheel held on, with waning success, for about fifteen years longer, when that went to keep the former company. Spinning spells were merged into church sewing societies, conducted under a president and officers similar to the present day, only the meetings were at the homes of the members, as there were no public meeting places.

The neighborhood "tea drinkings" were very enjoyable affairs. Perhaps a dozen ladies, with their sewing and knitting, would assemble about two o'clock and after tea the gentlemen would join them; light refreshments or fruit were passed around in the evening, and a general good time followed. Then in the winter there would be one or more general sleigh rides, according to the amount of snow. The whole town would turn out—heads of families as well as young people. They would go to some good public house or hotel, and have a supper, and the young people a dance. The good matrons would take to the parlors, with their "wine sangaree," while the fathers were busy with their "eggnog," and the youngsters were dancing in the ball room. Frequently some of the fathers would slip out and be found dancing with their prospective daughters-in-law—living young days over again. All would enjoy a bountiful supper and have a really good time. In the summer there were "barbecues" at the "head of the pond" (Lake Saltonstall), and sailing parties "down the river" (Mansfield's Grove). Wherever such gatherings were held, the inner man was bountifully refreshed.

In Connecticut and all over New England, the Lord's Day began according to the Hebrew manner, at sunset Saturday night, because "the evening and the morning were the first day," and ended Sunday at sunset. No sooner had the sun disappeared, than out came the spinning wheels, knitting kneedles, spooling reels and quill wheels; so much work had to be done by the female portion of the household that not a moment was to be lost. Sunday evening was also a time for recreation, especially with the young men. Hence arose the practice of the youngsters doing their "courting" Sunday evening. Although the law was very strict, forbidding any young man to inveigle or draw the affections of a maid without the consent of her parents or guardian, yet he probably knew of some family where he might meet a young lady with whom he had exchanged glances, from the opposite gallery of the meetinghouse, during the day, without opposition from her elders, and oftentimes was treated to the best the house afforded.

The story has been told of a very shrewd matron in East Haven, who had more than a half-dozen girls to marry off. The young men knew that if there was one among the number of callers who was distasteful to the good dame, there would be no refreshments forthcoming; but if all were acceptable, in a little time the smell of hot doughnuts would greet their olfactories, as she always kept the dough on hand to boil

as occasion required. Whether it was the hot doughnuts, cheese, etc., or not, all her girls were successfully
mated.

East Haven was not without its appreciation of
music: for as early as 1752 it was

"*Voted,* that Mr. Heminway shall name the Psalm in public;
Nathaniel Barnes shall tune the Psalm, and in his absence
Jacob or Isaac Goodsell."

The following extracts from the town records will
speak for themselves:

Feb. 5th, 1798. "*Voted,* that Capt. Hemingway & Joseph
Hotchkiss be appointed for to employ a singing master, two
months for to teach a singing school in this Town, and to
draw the money out of the Town Treasury, to pay the singing master for his service."

Jan. 1801. "*Voted,* Joseph Hotchkiss and Zebulon Bradley be a
Committee for to lay out $12 as they shall judge best advantage
to increase the singing. *Voted,* that the Treasurer be directed to
pay to the Committee $12 out of the treasury, and in addition
to the $12 as much as they have expended, for the support
of said school."

March 18th, 1805. "*Voted* that Eleazer Hemingway, Asahel
Bradley, Zebulon Bradley and Samuel Barnes be appointed
to superintend a singing school, and they, or the major part
of them be authorized for to draw $15 out of the Town Treas-
ury, to be appropriated and expended towards the support
of a singing school in the town." (*E. H. Town Rec.*)

East Haven kept up these schools from time to
time until 1819, called "Toleration year," when Connecticut's first constitution was adopted, abolishing the
support of Congregational churches and its inci-
dentals by taxation, thus making every denomination
stand equal before the law. East Haven was among
the very first Congregational churches to introduce

instrumental music into their worship. The instrument was a bass viol. Mr. Isaac Pardee was the performer and chorister for forty or more years, carrying his "big fiddle" (as the children called it), carefully wrapped in a green baize bag, to and from the church every Sunday. Previous to this time musical instruments were debarred from all New England churches, as sinful and unchristian, and nothing was used in any of them but the tuning fork. An organ in a church was a puritanical abhorrence, considered as an abomination of wickedness. How time has mellowed down prejudices even in music!

East Haven people have always been ready to take advantage of every improvement in their business, as well as municipal affairs, as soon as opportunity offered. When water mains were laid, pumps and wells were very generally discarded on the line; now there is scarcely a house but affords all the modern conveniences which water brings in its train. So also with gas; wherever the pipes have been placed, gas is introduced and very few houses are without their gas cooking range, if no more. Street lights sprang up as if by magic. Main street is lighted from border to border of the town, and other streets as far as practicable.

The people also have kept pace with the social changes of the times, gay or grave. In the forties, when the fashion of dances changed from the old-fashioned minuet, contra dances, etc., to quadrilles, cotillions and waltzes, East Haven had her dancing schools at the town hall. An accomplished dancing master was employed and the course was twelve lessons, one a week, followed by a quarter ball.

These were by no means promiscuous dances. Each member had a limited number of tickets, which were distributed to selected friends, agreeable to the whole company, which eliminated every unpleasant feature, and rendered the whole more like an invited party. These were followed by various temperance societies of their day, with weekly meetings, down to the present W. C. T. U. When club formations became the rule in social life, East Haven readily followed the plan, and several clubs were organized. The Woman's Club took up civic improvement for the benefit of the town, a work which has been recorded in foregoing chapters.

THE RADIUM CLUB.

The general object of the club is to bring the young people of the town together in a social way, in order that they may take up and discuss those affairs and incidents which will prove of practical importance in later years. It is composed of the younger people, none under sixteen years of age. It has weekly meetings, during the winter and spring, at the homes of its respective members. Two members are appointed each week to take charge of the literary work for the next meeting. The subjects are of a historical and educational character, and sometimes international affairs are considered. Good wishes and speed to the work, and may its shadow never be less!

THE MOTHERS' SUNSHINE CLUB.

This seems to be more of a benevolent and charitable cast, namely to do good as they have opportunity, carrying sunshine and happiness to the afflicted, the poor and the orphan, looking out for the benefit of the children and the helpless, that cannot take care of them-selves. Truly a noble work. All the clubs seem to have the one object in view—the broadening of heart and soul, going out of one's self to the uplifting and benefit of others, material and intellectual. This is the time of seed-sowing. Who can estimate the harvest in time to come?

PRESIDENT HAYES' VISIT.

During President Rutherford B. Hayes' term of office from 1877 to 1881 he visited New Haven, and also the home of his great-grandfather, Ezekiel Hayes of Branford, Connecticut. While passing through East Haven, he called at the home of Edward Ells-worth Thompson, where he was entertained and a short reception held.

Through the kindness and courtesy of our congress-man, N. D. Sperry, a list of postmasters was furnished.

EAST HAVEN POSTMASTERS.

Stephen Thompson, January 27th, 1824.
James Thompson, April 9th, 1829.
Ruel Andrews, September 9th, 1829.
Stephen Hemingway, June 9th, 1853.
Henry Hagaman, April 27th, 1861.
Ellen Hagaman, May 27th, 1862.
Daniel M. Church, Apr. 5th, 1867.
Stephen Hemingway, Aug. 4th, 1869.
Calvin C. Kirkham, July 29th, 1889.
Florence R. Andrews, Sept. 8th, 1892.

STATE SENATORS.

David Sullivan Fowler,	1852	Charles A. Bray,	1877
James Mulford Townsend,	1864	Charles A. Bray,	1879
	Dwight Williams Tuttle, 1897		

LIST OF REPRESENTATIVES FROM 1785.

Capt. Stephen Smith,	1785	Bela Farnham,	1823
Mr. Amos Morriss,	1786	Bela Farnham,	1824
Mr. Josiah Bradley,	1786	Eleazer Hemingway,	
Mr. Samuel Davenport,	1787	1825 to 1830 (inclusive)	
Mr. Samuel Davenport,	1787	Philemon Holt, 1831 and 1832	
Mr. Samuel Davenport,	1788	DeGrass Maltby,	1833
Mr. Samuel Davenport,	1788	James Thompson,	
Mr. Samuel Davenport,	1789	1834, 1835 and 1836	
Mr. Josiah Bradley,	1789	Wm. K. Townsend,	
Mr. Samuel Davenport,	1790	1837 and 1838	
Mr. Josiah Bradley,	1790	Hoadley Bray, 1839 and 1840	
Mr. Samuel Davenport,	1791	Hoadley Bray,	1841
Mr. Josiah Bradley,	1791	Wm. K. Townsend,	1842
Mr. Samuel Davenport,	1792	Harvey Rowe, 2nd,	1843
Mr. Samuel Davenport,	1792	Daniel Smith,	1844
Mr. Josiah Bradley,	1793	Wyllys Hemingway,	1845
Mr. Samuel Davenport,	1793	James Thompson,	
Mr. Samuel Davenport,	1794	1846 and 1847	
Mr. Samuel Davenport,	1794	Harvey Rowe, 2nd,	1848
Mr. Samuel Davenport,	1795	Stephen Dodd,	1849
Mr. Samuel Davenport,	1795	Jeremiah B. Davidson,	1850
Mr. Stephen Woodward,	1796	Wyllis Hemingway,	1851
Mr. Enos Hemingway,	1797	James Potter Smith,	1852
Mr. Enos Hemingway,	1798	Wyllis Mallory,	1853
Mr. Enos Hemingway,	1799	Stephen Smith 2d,	1854
Mr. Stephen Woodward,	1800	Samuel T. Andrews,	1855
Mr. Enos Hemingway,	1801	William H. Hunt,	1856
Mr. Enos Hemingway,	1802	James Thompson,	1857
Mr. E. Hemingway,	1803	Charles Holt Fowler,	1858
Mr. Enos Hemingway,	1804	James Thompson,	1859
Mr. Enos Hemingway,	1805	Charles A. Bray,	1860
Mr. Enos Hemingway,	1806	Nathan Andrews,	1861
Mr. Enos Hemingway,	1807	Capt. William Farren,	1862
Mr. Enos Hemingway,	1808	Alexander W. Forbes,	1863
Mr. Amos Bradley,	1809	Charles L. Ives,	1864
Mr. Amos Bradley,	1810	Samuel Chidsey,	1865
Mr. Amos Bradley,	1811	William E. Goodyear,	1866
Moses A. Street,	1812	Charles L. Ives,	1867
Amos Bradley,	1813	Charles L. Ives,	1868
Eleazer Hemingway,	1814	Joseph I. Hotchkiss,	1869
James Thompson,	1815	Capt. Joseph R. Bradley,	1870
James Thompson,	1816	Lyman A. Granniss,	1871
Eleazer Hemingway,	1817	Rev. Daniel William Havens,	
James Thompson,	1818	1872	
Bela Farnham,	1819	Leonard R. Andrews,	1873
Bela Farnham,	1820	Hiram Jacobs,	1874
Philemon Holt,	1821	John Woodward Thompson,	
Philemon Holt,	1822	1875	

Dea. Asa L. Fabrique,	1876	Dwight W. Tuttle,	1889
Horace H. Strong,	1877	Dwight W. Tuttle,	1891
Charles L. Mitchell,	1878	Grove J. Tuttle,	1893
Grove J. Tuttle,	1879	Charles W. Granniss,	1895
Lester P. Mallory,	1880	Francis Foote Andrews,	1897
Dwight W. Tuttle,	1881	Charles W. Granniss,	1899
Orlando B. Thompson,	1882	Edward Foote Thompson,	
Alexander W. Forbes,	1883		1901
Alexander W. Forbes,	1884	John S. Tyler,	1903
Justin Bradley,	1885	John S. Tyler,	1905
		Horace A. Smith,	1907

Biennial Sessions.

*James Smith Thompson, 1887

The two men who served the greatest number of terms in the State Legislature were Esquire Enos Hemingway, of North Quinnipiac street, and Capt. James Thompson, corner of Main street and Thompson avenue. Mr. Hemingway served continuously from 1797 to 1809 inclusive, twenty-one sessions in all. Up to 1806 there were two sessions per year, spring and fall. Captain Thompson was elected eleven different times of one year each.

COUNTY OFFICERS.

Sheriff, David Sullivan Fowler, elected in 1857 to 1860; second term, 1860 to 1864.

County Treasurer, Hiram Jacobs, 1893 to —

County Commissioners, Nathan Andrews, 1872 to 1876; Hiram Jacobs, 1879 to 1893; † Edward Foote Thompson, 1901 to 1905; second term, 1905 to 1908.

Town Clerks.

Samuel Hemingway ....1682 to 1702
Ebenezer Chidsey ....1702 to 1726
Samuel Hotchkiss ....1726 to 1727
Gideon Potter ....1727 to 1757
Isaac Holt ....1757 to 1763
Simeon Bradley ....1763 to 1768

* Appointed City Court Judge, New Haven, 1887 to 1891.

† Died in office, after the first part of this work had gone to press.

Abraham Hemingway ....1768 to 1769
Simeon Bradley ....1769 to 1779
Joshua Austin ....1779 to 1787
Josiah Bradley ....1787 to 1806
Dr. Bela Farnham ....1806 to 1846
*Ruel Andrews ....1846 to 1864
Charles A. Bray ....⸴1864 to 1879
A. L. Chamberlain ....1879 to 1881
Dwight W. Tuttle ....1881 to 1882
*Charles T. Hemingway ....1882 to 1894
Dwight W. Tuttle ....July, 1894 to Oct., 1894
*Augustus Street ....1894 to 1902
Calvin C. Kirkham 1902

EAST HAVEN INCORPORATED A TOWN 1785.

Town Treasurers.

Azariah Bradley ....1785 to 1787
Josiah Bradley ....1787 to 1806
Dr. Bela Farnham ....1806 to 1809
Eleazer Hemingway ....1809 to 1813
Dr. Bela Farnham ....1813 to 1846
Ruel Andrews ....1846 to 1852
Samuel T. Andrews ....1852 to 1854
Joseph Pardee ....1854 to 1856
Samuel T. Andrews ....1856 to 1858
Joseph Pardee, ...1858 to 1868
Augustus Street ....1868 to 1879
Orlando B. Thompson ....1879 to 1887
Ebenezer Gilbert ....1887 to 1894
*Frederick L. Hawkins ....1894 to 1907
Henry H. Bradley 1907

SELECTMEN.

1785	1786
Capt. Isaac Chidsey	Samuel Davenport
Capt. Samuel Forbes	Samuel Holt
Azariah Bradley	Amos Morris, Jun.
Joseph Holt	John Hemingway
Amos Morris, Jun.	Samuel Forbes

* Died in office.

1787
Dan Holt
Samuel Forbes
Amos Morris, Jun.
Joseph Russell
Jacob Bradley

1788
John Woodward, Jun.
Capt. Samuel Forbes
Amos Morris, Jun.

1789
Samuel Forbes,
Amos Morris, Jun.
John Woodward, Jun.

1790
John Woodward, Jun.
Capt. Isaac Chidsey
Capt. Enos Hemingway

1791
Amos Morris, Jun.
John Woodward
Dan Holt

1792
No record found.

1793
Dan Holt
John Woodward
Amos Morris, Jun.

1794
John Woodward
Dan Holt
Amos Morris, Jun.

1795
Enos Hemingway
James Chidsey
Stephen Woodward

1796
James Chidsey
Enos Hemingway
Stephen Woodward

1797
Enos Hemingway
James Chidsey
Stephen Woodward

1798
Enos Hemingway
James Chidsey
Amos Bradley

1799
James Chidsey
Amos Bradley
Capt. Isaac Chidsey
Dan Holt
Joshua Austin

1800
James Chidsey
Amos Bradley
Caleb Smith
Stephen Woodward

1801
Levi Potter
Ichabod Bishop
Daniel Tuttle

1802
Levi Potter
Daniel Tuttle
Ichabod Bishop

1803
Levi Potter
Daniel Tuttle
Dr. Bela Farnham

1804
Levi Potter
Daniel Tuttle
Samuel Bradley

1805
Dr. Bela Farnham
Capt. Samuel Chidsey
James Thompson

1806
Samuel Chidsey
James Thompson
Samuel Bradley

1807
Samuel Bradley
Samuel Chidsey
James Thompson

1808
Samuel Bradley
Samuel Chidsey
James Thompson

1809
Nicholas Street
James Thompson
John Russell

1810
James Thompson
Samuel Bradley
John Russell

1811
Samuel Bradley
James Thompson
Thomas Smith

1812
Thomas Smith
Jared Andrews
Eleazer Hemingway

1813
Eleazer Hemingway
Christopher Tuttle
Jared Andrews

1814
Jared Andrews
Christopher Tuttle
Amos Bradley

1815
Christopher Tuttle
Amos Bradley
James Thompson

1816
Amos Bradley
James Thompson
Samuel Chidsey

1817
James Thompson
Eleazer Hemingway
Christopher Tuttle

1818
Christopher Tuttle
Jared Andrews
Elijah Bradley

1819
Elijah Bradley
Wyllis Hemingway
Eleazer Hemingway

1820
Elijah Bradley
Eleazer Hemingway
Wyllis Hemingway

1821
Philemon Holt
Dr. Bela Farnham
James Thompson

1822
James Thompson
Dr. Bela Farnham
Philemon Holt.

1823
Daniel Smith
Eleazer Hemingway

1824
Eleazer Hemingway
Daniel Smith

1825
Eleazer Hemingway
Jacob Smith
Philemon Holt

1826
Philemon Holt
Jared Andrews
Eleazer Hemingway
Jacob Smith

1827
Eleazer Hemingway
Wyllis Hemingway
Amos Morris

1828
Eleazer Hemingway
Wyllis Hemingway
Philemon Holt

1829
Eleazer Hemingway
Wyllis Hemingway
Philemon Holt

1830
Eleazer Hemingway
Wyllis Hemingway
Jeremiah B. Davidson

1831
Eleazer Hemingway
Wyllis Hemingway
Jeremiah B. Davidson

1832
Eleazer Hemingway
Wyllis Hemingway
Jeremiah B. Davidson

1833
Jared Andrews
Jeremiah B. Davidson
James Thompson

1834
Jared Andrews
Jeremiah B. Davidson
Jacob Smith

1835
James Thompson
Hoadley Bray
Russell Hill

1836
Hoadley Bray
Russell Hill
Ruel Andrews

1837
Hoadley Bray
Ruel Andrews
Daniel Smith

1838
Hoadley Bray
Ruel Andrews
Daniel Smith

1839
Ruel Andrews
Daniel Smith
Hiram Rowe

1840
Ruel Andrews
Daniel Smith
Hiram Rowe

1841
Ruel Andrews
John Bishop
Hiram Rowe

1842
Ruel Andrews
Hiram Rowe
Jeremiah Woodward

1843
Hiram Rowe
Ruel Andrews
Jeremiah Woodward

1844
Ruel Andrews
Hoadley Bray
Daniel Smith

1845
Ruel Andrews
Hoadley Bray
Daniel Smith

1846
Daniel Smith
Hoadley Bray
Samuel Chidsey, Jr.

1847
George Thompson
Alvin B. Rose
Hoadley Bray

1848
Daniel Smith
Hoadley Bray
George Thompson

1849
Jeremiah B. Davidson
Justus Kimberly
Samuel Chidsey, Jr.

1850
Jeremiah B. Davidson
Levi Rowe
Samuel Chidsey, Jr.

1851
Thomas Granniss, Jr.
Joseph I. Hotchkiss
Joseph Pardee

1852
Alvin B. Rose
Joseph I. Hotchkiss
John Thompson, 2d
(excused)

1853
Thomas Granniss, Jr.
John Hemingway
James Wedmore, Jr.
Edward Hemingway
William Jacobs
Town Agt. James Williams

1854
Hoadley Bray, 1st Select-
man and Town Agent
Henry Smith
Asahel Thompson

1855
Hoadley Bray
Henry Smith
Asahel Thompson

1856
George Hultz
Alfred Hemingway
Joseph I. Hotchkiss
Asahel Thompson
George W. Baldwin
Edward E. Thompson
Zina Mallory

1857
George Hultz
Joseph I. Hotchkiss
Alfred Hughes

1858
James C. Woodward
Joseph I. Hotchkiss
Willet Hemingway
Bradley Pardee
John Farren
Jared Smith
Jonathan B. Huntley

1859
Bradley Pardee
William H. Shipman
William R. Street
Lucius Elliot
Willis Bailey
George Hultz
Timothy Andrews

1860
Bradley Pardee
William H. Shipman
William R. Street
William W. Bradley

Willis Bailey
Willet Hemingway, Jr.
Charles A. Thompson

1861
George Hultz
Willet Hemingway, Jr.
John Russell
Alpheus Young
John Hemingway
Francis D. Kellogg
Charles W. Bradley

1862
Charles A. Bray
Alpheus Young
Bradley Pardee
Samuel Linsley
Alfred Hughes
S. M. Tuttle
Henry Smith

1863
Charles A. Bray
Alpheus Young
Bradley Pardee
Samuel Linsley
Alfred Hughes
S. M. Tuttle
Henry Smith

1864
Bradley Pardee
Alpheus Young
Edwin Granniss
Chas. A. Bray
Zadoc R. Morse
James F. Babcock
Edward B. Thompson

1865
Bradley Pardee
Chas. A. Bray
Alfred Hughes
Henry Smith
Zadoc R. Morse
Alpheus Young
Edward E. Thompson

1866
Bradley Pardee
Charles A. Bray
Zadoc R. Morse

1867
Samuel Chidsey
Charles A. Bray
Alfred Hughes
Zadoc R. Morse
Julius H. Morris

1868
Lyman A. Granniss
Alvin B. Rose
Charles A. Bray
Henry P. Bradley
Alfred Hughes
Hudson B. Forbes
Timothy Andrews

1869
Lyman A. Granniss
Charles A. Bray
George Hultz
Henry A. Stephens
Hudson B. Forbes
Lyman Hotchkiss
Albert Forbes

1870
Lyman A. Granniss
Andrew Barnes
Charles A. Bray
James R. Hunt
F. Foote Andrews
William A. Woodward
Edward B. Thompson

1871
Lyman A. Granniss
Charles A. Bray
James Thompson

1872
Lyman A. Granniss
Horace H. Strong
James Thompson

Nelson Linsley
Julius H. Morris

1873

Lyman A. Granniss
Horace H. Strong
James Thompson
Dr. Henry E. Stone
Julius H. Morris

1874

Lyman A. Granniss
James Thompson
Julius H. Morris
William M. Lancraft
John C. Bradley

1875

Albert Forbes
William M. Lancraft
John C. Bradley

1876

James Thompson
William M. Lancraft
John C. Bradley

1877

James Thompson
William M. Lancraft
John R. Kingsbury

1878

James Thompson
William M. Lancraft
Hudson B. Forbes

1879

Hudson B. Forbes
James C. Woodward
Alonzo D. Jacobs
Levi L. Bradley
Ruel S. Thompson

1880

Hudson B. Forbes
Samuel Chidsey
John C. Bradley

1881

Hudson B. Forbes
Samuel Chidsey
John C. Bradley

1882

Reuben H. Coe
Ruel S. Thompson
Henry Smith

1883

Leonard R. Andrews
Ruel S. Thompson
Henry Smith

1884

Leonard R. Andrews
Ruel S. Thompson
Henry Smith

1885

Albert Forbes
Ruel S. Thompson
Lyman A. Granniss

1886

Leonard B. Smith
Ruel S. Thompson
John S. Tyler

1887

Henry Smith
John S. Tyler
Ruel S. Thompson

1888

Leonard R. Andrews, Agt.
Frank M. Sperry
John S. Tyler

1889

John Ives Bradley, Agt.
Frank M. Sperry
John S. Tyler

1890

Leonard B. Smith, Agt.
Ruel S. Thompson
John S. Tyler

1891
Reuben H. Coe, Agt.
John S. Tyler
Ruel S. Thompson

1892
John S. Tyler
William S. Chidsey
John Jackson

1893
John S. Tyler
William S. Chidsey
Eugene S. Thompson

1894
John S. Tyler
Leonard R. Andrews
Eugene S. Thompson

1895
John S. Tyler
Leonard R. Andrews
Edmond B. Woodward

1896
John S. Tyler
Leonard R. Andrews
Henry T. Thompson

1897
John S. Tyler
Edmond B. Woodward
Henry T. Thompson

1898
John S. Tyler
Henry T. Thompson
Sidney B. Smith

1899
John S. Tyler
Edmond B. Woodward
Henry T. Thompson

1900
John S. Tyler
Edmond B. Woodward
Eugene S. Thompson

1901
John S. Tyler
Edmond B. Woodward
Eugene S. Thompson

1902
John S. Tyler
Edmond B. Woodward
Eugene S. Thompson

1903
John S. Tyler
Edmond B. Woodward
Eugene S. Thompson

1904
John S. Tyler
Eugene S. Thompson
Edmond B. Woodward

1905.
John S. Tyler
Edmond B. Woodward
Eugene S. Thompson

1906
John S. Tyler
Edmond B. Woodward
Eugene S. Thompson

1907
John S. Tyler
Edmond B. Woodward
Eugene S. Thompson

RETROSPECTION.

Now as we take a retrospective view of the two hundred and sixty-eight years, so briefly and imperfectly noted within the covers of this work, what do we see? First, a little handful of men, landing upon the wilds of a hitherto unknown, unexplored, and savage land, to build homes and found governments, whereby they might enjoy their own liberty of conscience in the worship of God, as they expressed it. A company of pioneers, strong in will power, firm in resolution, unflinching in courage, indomitable in perseverance, impregnably fortified by principle, taking the Scriptures as their guide and following its precepts, as revealed to them. They acknowledged with gratitude the law; they believed order was Heaven's high decree; they made integrity their watchword, and their ambition knew no bounds—masterful in spirit and practice.

We see the little colony of Connecticut holding out the beacon light of liberty as a torch to the world, in the first written constitution guaranteeing the whole rights of man that the world ever saw—one of their very first acts. Other constitutions had been given in foreign lands, but none which placed every man equal before the law. They continued to sow and to reap these first principles, until New England became the seed bed of the nation, if not of the world. They came with the Bible in one hand and a gun in the other, and to which was given the right hand would be difficult to determine.

We follow its growth, until to-day it stands a giant among all the nations of the earth. From the little companies of emigrants dotting the seacoast, arises the prosperous homes of 80,000,000 of freemen, citizens of the United States, stretching from ocean to ocean. Instead of a wilderness, the whole land is dotted with cities, towns and villages, all enjoying the advantages which the highest civilization of culture, education and religion can give. Not only its size and population, but its resources are equally astonishing. Taken as a whole, this young nation astonishes the world by its rapid development of wealth, intelligence, culture and power.

In the Union, our own little state of Connecticut has always stood in the front rank. True, she has never filled the presidential chair directly, but the descendants of her sons have in the persons of U. S. Grant and Rutherford B. Hayes. She has furnished statesmen of the first order of ability, from the signing of the Declaration of Independence by Roger Sherman and Oliver Wolcott down to the day when Orville H. Platt passed away, whose memory will pass on to generations as one of the greatest statesmen of the age. Connecticut is small in stature, but mighty in intellect, education, industries and inventions.

The nineteenth century will be styled the century of inventions. We may commence with the little stick of a match, now a household necessity, which was not in use at the time the nucleus of this book was published in 1824. This was about the beginning of manufacturing, although steam as a propelling power had been used to a limited extent. Observe the change from Robert Fulton's little steamboat to the great leviathans of to-day, now swiftly crossing the ocean, bearing thousands of lives and millions of treasure daily. Contrast the little wooden ships with the ponderous engines of war now plowing the waters of the Pacific, the most powerful fleet that ever navigated those waters, whose naval discipline and strength are acknowledged throughout the world. Witness steam applied to mechanical arts, turning millions of wheels and spindles all over the land. Behold the wilderness of two hundred and fifty years ago now completely girded and bounded in every direction, with the iron tracks of its trolley and steam railroads, bearing its millions of travelers and freight from ocean to ocean. Notice the little, often unpainted school-house standing by the roadside, void of every convenience, and now the vast universities all over this broad land supplied with every appliance of science, numbering its students by the thousands. Regard with thankfulness the elegant churches, of every material, belonging to every creed, some of great architectural design and beauty, furnished with every convenience and garnished with much elegance, rearing their lofty towers and spires heavenward; many at a cost reaching the million point, and some much beyond.

Inventions quickly followed one another, in all the varied industries of life, until there seemed to be nothing more to come, particularly during the last half of the century, but each year sees improvements and new wonders. The electrical spark which Benjamin Franklin brought from the clouds with his kite and key was left for Prof. S. F. B. Morse to develop and bring into use in 1844. He called it the "magnetic telegraph." No one seemed to comprehend his ideas, and he was the subject of much doubt, many

Lightning Source UK Ltd.
Milton Keynes UK
UKHW012033100220
358504UK00002B/542

9 789353 977238